VIDEO ART for the CLASSROOM

Edited by George Szekely & Ilona Szekely

2005 National Art Education Association

About the National Art Education Association

The National Art Education Association is the world's largest professional art education association and a leader in educational research, policy, and practice for art education. NAEA's mission is to advance art education through professional development, service, advancement of knowledge, and leadership.

Membership (approximately 40,000) includes elementary and secondary art teachers, (and middle and senior high students in the National Art Honor Society programs) artists, administrators, museum educators, arts council staff, and university professors from throughout the United States and several foreign countries. It also includes publishers, manufacturers and suppliers of art materials, parents, students, retired art educators, and others concerned about quality art education in our schools.

The Association publishes several journals, papers, and flyers on art education; holds an annual convention; conducts research; sponsors a teacher awards program; develops standards on student learning, school programs and teacher preparation; and cosponsors workshops, seminars, and institutes on art education. For further information, contact our web site at www.naea-reston.org.

© 2005 National Art Education Association
1916 Association Drive
Reston, VA 20191

Order No. 215
ISBN 1-890160-27-X

This book is dedicated to our third generation art teacher,
Emilie Szekely-Tackett, who will be an innovator in video art and teaching...

Illustrations featured at the beginning of each
section were created by students of Renee Shaw.

Table of Contents

Introduction

Assembling the Anthology

My students and I took a trip to the National Gallery of Art. On the way, students noticed my video camera and asked if they could use it. Worried, I weighed the risks. I imagined the camera plummeting out of their small hands and sliding down the aisle of the school bus—or worse, watching it fall out the window. I thought of the money it would take to buy a new one, of being sued by the school. But seeing my students' obvious need to explore, I handed the camera over to my most trusted student. The bus quickly transformed itself into a stage. The children began to perform for one another, turning the school trip into a television show. When the camera changed hands and was given to a quiet child, she formed a close relationship with the camera, describing scenes outside the bus as she recorded. Talking about the sights and sounds of our journey made for a perceptive half hour even before seeing artworks. Once at the museum, the students asked to use the camera again and, without prompting, started to document their experience. They comfortably described each artwork in detail, as if the video camera was a friend. I realized how having this "thing" with us changed the children's experience. The funny part of all of this was that the camera did not even have to be turned on.

Back at school, I decided that I would use this "looking glass" as a tool for a larger group. Two obstacles to overcome were obtaining enough cameras for everyone in class, as well as training large groups of students to handle the cameras without dropping them. Then I remembered when I was 3 years old and had just started playing the violin. No one put a Stradivarius in my tiny hands. I began with a margarine box on which my parents had drawn strings. A sponge was fixed beneath the box for a shoulder rest. My bow was a ruler. I don't think my wooden violin was ever as magical as that dressed up box. It gave me the feeling of the violin, but allowed me to play and freely experiment with it like my toy friends.

I started video lessons in the classroom by using the same solution my parents used when they gave me my margarine box violin. Children designed their first video cameras out of boxes, sponges, and paper rolls, adding machine tape for film. Soon they recorded their own variations on scenes, "cropping," and focusing in on subjects. The children recorded what they thought was important in an object, scene, or event. Using our video cameras, the children gained an understanding of the artistic experience involved in video and developed a bond with the camera. It all led to great excitement when one day a real video camera appeared in our art class.—Ilona Szekely

Children, who have been on the forefront of every new art idea, have had a unique interest in video ever since cameras came home. As Earthworks were tested in the sandbox, children who borrowed the family video camera used it for more than "snapshots." It is with an appreciation for children's unique contributions to this media that we have focused on children as video artists. With audience interest in adult video art at an all time high, with paintings and drawings in museums now sharing their walls with video projections, we did not wish children's contributions to this media to be neglected. We knew of many video art programs throughout the country whose contributors felt as if they were working in isolation and not as well recognized as those in traditional media programs. It was our intention to demonstrate the wealth and well being of video art instruction in the United States and Canada, to encourage broader participation, and to bring video art into the mainstream of the art curricula.

We did not approach this anthology with the traditional editor's role of asking for specified concepts to fit into predetermined chapters. We wanted an open forum for diverse voices, to use the anthology format as a means of discovery, to get an authentic sense of the field without trying to control the flow of ideas or information. Since little has been written about video art programs in art education, this anthology is a ground-breaking venture.

The responses to our call for papers would themselves fill a chapter. Reply e-mails to us were filled with inquiries and comments such as, "Do you mean digital?" "I use Super-8 cameras I find at garage sales; it's old equipment but we make amazing films with kids...would you be interested?" "Our art department doesn't do this...I teach technology and we make wonderful videos." "We just moved into an old fire station converted into a video lab-studio, but we are not a school program...could we be included?" "I do what I call moving paintings with the kids, would that count?" "We don't do 'the morning news' in school, or television-style videos, would you have room for us?"

What we began to discover is that video is taught by many creative teachers with different backgrounds, in different areas of schools, using different equipment. It is taught in school, after school, and by different community organizations. It is explored as animation, filmmaking, documentaries, coverage of school events, and yes, even by replicating the morning news. So what is video art? Who does it? When and where do they create their art? This anthology is a process, a sampling, a journey to find out. Meanwhile, video art keeps expanding even as we read about it.

After inviting an all-star line up of video artists, filmmakers, and experienced teachers representing all levels of schooling, papers started arriving. We were delighted to discover so many additions to using and thinking about, the media. We learned how video can facilitate sculpture or bring paintings to life. We discovered how it is used by traditional art programs to take a new look at the environment and one's own art. One contributor said when he created video he was like a filmmaker who didn't need a studio or studio budget. Video offered this teacher independence and a way to get started in film. Others described the power they felt video gave them as a means of gaining control of the media to direct it and be part of it instead of passively watching it. In the hands of contributors, creating a video became a method for collecting, a way of teaching camera arts, and an incentive for children to perform. In the hands of children, a video camera became a magic box.

We hope this volume offers encouragement to teachers contemplating using video in their classrooms. We think that many pages will offer new ideas and inspiration to veteran video teachers. Our hope is that this book will serve not only as a reference, but also as a significant building block for the growth of children's video art education—and as a means for building a video art community among art teachers.

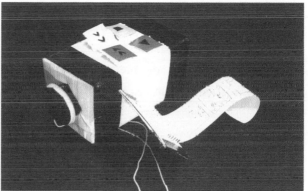

Cameras and projectors made by George Szekely's students.

The Cast

Ralph Raunft is Professor of Art at Miami University, Ohio. He traces his interest in animation back to his childhood in the Bronx, New York. According to Raunft, animation brings together the traditional arts of sculpture and drawing with the new media of video. In his paper on animation, we are taken on an elegant voyage of the history of this art form, the special role it has in young peoples' lives, and the social aspects of the media. According to Dr. Raunft, animation teaches sequential thinking, patience, technical knowledge, and storytelling skills. His chapter is filled with useful resources on how to teach animation, how to study it, and how to appreciate it.

Donna Learmont administers one of the most technically advanced and comprehensive high school video programs in the country. In the Bloomfield Hills, Michigan program, students receive a state-of-the-art foundation and are encouraged to use their advanced skills to make art videos and commercial videos. Learmont's comprehensive program is built on a ladder of skills, with each rung emphasizing a mix of technology, visual aptitude, and creative judgment. Donna Learmont has pioneered a sequential approach to video teaching that recognizes students will ultimately use the media in different ways. After "basic training" and the development of confidence, students work on both personal art statements and client-driven projects. Learmont's approach has allowed program graduates to successfully enter the corporate video world as well as contribute to the video art scene.

Marshall Weber, John Toth, and Renee Shaw are notable video artists who were interviewed for this anthology. They speak with wisdom and passion about video, children, and teaching. These artists share their thoughts from the context of their unique experiences with school-aged children. **Dipti Desai** spoke to Marshall Weber about his video teaching at the Heritage School in New York's East Harlem. John Toth was interviewed by Ilona Szekely in Central Park, New York. Ilona Szekely also spoke to Renee Shaw at her Washington, DC studio.

Digital artist and art teacher **Harold Olejarz** understands that video can be integrated into even the most ordinary aspects of school culture, such as the ubiquitous morning announcements. Olejarz uses his art teaching skills and design education to make video an art experience for students. Besides providing a useful review of the history of the field, Olejarz highlights an array of innovative video projects and shares solid advice with students and teachers— all from a recognized master of video art and a long-time digital art teacher.

In art history we teach about painters, sculptors, and architects. Video has its own benchmark artists. **Erin Tapley** of the University of Wisconsin, suggests some of the artists a lesson in video history and appreciation should include. Tapley also discusses how to use video in an art room in artistic and experimental ways. Her program is not overwhelmed by equipment and technical skills, but instead she focuses on student inventions with the camera and in performances before the camera. According to Tapley, future art teachers have to find creativity and joy in their introductory video experiences, so they can carry these feelings into their teaching.

Panasonic Corporation has an extensive outreach program to schools, lending equipment and expertise to video programs. When I asked the public relations department who to contact as a contributor, without hesitation they recommended **Susan Lehman**, a veteran video art teacher at the John Still Center for Creative Expression K-8, in the Sacramento school system. Susan was generous and candid in our first phone meeting, as she was in her paper, and shared a wide range of her experiences in teaching preadolescents the skills and art of video. Susan not only takes you through some crucial steps for getting started, but she also acknowledges her initial hesitation, fear actually, of being involved in a technology-based media. This is a very useful chapter to read if you are an art teacher thinking about starting a video program.

Video projects can be school-wide initiatives. Working on the elementary level in Pickerington, Ohio, art teacher **Mary Sheridan** is project director for *Changing Places*.

The project is a school-wide, arts-inspired integrated curriculum, which marshals everyone's talent in the school and uses filmmaking to explore community issues. In this unique project, art and video lead the way in a long course school effort, recognized for its excellence by the United States Environmental Protection agency.

Joanna Black, a CyberArts instructor at the University of Manitoba, Canada, addresses several important subjects. Her first chapter is a moving account of making an award-winning film with high school students called *The Last Dynasty*. The film won honors at the Sprockets Children's Film Festival, one of the most prestigious film awards in the world. Black describes the monumental adventure, including words from student participants, while pointing out important steps in organizing a major student film production. In the project, still images are employed as an impetus for moving images to build a narrative video. Examples of well-known artists, photographers, and filmmakers are used to inspire each step of the process.

When teaching the technology of video art, students are often more familiar with computer editing programs than the teacher. In a second paper, Black has researched this "topsy-turvy" relationship of tech-savvy students, who often take on the role of teachers in a video class. In her chapter we find important suggestions for working with the new teachers in our classrooms, our students

Joanna Black focuses on the voices of students. In her piece dealing with student videos for the Ontario Science Center, we hear from young filmmakers conducting interviews with notable scientists and speaking about every aspect of video making. The student's comments present an important background for video art teaching, which is profound when adults listen to students' ideas and experiences.

A new kind of art requires new modes of appreciation. If you have no idea what "single, communal hypertext computer Web" means, and I did not, **Pamela G. Taylor** of Virginia Commonwealth University explains it in her chapter. Starting with a traditional art project illustrating the layers of meaning in an artwork, students are led through an examination of layered meanings which often occur in video. Looking at music videos for art and meaning serves as an example for student use of video as an element in art appreciation. Taylor shows how video can give art appreciation a new look, taking it out of dark projection rooms.

Karen Lindholm-Rynkiewicz talks in loving terms about making her first video. She describes in detail the importance of that experience in her life and how she is still excited about the videos she creates and shares with students. Being an artist-teacher is the theme of this contribution. For Rynkiewicz keeping up with your own art is not only a way to keep up with technology and equipment, it is a way to share a lifelong fascination with the media. Presenting one's video and artist self in class earns great respect from students.

"Our program fosters community leadership, transformation, and new technology access to urban youths," says **Deidre Searcy** of Street Level Youth Media, based in Chicago. Street Level has become a nationally recognized model for community-based action and the creative healing potential of video art. Its many important achievements include "Video Dialogues," which hands cameras across gang lines to create video letters between gang members. Through its many studio, mobile, and outreach programs in neighborhoods and schools, Street Level organizes street video events and opportunities for inner city youths to create and share their videos. The organization is also a training group for the professional development of video teachers and is known for its partnership programs with the Chicago schools.

Rikki Asher of Queens College, the City University of New York, feels that murals and video have a great deal in common. Both art forms are crafted by a dedicated group. Both are a public art, created to share with a wide audience. Both bring awareness to a personal idea and the school art program. When students document mural artists' work and thoughts on video they make the intent of a public art even more public.

The descriptive study of a powerful video made in the Bronx, New York, parallels a tragic school event and the art response by student muralists. It is the story of how powerful art forms can inspire hope, healing, and recovery. Asher believes video is an important media to record the process of art being developed in another media. Video fosters understanding of the other media and is able to capture the art making process and reactions to it by its planner and "recipients," its audience. Video can be used to share and distribute other forms of children's art.

Digital opera, Shakespeare, and video—what other strange mix will follow? You never know when it comes to **Arlene Jordan's** kitchen. Ms. Jordan was an inspired art supervisor from Queens, New York, where students in the schools spoke over one hundred different languages but found a common language in art. She then moved on to work as the Education Director in the non-profit world. In both roles, Arlene Jordan has inspired her teachers to use video across the curriculum, to make it a standard among educational standards. Award-winning videos have been screened in movie theaters and their daring weave of different art forms have received enormous praise.

Windsong Pictures, based in Fort Wayne, Indiana, is one of the nation's most comprehensive filmmaking programs. Directed by **Michael Floyd**, this nonprofit organization of students creates full length motion pictures. Floyd is involved in teacher education and coordinating a film festival and a summer film camp. Windsong's many activities are designed to encourage students of all ages to explore the limitless potential of creative film production. Windsong pictures strives to build a vast community of filmmakers through its many outreach programs and by supporting film artists and film programs all over the world.

Hollywood may seem a long way from a public school video program, but **Darrin Fletcher** was determined to bring them closer together. Starting with helping students to make films, Fletcher, a professional in the film industry, realized that teachers need to be inspired, if great film programs are to take root in a school. And what could be more inspiring than bringing teachers down to the film lot at Universal Studios and Warner Brothers and working alongside teams of filmmaking professionals? In each of his innovative programs, Fletcher works to bring the best of the industry to schools. Many young filmmakers across the country have benefited from Fletcher's on-site and Web site training programs.

In an old converted fire station downtown, in the heart of Poughkeepsie, New York, resides a thriving video art program. The staff is bravely dedicated to preserving the creative visions of local youths, by involving them in exciting video productions. **Corinne Militello**, former director of strategic planning and development at the Hamptons International Film Festival, set out to chronicle the work of a group of young video artists, striving to make a difference in the way inner city children view their world and themselves. In the Children's Media Project, video artist-teachers share their creative knowledge and experience in an enduring mentoring relationship.

PART ONE

Developing Video Art Programs

1

Talking Animals, Human Machines, and Telling Stories of the Phantasmagoric –

Animation and Light Media for Preservice Teachers

Introduction

For a 10-year-old growing up in the 1950s in the Bronx, New York City, Saturday mornings were spent imploded on the couch watching cartoons such as Tom and Jerry, Bugs Bunny, Porky Pig, and eventually Yogi Bear. They spoke directly to a young boy's love of movement and action, slapstick humor, wacky and absurd characterizations. While watching a kid's television show I discovered how such movies are made. With the help of my father's 8mm Bell and Howell movie camera used primarily to document family excursions and events, I set out to create movie magic.

Soon I began tinkering with 3-D animation called stop motion photography. Through trial and error, a small corner of my parent's bedroom became the set for extensive miniatures made from cardboard, tempera paint and toothpicks. Here clay dinosaurs and crocodiles, supported by clothes hanger armatures, were coaxed to life. What I remember most from this experience was the excitement of creating, transforming, testing, and inducing imaginative worlds that I could shape, alter, and tell stories about. I learned technical skills, sequencing, and patience by moving the 3-D object to be animated a little at a time, keeping track of what parts moved and what parts still needed

moving for each frame of film. My father allowed me to use 5 minutes of film at the end of family movies. When he brought back the developed film, our small apartment living room became a theater where roars, flashing lights, and animated images of my creations came to life. Unfortunately, the lack of a supportive school art program and financial constraints in buying and developing film, brought this childhood creative pursuit to a premature end.

In art school, two of my fellow classmates, Peter Wallach and Dexter Reed, were destined to become innovators in this field, winning accolades for their work in such movies as *Joe's Apartment* and *The Simpsons*. Although I enjoyed this creative process, my goal in art school was to hone more traditional artmaking skills and to become an art teacher. My first opportunity to share this interest with young people took place during my student teaching at Conwell Middle Magnet School of the Philadelphia Public Schools in Kensington, Philadelphia. With the support of my cooperating teachers I was able to bring my interest in animation to inner city children. Interestingly, this school was near the set of a low-budget independent movie, with an unknown actor in the lead, about a poor underdog fighter that came to be known as "Rocky." At the same time my young students at Conwell, many who also felt like underdogs, made and starred in their first animated and stop motion photography film called "Welcome to Conwell Middle Magnet School." The students created this theme enthusiastically with hand drawn animation, collage, photo animation (reminiscent of the work of Terry Gilliam's opening animations of the Monty Python Flying Circus), claymation, and also including the interjection of live action. Since those days long past, I've largely moved on from feeling like the underdog kid myself, who was transported from that small apartment through the infatuation with cartoons and fantasy and the enthusiasm of making surreal animated movies. However, I am still thrilled in sharing this interest with children, adolescents, and now preservice teachers.

Preservice students looking to develop knowledge in light and moving media such as film, computer created designs, and animation usually take specific film theory or studio media classes when available. Incorporating the practical and theoretical aspects of animation, as an important popular art form, into a more specialized child art/adolescent theory and practice class, where students can more easily see how such media can be taught to young people is presented in this chapter. Incorporating such an emphasis into a preservice art education class gives students opportunities to learn its history and aesthetics; explore its tools and techniques; understand its language and engage its meaning as critique, while also recognizing its potential impact on the development of children. It is the medium's potential for expression, as a way for people to make sense of their world, and in the context of popular media, as a socialization force whose values can be recognized, contested, negotiated and challenged, that becomes the emphasis in such a class. Through simple and more complex studio activities of an individual and collaborative nature, as well as reflective, critical and transformative activities, preservice students discover animation's potential in the context of the expression and identity formation of young people.

A Brief History of Animation

Film is a powerful, valuable, and emotionally seductive medium that at its most creative, can transform, renew, and empower the filmmaker and audience. A specialized form of film is animation. Animation existed before film, motivated by a desire to express, to make something special and foremost to depict movement.

Deep in the caves at Altamira and Lascaux, our ancient ancestors captured the energetic movement of bison and horses, momentarily freezing them while at the same time suggesting their movement (Halas & Manvell, 1976). The moving figures in the Rock paintings of Neolithic herdsman in Africa show an even more stylized movement containing quick and difficult action. These images are more geometric and compared to the works of their Paleolithic ancestors, who through necessity and the lack of access to domesticated animals, captured or depicted these moving images more realistically (Feldman, 1970, pp. 168-169). Exaggerated and stylized images with rhythmic movement and dramatic action is also venerated by today's young people, who relish stylized media images, that primarily contain rapid, agitated, and deliberately erratic movement as found in cartoons and other related media.

More asserted efforts at animation did not occur until the 1760s and in the 19th century, coin-shaped spinning toys for children magically combined two images into one. The Thaumatrope, followed by the Phenakistiscope and eventually the Zoetrope, perhaps came closest to the rhythmic and sequential movement found in film. The history of animation has gone through five main periods beginning with a formative period of trick work, magic, and explorations of the phantasmagoric; a period where the cartoon became an ancillary form of entertainment; a period of experimentation with technique and the establishment of full length feature animation that compete with live action movies; a period where animation was produced for television, for commercials, and for educational purposes; and lastly, the period where computers are used to create animations and where these animations are often seamlessly integrated with live action work.

Emile Cohl began working on the first animated series called "Phantasmagoric" which contained stick figures, as a short hand for experimentation—utilizing crude animation techniques, but nevertheless revealing the magic and awe of such medium to audiences. Ninety years later, one of the first computer games for adolescents named "Phantasmagoria," creatively combined live action and computer animated images and explicit story line, while at the same time ushering in a new era of computer animated interactive games for children and adults. By 1911, the first truly animated film named "Little Nemo," by Winsor McCay was produced and was later followed by a work he did in response to real world events titled, *The Sinking of the Lusitania*. Like Daumier's political cartoons 60 years before, this work reflected one of the first uses of animation as not only entertainment, but as an educative, critical or social commentary.

In the 1920s, Walt Disney excelled in synchronizing picture and sound in animation (called "Mickey-mousing" by animators) and introduced Mickey Mouse in *Steamboat Willie*, and thus created one of the first visual and imaginatively conceived-popular cultural icons. Animations from Disney and other producers such as Max Fleischer and Walter Lantz, were not only popular among the masses, but were also acknowledged by filmmakers and critical social theorists.

Sergei Eisenstein, the renowned Russian theoretician and movie maker during the formative years of motion pictures, visited the Disney studios as did revolutionary thinkers such as Theodore Adorno and Horkheimer. Adorno and Horkheimer looked at Disney and other cartoons negatively, as part of a larger cultural commodity production, where such entertainment teaches social conformism, inauthentic being, and violence to children. Rather than bridging the gap between high art and popular art, their negative critique thus perpetuated this division even more (Tavin, 2003). At the same time they designated it as a special form of technological and media culture ripe for criticism (Leslie, 2002) and challenging more recent critical social theorists (Giroux, 1999) to look at the Disney phenomenon not as domination and corruption of the identity formation of the young, but within a context of struggle and resistance. Through dialogue and critique focused around what's meaningful to students (i.e., perhaps start-

ing with what stands out such as bubbly characters, zany and violent humor, frantic stories and other things apart from aesthetic value), teachers can guide students to understand how such interests can be explored and even contested in the larger framework of the self and others, economics, history and the larger domain of culture. By focusing on the design, subject matter, targeted audience, message, and hidden assumptions about animated films, students can develop a greater sense of understanding of what such works mean with regard to power and influence in the shaping of their consciousness. For example: How and why is the "ogre" in the computer animated movie, *Shrek*, considered to be an outsider, separate from the community? What does it mean to be an outsider? What people in the real world are made to feel like they are outsiders? What other characters in this movie or other animated movies are perceived to be isolated for being different? The producers of this movie believe that some moral exists in this story that reiterates the language of fables and is "about self acceptance and that things aren't always as they appear" (Inside cover of *Shrek* production notes). Teachers can push the movie's theme further by dialoguing and engaging students to debate or express their ideas with regard to such issues where society at one end supports uniqueness while at the same time chastising, or marginalizing those people who are different because of how they look, speak, or come from socioeconomically.

During the 1930s and into the 1940s, Oskar Fischinger experimented with and won awards for more abstract, non-objective and nonlinear forms of animation complementing the modernist trends at the times. Sadly, these works were not viewed by large audiences, which instead sought wacky stories or more illustrative themes in animated works (Moritz, 1988, pp. 21-22). Ironically, Fischinger later worked for Disney where he tried to influence the work in that studio.

As an excepted art form, yet predominately found in the commercial arena today, children fully relate to cartoons and enjoy watching them at home, on video, on DVDs, at the movies and even in the back seat of the family van which now comes with the option of a DVD player attached to the ceiling. Animation, as with some other visual media at one level, becomes a socializing and surrogate influence in the context of family life today. Families bond through participating in viewing feature length contemporary animated cartoons such as *Toy Story*, *Shrek*, or *Ice Age*, which reinforces a type of multi-dimensional bonding that prepares children to accept the story and characters as babysitters when parents are not available to help in their becoming. Other forms of animation, such as three dimensional approaches using stop motion photography as in *James and the Giant Peach*, allow animators to give 3-D sculpted characters movement through successive changes of the image filmed one or more frames at a time. Apart from grand theatrical cartoons, or even those made exclusively for television, animations are also used and embedded in advertising and in selling products; in information or educational productions and to visually depict what can only be at first imagined in science; and on web pages where moving images sell and get more attention.

Animation is a pervasive part of children's and adolescents' lives. It is one aspect of popular culture, and with the help of teachers, it can teach them about concepts of time/duration, strategies for representing movement, and design, while giving them opportunities to express themselves playfully through the medium (Jackson, 1997). Once they have experimented with its disciplinary ground, they could then use this medium's narrative capabilities, to tell stories about what is, what was, and what could be in their lives and in other imaginary worlds. Studying animation not only promotes children's creative and expressive becoming, but can be a form of socio-cultural learning which through critique, can reveal the political, historical, and hegemonic undercurrents of such popular art forms. Such enterprises take courage and patience, but the rewards are plentiful as children become more active, informed, thoughtful and civic minded readers of such visual forms of communication.

Defining Animation

All films show movement and are the result of a sequence of closely related photographic images which when projected at a continuous speed will give the illusion of movement (Halas & Manvell, 1976). The illusion created by picture change is made possible by the retina's capability to retain an image for a tenth of a second, and the phi phenomenon which gives us the ability to see those after images, as connected, moving, and real (Rubin, 1984). Film animation, on the other hand, is considered a separate art form which employs visual and graphic communication techniques to create complex, surreal, or informative worlds. The word animation is derivative of the word anima or animate which means give life to (*Microsoft Encarta World English Dictionary*, 2001). Animation incorporates the techniques of stop-frame or stop motion photography, where the camera or video device exposes single or multiple frames of drawn, painted, or sculpted images into a series of continuous movements (Halas, 1976). Computer generated animations, besides creating pure fantasies, allow animators to seamlessly integrate synthetic-animated images into live action. Nevertheless, the challenges for both the graphic animator and computer artist are unique and equally challenging. Animators often work collaboratively and use their technical knowledge creatively in telling stories, articulating concepts, and informing educationally. Many of these efforts require much "thought, time, creativity, and love to become reality" (Solomon & Stark, 1983, p.7).

Why Children Enjoy Animated Cartoons

Animated cartoons depict action and dynamic movement which support and reinforce children's first expressions that evolve around feelings of movement, responses to being moved, responses to how the eyes move and responses to the movement depicted in other graphic or real world images (Czurles, 1975). In adult life, this kinesthetic way of being—the rhythm, tempo, gate, of their entire body and is just one aspect of their aesthetic and unified being affected by early childhood experiences in cultural contexts. As a child becomes an integrated human being, their sense of self is reflected and extended in how they move, act, and interact with people. Children express these movements during the scribbling phase as a response to this way of relating to their world.

It is this rudimentary tendency towards movement, action, and something humorous that grabs the young viewer's attention. Even live action movies, such as *Star Wars*, *Raiders of the Lost Ark*, and more recently *Tomb Raider*, have quick pacing and exaggerated story lines that now model themselves after cartoons, video games, music videos and other multi-media. Outlandish and phantasmagoric cartoon animation, with its exaggerated movement, quick pacing, bizarre or unexpected humor and whimsical characters drew children into a fantasy realm for many years and still do so to some degree. In trying to develop a larger market and to push animation's potential and competitiveness with live action, Walt Disney first brought in larger production values (i.e., *Snow White and the Seven Dwarfs*, and *Fantasia*) and tried to raise the bar with regard to quality images and stories—combining the outlandish, the whimsical, mythical, and the stylized in a grand way.

Today, children have become somewhat more sophisticated in their viewing of animation, demanding more evocative eye candy and dynamic action/movement, better story lines and characterizations, and music which reiterate what they experience on television and on the radio. Nevertheless, when this expensively orchestrated and highly refined form of animation works, it perhaps more than other media still provides ample opportunities to stir, motivate, and instill in young people not only the "phantasmagoric," but issues about the self and others. What child doesn't come to grips with his/her own fright of scary things through viewing with their parents, siblings, friends or babysitters the monsters in *Monsters Inc.*, and perhaps becoming more able to gradually deal with challenges of the real world.

At their best, when animated stories stir or tap into primal feelings and thoughts, children and grownups are momentarily swept away, not just as escapist entertainment, but through it towards a greater reaffirmation of what it means to be human. At their worst, animated films can have weak production values, poor or inappropriate stories, banal manipulations of the emotions, commoditizing or stereotyping of people or images and overall aspirations that fall short in challenging all children's growth as a reflective,

critical, social and civic minded persons. Animated stories that are not only enjoyable to watch for their aesthetic merits, but which are embedded with mythical drama that alludes to honor, fairness, thoughtful reflection, and civic pride in the context of community are worthwhile contributors to children's sense of self.

Sadly, animated cartoons have to some degree replaced the storytelling narratives once evident in households where family members of all generations interacted and told stories to youngsters which were embedded with such tales of honor, work ethnic, sacrifice, love, and compassion. Examining these works critically for their technical, aesthetic, and cultural value is imperative for parents and teachers. When children are left on their own, Mickey Mouse is, ".....but an abstract idea in the process of a (young?) person's becoming" (Leslie, 2002, p. 30).

Why Teach Animation to Preservice Teachers

An animation film unit for Preservice teachers should contain a wide range of theoretical and hands-on experiences that will give them the necessary knowledge as future teachers who will also have the option to teach similar concepts to their students. Film animation is important in a public school art curriculum because it bridges the gap between hands-on experiential and sensory approaches to personal or collective expression, with that of knowledge and experiences with developing technologies such as computers.

Given opportunities to study this popular medium and understand its history, the personal transformation of ideas involved in the making of them, and criticism directed to their significance are important aspects related to their development. Animation teaches sequential thinking, patience, technical knowledge, and supports storytelling skills. For children, the structure of their early childhood development is reiterated, complemented, and enlarged in their creations that have impact on them in transformative and celebratory ways (London, 1992). The expansion from individual expression to collaborative ventures that support bonding in an entertaining, challenging, and authentic context is an essential outcome of such activities. Children have opportunities to experience, express and empower themselves through materials and processes which are multi-dimensional and which become the basis for cultural exchange (Burton, 2000).

Such studio processes are flexible in accommodating different learning styles, particularly the kinesthetic and visual while at the same time developing their processes of discrimination and critique. Through group planning (interpersonal skills); writing scripts (linguistic); simulating and creating basic and exaggerated movement (visual-spatial-kinesthetic); filming and editing (logical-mathematical); understanding character development and characterizations (intrapersonal); and adding music (musical) gives wonderful opportunities to children and adolescents with several different learning styles (Gardner, 1993). Conceived as a type of play, animation gives children opportunities to create different imaginative worlds (Goodman, 1978) and characters that at times may personify their surrogate selves and which gives them opportunities to act out possible, outlandish, and future situations (Wilson & Wilson, 1982). During any of the collaborative experiences such as filming an animation, students also have to suspend or regulate their desire to resolve an idea immediately, by freezing their impulsivity (i.e. stop motion requires the freezing of one frame or more at a time) in support of a larger creative and fun enterprise. Through such means, students learn not only self-regulating skills, but also reflective and critical skills since they will have time in between shots, setups, light changes to think about what is, why it is so, and what should happen next (Flanders, 2002). The development of coping skills and patience in the context of work with others and the withholding of pleasure, of wanting to do or see something resolved immediately, is one of the most important growth experiences for children and adolescents that can be supported and nurtured through such an experience.

How Art Teachers Have Been Trained in the "Art of Animation"

Art teachers have been mostly trained in the art of animation in summer or special workshops, at university art departments or media centers, or in some preservice classroom where they explore animation themselves and learn to use that knowledge with their students (Berarducci, 1971; Ehrlich, 1995). One would think that such efforts have been accelerated today, in the context of a technologically driven educational system that often times favors computers and light media in the art room, over the more basic, but nevertheless beneficial longstanding and multidimensional art materials.

Leading art education material and method text books, both in the past and some in the present (Chapman, 1978; Hurwitz & Day, 1991) devote at least one section to photography, film, television and newer media, with only a relatively small component devoted to film animation for children. Ironically, even though these major texts believe it to be an important vehicle for personal expression, and suggest that it is valuable, "because it teaches patience, satisfies the desire to learn purely technical processes, and develops narrative skills," (Hurwitz & Day, 1991, p. 268) few teachers actually seem to instruct their students in this medium.

Some teachers have experimented with animation created solely on the computer using iMovie as well as more sophisticated programs through self instruction. Commercial publications devoted to animation are available but not abundant and lend themselves as teacher resources. However, few directly address how animation can be used to address the needs of teachers of young children. Most of these books have an introductory history of animation, a section on animation techniques, how a studio animation is produced, and the materials and equipment needed (Grush, 1981; Rubin, 1984; Halas & Manvell, 1976; Canemaker, 1988; Perisic, 1978; Hobson & Hobson, 1976). Some may even have sections devoted to interviews with filmmakers, the performance of animation, (Hooks, 2000) career options, and an overview of international animation (Solomon & Stark, 1983). Articles devoted to animation in art education journals or educational magazines seem to appear sporadically (Berarducci, 1971; Ehrlich, 1995; *Scholastic*, 1997; Palmer, 2002) while research with regard to animation concepts, its application, or effectiveness as a viable disciplinary focus in the classroom are even less evident and are often of an ethno-graphic nature (Bickley-Green 1997; Stokrocki, 2002). Web sites devoted to the animation arts, with some emphasis on children's animation productions and workshops in the United States present some of the most exciting uses of this medium (Jackson, 1997). Nevertheless, there are few if any sources that comprehensively describe specific strategies and uses of animation in the classroom.

Introducing Future Teachers to Animation

Art teachers can teach this art form and guide children and adolescents to experience animated films, seen not only as powerful influences, but also as a resource which would allow them to gain greater understanding of how visual images can be read and created (Golubieski, 2003; Buckingham & Sefton-Green, 1994). Teachers can learn the history of animation, the artistic conventions of this particular art form, while also developing a critical awareness of the qualitative differences of animation's ability to empower, entertain, or educate students. In discovering its history, its processes, and how to read those images they will get a better understanding of their various levels of intent, purpose, and deep structure. While becoming familiar with the technical and conceptual processes shaping such images, as well as reading them at various levels of understanding, they are also forming the basis for their own creations. Once preservice teachers have engaged such an art form at various levels of understanding, response to it, and personal or collaborative expression, they can then more fully structure and incorporate those ideas into their own classroom.

Curricular Considerations

A hands-on media and animation unit, complementing a theoretical focus on child and adolescent development, is presented in a 3-hour class modeling itself after a studio class, and which meets for 2 hours—three times a week. Animation is seen as the starting point or beginning for more in depth explorations of media/film and computers in other classes. Such a unit gives the preservice student the theoretical and pragmatic basis for animation and related experiences that would enable them to teach such a

unit to children. The structure of the class and techniques used involve individual and cooperative learning experiences that complement and are appropriate for elementary, middle and high school students. In a broad context, this unit should make teachers knowledgeable to: 1) understand the role of animation in people's lives, particularly young people, 2) be able to communicate and express their own ideas through the animation arts in order to know its expressive potential, 3) develop the ability to critically respond to a variety of animation work found in popular culture as well as in fine art, and 4) to understand the value the animation arts have in society. These four parameters, for example complement and support the Comprehensive Arts Education. They can also be modified to support other local or state curriculum guidelines: Ohio's Model Competency Based Program Curriculum guide, 1996 for pre-K through 12th grade). These goals also have indicators for assessment focused on the preservice students' skills in 1) accessing and integrating knowledge of animation and related media coherently, 2) the disciplinary and related knowledge of animation processes and the factors that shape its use, 3) the deep structure of thought processes in decision making with regard to film and animation processes and how they relate to the needs of children, 4) fluency of integrating disciplinary skills into successful performance exemplars, and 5) at a meta-cognitive or self-regulatory level —how they use different strategies to raise critical questions and to make questions posed with regard to film animation understandable in the verification and support of their own conclusions.

Also considered are sequential instructional and performance objectives for each grade level; strategies for remediation and intervention; organizing principles which guide or direct visual art inquiry; and what is important in this particular model, a statement of belief in how such learning should thoughtfully and holistically be integrated into life world of students. The discipline of art, and more so the discipline of animation, becomes a mode of inquiry where students should have choice, experience diversity, and where the art content is a means of understanding their world and the world of others. Because preservice teachers are asked to consider their instructional goals and disciplinary directives in the context of the relevancy of those issues in the lives of their future student needs, it is then also logical to give the preservice student such considerations in their education. Thus, the instruction for the preservice teachers is also built around their ideas, concerns, and feelings as they develop their repertoire for expression and response.

The Format, Order, and Sequencing of Animation Concepts and Experiences

The guiding principles and format for this unit involves four areas of focus with six sequential steps. The guiding principles suggest the importance of historical as well as disciplinary knowledge of the medium; the importance of individual and collaborative exploration and more complete expression with the medium; the importance of reflection throughout such a unit; and the importance of the development of critical abilities and awareness of the applicability of such ideas with regard to teaching children and adolescents to engage popular culture through such works more meaningfully. There are seven sequenced foci of what specific concepts are introduced under each principal that conforms to a 16-week semester with approximately 2 weeks devoted to each area. Not all areas necessarily need to be covered and new components may even be added based upon the background and interest of students enrolled in such a class.

The following matrix outlines this curriculum unit which emphasizes teacher preparation and responsibilities as well as what students may be expected to bring into the class with regard to performance and response. Questions engage students, and are directed to all aspects of animation and reflect what is, what was, what could be and of course why certain things are the way they are. This planning matrix exemplifies a more extensive curriculum. Throughout this experience students are asked to keep journals of their thoughts and feelings with regard to their involvement.

Animation Unit Matrix

Historical Reflection & Disciplinary Processes	Individual & Collaborative Expression	Reflective Response	MetaCognitive/Critical & Transformative Response
A history of Animation Teacher Questions When, where, and how did Animation historically evolve? When and what processes were explored and by whom? How is it similar to other art forms? How is it different? What is an animation aesthetic? *Focus* When did students become interested in animation? What types of animated works interested them? How has their feelings and thoughts about animation changed over the years? What still excites them?	*Telling a Story Through Movement and Light* Early explorations of symbolic play through light: Students are asked to work in groups with small flashlights that have different colored lenses. An alternative is to work with glow sticks of different colors. They are to tell a story with the movement of the flashlights of different colors, focus, and size. Emphasis on movement, rhythm, interval, and overlap are suggested in telling a brief story through an abstract idea.	*Previewing Animations* Several vignettes from such animated works as (Elmo the Dinosaur, Snow White and the Seven Dwarfs, Toy Story) an animated add and a section of an informational animated film is previewed. *Focus* How are these works similar and how are they different with regard to imagery, development, and characterization? How does the purpose of the work affect your response to it? What are the qualitative differences of the works?	*Examining the History of Animation Critically* How has the knowledge of the history and purpose of animation changed or altered your view of it in the context of art, entertainment, advertising, and education? Why teach children animation? What animated works are worth sharing with young children and adolescents? What makes these works worthwhile? What questions could you ask children after their experiences with such films? What questions of a non-critical nature could be asked? Of a critical nature?
Overview of Early Animation Processes Introduction to simple animation processes through playing with historical and related devices or processes. • Flip Books • Zoetropes • Thaumatropes • Phenakisticope (fantascope) *Student Focus* What are ways of experimenting with the principles of animation? What types of concepts of movement could be attempted? What materials could be used in exploring these processes? What is the physiological basis for how these devices work?	*Demonstrating a Sequence of Movements Through Flip Books/Zoetropes* Student focus is on creating movements of a visual image through sequential drawings on index cards—reflecting transformation, emotion, and a change in time. An alternative is to use a Zoetrope and create a film strip that takes the flip book idea to a more mechanical and easier to view realm. Zoetropes can be made from a large ice cream container and spun on a lazy Susan. An old phonograph turntable that rotates at different intervals could also be used.	*Challenges and Rewards of Basic Animation Processes* Student work is examined for its ability to depict a movement successfully through such simple processes as flip books and Zoetropes. Basic goals, objectives and rubrics are presented. *Focus* Variety of ideas and variety of processes in the work: How are the works different? What makes for a successful work? What other strategies could be used to create variations of movement in the work? In telling stories, what other considerations could there be when working with such material?	*The Animating Nature of Animation* How has the experiential knowledge of simple animation helped the student to understand the concepts? What potential do these concepts have when working with children? How can the flip book project be introduced to a class of 5th or 6th graders? How does one teach basic animation to students with different ability levels, learning styles and interest? How could a flip book be a no fail experience for students? How can teachers help students to achieve higher levels of understanding of the affects of popular media through such endeavors?

Historical Reflection & Disciplinary Processes	Individual & Collaborative Expression	Reflective Response	MetaCognitive/Critical & Transformative Response
The Telling of Stories Viewing animated films that exemplify good story telling and more advanced animation techniques. • Storyboarding as a precursor to creating animations. *Student Emphasis* What makes for a good story? What makes for a good animated story? *Exercise:* Play the "Constructing Dramatic Plot," game. Why tell stories? What is the significance of stories? What types of stories are worthwhile telling? How are good stories shaped visually? How could such stories be told through animation? How can collaboration in story telling be done? What do they need to know in working collaboratively on the development of a visual story?	*Slide Narratives – Storyboards, and Visually Telling Stories* *Student Focus:* Creating a visual story board of a dramatic plot: • 30 still pictures • Markers • Paint • Workable Acetate • Related Processes An alternative is to create the narrative of each scene on 2"x 2" slide mounts with acetate insets. Students are: encouraged to experiment with variations of process —with different textures, materials both of a transparent and opaque nature. *Additional Focus:* • Music • Sound Effects • Voice Over *Challenges:* Continuity of characters, background, props, etc. needs to be carefully considered in such a collaboration.	*Working Collaboratively, and Presentations* *Focus:* The works are presented and colleagues from other classes are invited to the "Premiere." Students are asked to reflect upon the development of the endeavor: What is challenging about such explorations? How are obstacles overcome? What conceptual and physical strategies work best in creating the storyboard? How were transitions handled from frame to frame? How does the music or voice over help the viewer to understand what is happening? What unique or different approaches can be taken? What variations of plot development are possible?	*Interdisciplinary and Creative Endeavors/ Challenges and Risks* What is involved in the democratization of the classroom through individual and group decision making towards a purposeful end? How are individuals empowered through collaborative disciplinary creative experiences? How are voice, direction, and unity of the task determined in such a context? What problems could one expect from middle school students working on such an endeavor? How can children be prepared to work collaboratively? How can such work be looked at in a non-critical way? In a more critical way with regard to effective emplotment, characterization, continuity, and other productive disciplinary skills?
Reference Films/Video Animations Students have become familiar with the history of animation; some basic processes; how to emplot a story; how to develop characters; and how they might introduce these ideas to children. Further challenges lie ahead in film/video animation production, with	*Creating Sampler Animations* Students are challenged to make several small-exploratory reference or demonstration films: With consideration for different ways of depicting movement, timing, and creating depth.	*The Potential for Meaningful Expression* As students become familiar firsthand with the actual processes of animation, they keep journal entries of their successes, problems, and changes they made in their explorations. Focus for entries are on ideas they may have for telling stories; challenges they confronted and	*Visual Codes and Meaning of Animated Works* As students develop a greater understanding of animation history, processes, and contemporary approaches to such processes, they are asked to become more critical of identifying animation not only as an expressive medium, but also

Historical Reflection & Disciplinary Processes	Individual & Collaborative Expression	Reflective Response	MetaCognitive/Critical & Transformative Response
emphasis on actual animation procedures; knowledge of equipment such as animation stands, cameras, lights, and technical processes of 2-D and 3-D animation. Vignettes from 2-D and 3-D films and videos are shown as examples of the art of animation, including some videos and DVD's of behind the scenes in studios and what animators actually do.	Both 2-D and 3-D animation techniques are utilized. *Processes:* • Collage-Photo/Cutout • Animation • Photokinesis • Object Animation • Puppet Animation • Clay Animation • Pixilation (Drawing on bleached 16 mm film from physical education department's films of athletes in training in the 1960s or 1970s) • Cell animation • Group Animation Games such as an Animathiaton	how they overcame them; limitations of the medium; differences between 2-D and 3-D animation and their own preference or comfort level. Brainstorming in groups for ideas which are interesting to explore in a larger animation focus suggested.	with regard to its potential as a critique for deconstruction. Vignettes of popular animations are examined for their messages. What message or themes are overt and what are covert? Students are challenged to become critical viewers of animation, through questioning, in an endeavor to demystify them as carriers of social ways of being.
Creating an Animated Film Processes of making animated stories are described, demonstrated and discussed with students based upon their familiarity with its history, conventions, processes, and collaborative experiences. A more thorough outline of the production end is presented through behind the scene videos of animation teams working in studios. Emphasis on computer editing, sound and music, and the overall production process is outlined. Emphasis for this component is on: • The Animation Team • Interchangeability of Roles • Production Processes	*The Animated Narrative* Students are placed in groups and challenged to brainstorm ideas for an animated story that all would be willing to invest time in. They can refer to their journals for ideas. The approach they take (2-D, 3-D or combined) should support their overall idea. The story then is developed into a script and visually depicted as a story board outlining the plot, characters, and backgrounds. (For 3-D animation building sets) Students learn to take turns in responsibilities and use of equipment.	*Reflecting on Experiments and Basic Expression* Students negotiate which ideas and processes could work. What problems do they need to find solutions to? How are problems resolved? What creative challenges did they discover in the production? What problems if any are involved in the actual production? What compromises are made in such a production? What resources are available to solve problems?	*Metaphoric and Structural Aspects Embedded in Stories* In the production of a narrative, how is meaning embedded in the structures of the story? What symbols are used? What is the overall emplotment of the work with regard to visual tone and uses of metaphor? Is it an ironic story? What metaphoric symbols permeate the story? What's the relationship between symbols and meaning in such a work? What visual or auditory symbols convey changes in tempo, rhythm, and support the overall story?

Historical Reflection & Disciplinary Processes	Individual & Collaborative Expression	Reflective Response	MetaCognitive/Critical & Transformative Response
Learning From Directors About Editing How are animations successfully edited: • Video Capture • Continuity • Transitions • Cross-Cutting • Patching • Pacing • Adding sound, music and other effects	*Video Editing* The learning curve in video editing can be high. Students make decisions together demonstrating: • Continuity • Matching Action • Maintaining axis of action • Dissolve • Appropriate pacing for theme • Sound • Music • Effects	*Problems Associated with Achieving One Voice* Strategies for achieving one vision: How is a unified narrative best achieved? What considerations were made by team members that helped in the success of the animation? What technical problems of editing proved challenging?	*A Critical Look at the Work* What is the work's significance? Social significance? How does the work relate to other animated works? What influences from media are evident in this work? What type of media was most influential in the conception of this work? What makes this work different in its visual content and idea than other works?
Review and Closure to Unit What can students learn about animation—it's history, processes, and criticism? What are the career options for students interested in animation?	*What 's Next* What other stories can be told through animation? What is the relationship between making an animated movie and a live action work?	*Looking Back While Moving Forward* What categories, patterns, or themes are evident in the student's personal journal-reflections?	*Animation: What's Expressive and What's Critical?* Why is this art form worthwhile teaching? How can a teacher maximize involvement from students? What are obstacles for implementing such a unit?

Example of A Class Focus

At the end of the 4th week, the preservice teachers are given opportunities to display and express their knowledge of light media and animation. They have up to this point learned about the history of animation through viewing a sampling of such works; found ways of telling stories with simple light media; had some opportunity to reflect upon their own preferences in animation; have some knowledge of the different purposes of animation; have become familiar with simple animation processes through the use of historical equipment and the qualitative differences amongst these materials; and have become aware to some degree of the developmental considerations of the use of these materials with children.

Students also have an understanding of their performance in class through a "Portfolio Review," which includes notebook and journal entries; a research compilation of reference books and materials on animation; written commentaries, and critiques; early studio explorations of their involvement with the medium; and various other assessment materials related to the structure of the class such as tests and a case study with a child or adolescent that involves the teaching of some of the concepts, processes, or forms of criticism to children or adolescents.

At the beginning of the 5th week, students will basically learn about how to tell stories pictographically and how to create "Storyboard Slide Narratives," as part of a team. Hurwitz and Day (1991) believe that a storyboard is, "a transdisciplinary activity that draws in varying degrees on narrative skills, the linking of image to story...." (p. 268). Once involved with such a narrative, they are asked to reflect upon their team's successful working and decision making processes with regard to story development; selection of characters; stylization of imagery; types of music selected; voice, or effects they're using; as well as how they perceive themselves and their colleagues in a collaborative enterprise. A team leader keeps track of the participants' involvement and a responsibility sheet will be handed in at the end of this unit. On a higher level, students are asked to reflect on the challenges envisioned and risks involved in such an endeavor.

Rubin, S. (1984). *Animation: the art and the industry*. Englewood, Cliffs, NJ: Prentice-Hall, Inc.

Individual teams develop thoughtful responses to each others finished work, based upon a critic guide that examines each team's work in a non-critical (i.e. the recognizable aspects of storytelling and processes involved) and then in a more critical way (i.e. how was success achieved? What are the narrative's strong points? What are its weak points?) A worksheet with rubrics, outlining the qualities that are sought is given to each class member at the beginning of this endeavor. In addition, students are also asked to develop questions with regard to personal issues that might have come up about the narrative, the production, the processes, and the collaboration. An important question raised by students has been how such a collaboration of a creative nature can still maintain a unified vision or "visual voice." Other questions that are asked are "How such work after it is created, then examined for its aesthetic qualities, then deconstructed within a larger arena of popular culture and myth, could be placed in some context within a story telling tradition? What conventions have been successfully employed? How does the work reflect the ideas and interests of all the team members? How does the work reflect their history? How is the work influenced not only by story telling traditions, but by images and concepts found in everyday popular contexts as well as in fine art culture? And does the narrative challenge the viewer with a new, different, or challenging vision? What is unique (What is stereotypical?) about the story, the imagery, or the handling of the materials? What types of audience does it exclude? What type of audience does it include? How does it marginalize people? How does it include different people, or different symbols that represent personal, political, social, or economic issues?"

To begin with, the preservice teachers are each asked to splice a 5-minute vignette from their favorite animated film for the class and to summarize the story in a paragraph. Focus here is on story development. Students are continuously asked "why" they choose things in addition to what they choose. They are asked to analyze what they envision to be the different emphases of the emplotment of the story and how does the animated movie build the audience's expectations of what will come next? What cinematic strategies are used in preparing audiences for the varied points of emphasis or importance? How did the filmmakers tell the story and how do they build interest, keep interest, and bring the story to some acceptable conclusion? These questions aim for a more informed and reflective understanding of the animated story such as: What is the intent of the movie maker? Is it to entertain or tell something worthwhile about people? Who is the target audience? What audience is excluded or not considered by the film maker and why?

The vignettes of examples of animations from students are examined with discussion focused on the structure of plot development and how expectancies in development could also be broken—for a more riveting or unexpected effect on the audience. As an exercise in creating a plot, a historical and helpful CEMREL game called "Constructing Dramatic Plot," (CEMREL, 1973) is played. In this game students are asked to pick cards with different aspects of a plot and each consecutive student is asked to follow that story further. This game is an excellent way of introducing adults and even more so children to the dramatic elements of stories. Students learn the basic structure for plot development through this game involving characters, settings, incidents, conflict, crisis, and resolution. There are also opportunities to use wild cards that may throw a wrinkle into the structure of the story and challenge the expectancy level for the audience. What audiences expect in a narrative film and how a film maker may deviate from that convention creatively is a major point of discussion for the class as teams are preparing to create their own storyboard narrative.

In planning an animated video, especially one that tells a story, sequential planning is essential and the storyboard becomes an important tool for the director or filmmakers. Storyboards allow the filmmakers to see the transitions between scenes in a logical way, particularly when scenes are broken up into smaller units from extreme close-ups, to long shots, to medium shots. Some animation conventions could also be explored in a storyboard that anticipates what students will be doing when creating their own animated film. One such convention is "anticipation of action," where a figure or object is about to do something

and how the character gets ready to do that in the previous scene could be considered. "Squash and stretch" and other forms of distorted, exaggerated, or imaginative movements of characters or props could also be depicted in a storyboard narrative. Usually a storyboard is not followed to the extreme by the actual animators, and becomes merely a guide.

Students are asked to work in groups and to create a narrative story that will be an end in itself with at least 30 slides—sort of a larger than life "comic book" when projected. They must work out a meaningful plot in written form, as a type of script, before beginning the visuals. They can work on regular 8.5" x 11" sized paper which will then be photographed and made into slides and projected on a large screen. The impact of projecting this work is far greater on the audience and is more stimulating for the storyboard/filmmakers. Younger students can also work on 2"x 2" inch slides, on workable acetate mounted in those slide casings with very pointed permanent markers, ink or paint, and other graphic media. The end product is usually limited in detail, but such a process doesn't require as much drawing skills and is often more interesting when it is projected on a large screen. Small wire figures become giant "elastic" bubble figures when projected on a large wall.

Students can keep the imagery simple, or make it more complex, depending on the teams drawing or mark making abilities. Students that are not particularly good at drawing—often have opted for more stylized works. One group for example did a take-off on *Romeo and Juliet*, where all the characters were pasta and their clans were the "Tortellinios and Macaronios." Simple drawings of this pasta, with basic variations, reinterpreted that story in an interesting and humorous way.

Different mark making equipment can be used from pen, pencils, crayons, paint, spray paint, paper cutouts, oil, acetate, stencils and other materials. Different people with different skills can work on different parts (i.e., background, ancillary items, sound, etc.) but all contributors to such an endeavor are important to the finished product. The task is to create a dramatic plot, with consideration for cinematic tools such as shot ranges (close-up, extreme close-up, long shot, medium shot); shot angles (low-angle, high-angle, medium angle); types of sequences (linear sequence, associative sequence and episodic sequence) which they learned about in previous lessons and classroom activities. Furthermore each group will consider the major transitions or scene changes between slides and how to use materials that may suggest fade (i.e., darker elements on one side; dissolve; metaphorical dissolve; or form dissolve). Voice, music, and special sound effects may be added on a separate recording device. The sound will be a random sync sound recording and students will have to work on the timing of how long the slides will be in view with a particular voice over narrative, musical sound, special effects sound. A 35mm projector with a timing device could help in this process, although the entire work including the slides could also be captured on video utilizing several frames of film at a time. Furthermore, if each slide becomes a jpg., then it could also become a powerpoint presentation and be projected with a media projector. After the work is completed, it is shown on a "large movie screen," where students can see the fruits of their labor. Students are given an opportunity to self evaluate their work before the Instructor evaluates it. Once they are able to tell a story through such means, they are often interested in applying those skills in more sophisticated ways through actual animation work with a digital camera.

Summary

Teaching light media and particularly animation to Preservice art education majors, gives them knowledge of its history; some of its disciplinary processes and conventions; an understanding of its impact as a popular media, and theoretical knowledge of the developmental appropriateness and applicability of such approaches with school- age children. Animation and related light media is looked at as important expressive media that is transdisciplinary. It mediates between experiential or collective expressions using traditional artmaking materials, with that of knowledge and experiences with newer digital based technologies. It supports multiple learning styles and high order thinking both in the production process, as students analyze streams of movement and recombine images through synthesis (Bickley-Green, 1997) and during critique when they are challenged to negotiate the meaning of a wide range of popular media in the context of questions and challenges. Animation is a unique medium, being largely associated with commercial enterprises, yet in the hands of thoughtful teachers, can give students opportunities to transform, empower, celebrate, and express their personal and collective lives.

References

Berarducci, V. (1971). Animation in the elementary school. *Art Education, 24*(4), 11-15.

Bickley-Green, C. (1997). Interdisciplinary Desktop Video in a secondary art program. In D. C. Gregory (Ed.) *New technologies in art education: Implications for theory, research, and practice* (pp 63-71). Reston, VA: National Art Education Association.

Buckingham, D. & Sefton-Green, J. (1994). *Cultural studies goes to school:Reading and teaching popular media*. Bristol, PA: Taylor & Francis Publishers.

Burton, J. (2000). The configuration of meaning: Learner-centered art education revisited. *Studies in Art Education, 41*(4), 330-345.

Canemaker, J. (Ed.). (1988). *Storytelling in animation: the art of the animated image* (Vol. 2.). Los Angeles: The American Film Institute.

CEMREL, (1973). *Constructing dramatic plot: Student materials*. New York: The Viking Press/Lincoln Center for the Performing Arts.

Chapman, L. (1978). *Approaches to art education*. New York: Harcourt, Brace, and Jovanovich Publishers.

Czurles, S. A. (1975). The broader and earlier foundations of visual art development. Bulletin *New York State Art Teachers Association*.

Ehrlich, L. C. (1995). Animation for children: David Ehrlich and the Cleveland Museum of Art Workshop. *Art Education, 48*(2), 23-24, 33-36.

Feldman, E. B. (1970). Becoming human through art: *Aesthetic experience in the school*. Englewood Cliffs, N.J.: Prentice-Hall, Inc.

Flanders, L. (2002). *Classroom circles and the art of making movies*. Paper presented at the third international conference on conferencing circle and other restorative practices, Minneapolis, Minnesota.

Gardner, H. (1993). *Frames of mind: The theory of multiple intelligences*. New York: Basic Books.

Golubieski, M. (2003). *Teaching for visual literacy: Critically deconstructing the visual within a democratic education. Unpublished doctoral thesis.* Miami University.

Goodman, N. (1978). *Ways of world making.* Indianapolis and Cambridge: Hackett Publishing Company.

Greene, M. (1973). *Teacher as stranger.* Belmont, CA: Wadsworth Pub. Co. Inc.

Grush, B. (1981). *The shoestring animator.* Chicago: Contemporary Books, Inc.

Halas, J. (1976). Film animation: *A simplified approach.* New York: UNESCO.

Halas, J. & Manvell, R. (1976). *The technique of film animation.* New York: Hastings House Publishers.

Harris, J. (1997). Art education and cyber-ideology: Beyond individualism and technological determinism. *Art Journal.* 39-45.

Hobson, A & Hobson, M. (1976). *Film animation as a hobby.* New York: Sterling Publishers Company, Inc.

Hooks, E. (2000). *Acting for animators*: a complete guide to performance animation. Portsmouth, NH: Heinemann.

Howlett, M. (1997). The art of animation: From cels to computers, *Scholastic Art, 27*(6).

Hurwitz, A. & Day, M. (1991). *Children and their art: Methods for the elementary school.* New York: Harcourt College Publishers.

Jackson, W. (1997). Kids making animation: A sampling of children's animation workshops around the world. *Animation World News, 1* (12), 1-6.

Leslie, E. (2002). *Hollywood flatlands*: animation, critical theory and the avant-garde. London: Verso.

London, P. (1992). Art as transformation. *Art Education, 45*(3), 8-15.

Keifer-Boyd, K. (1997). Interfacing hypermedia and the internet with critical theory in the arts: Preservice training. In D.C. Gregory (Ed.), *New technologies in art education: Implications for theory, research and practice* (pp. 23-31). Reston, VA: The National Art Education Association.

Microsoft (2001). *Encarta World English Dictionary*.

Moritz, W. (1988). Some observations on non-objective and non-linear animation. In J. Canemaker (Ed.), *Storytelling in animation* (pp. 21-31). Los Angeles: The American Film Institute.

Palmer, M. (2002). Byte-size animation. School Arts, 101(9), 43.

Perisic, Z. (1978). *The focalguide to shooting animation.* London: Focal Press.

Schreiber, R. (1996). New, newer! Newest!: Teaching new media. *New Art Examiner.* 30-33.

Sisley, J. B. (1966). Filmmaking in the art curriculum. *Art Education, 19*(4), 11-13.

Solomon, C. and R. Stark. (1983). *The complete Kodak animation book.* Rochester, NY: Eastman Kodak Co.

State Board of Education (1996). *Comprehensive arts education: Ohio's model competency-based programs.* Columbus, Ohio: The Ohio Department of Education.

Stokrocki, M. (1997). How an art teacher instructed students with discovery based Electronic technology. In D. C. Gregory (Ed.), *New technologies in art Education: Implications for theory, research, and practice* (pp 95-103). Reston, VA: The National Art Education Association.

Stokrocki, M. & Buckpitt, M. (2002). Computer animation at an Apache middle School: Apache children's use of computer animation technology. In Y. Gaudelius and P. Speirs (Eds.), *Contemporary issues in art education* (pp 264-274). Upper Saddle River, NJ: Prentice Hall.

Surplice, M. (2003). Stop-motion movies. *Camcorder and Computer Videos* 2003, 70-74.

Tavin, K. M. (2003). Wrestling with angels, searching for ghosts: Toward a Critical pedagogy of visual culture. *Studies in Art Education,44*(3), 197-213.

Wilson, B. & Wilson, M. (1982). *Teaching children to draw: A handbook for parents and teachers.* Englewood Cliffs, NJ: Prentice-Hall, Inc.

Web Sites

Paper or Cel Animation
Some information about stop motion photography and related links: www.stopmotionanimation.com
www.egroups.com/group/stopmotion

Three Dimensional Animation
www.egroups.com/group/clayanimation

Computer Editing Program Sites
www.stopmotion com
www.thirdwishsoftware.com
www.adobe.com

Children and Animation
An excellent source for other sites about animation: www.animation.about.com/library/weekly

Animation world network that presents kids making animations in workshops. Also it contains materials from the Animation World Magazine: www.awn.com

An excellent library of articles on process, books, and animation workshops for children and adults: www.animationtoolworks.com

Societies
A society based in Hollywood for the advancement of animation: www.asifa-hollywood.org

Technical Notes

The following are some recommended hardware and software to create animations. Before investing in such hardware and software, it is recommended that research must be done since the model numbers and software designations change with the addition of new features every few months. These are just the basic materials and should not be looked at as the definitive resources to be used. The author has mainly worked with Windows based software, but Mac users utilize similar equipment and resources.

The Camera

The most important aspects of purchasing a camcorder is that it should be a digital camcorder, since it allows for non-linear editing on the PC or Mac and should have:

- Features to be able to do single frame or stop motion photography

- A firewire (IEEE1394) or USB

- The ability to not only put video in, but also to put it back out in edited form for playback on television

- Some ability to put Analog video in for editing and then taking it back out in Digital form

- A video out and video in port

- Image stablilization

- A big color LCD monitor

- Mike/Earphone Jack

- The following are two cameras that are recommended, although the model numbers change each year and something comparable should do: Sony DCR-TRV30; Panasonic DSI DV

Computer Hardware

Most schools will have some aspects of the following equipment either in the art room, or in a computer lab. A computer must have capabilities for capturing video from a camcorder through either a firewire card or USB port. It must be a fairly high end system such as a Pentium III or better with at least 512MB Ram and an 80 gigabyte hard drive or greater to be used exclusively for such endeavors. Editing video takes up a tremendous amount of hard drive space and even an external hard drive just for that purpose would be even more efficient. Mac users should have a G4 series or higher with maximum computer pro-

cessing speeds beyond 700MHz. i-Book Macs may work with regard to editing but are slower and not as efficient. A CD recorder is helpful and would allow some form of video to be transferred for storage to CDs (they would have to be compressed) and then played back on computers. A DVD recorder would be ideal for saving several finished works rather than storing them on tapes or on the hard drive on the computer. Sony internal and external DVD recorders have been proven to be the most efficient, reliable, and versatile. A high end graphics card, such as those produced by NVIDIA Radeon allows smoother video for viewing and editing, taking some of the load off the main processor. Many of the video cards come with inputs and outputs and even firewire ports built in.

Software

Software is very specialized for editing animation. Most schools don't have this type of software, but school discounts are often available from the manufacturers. Some packages which include software and a video input card are available from such companies as Pinnacle. The following are recommended software for video editing. The top two support the MPEG-2 file format or greater which allows compression of video for smaller storage space on the hard drive and could be easily transferred to DVDs for storage and playback on DVD players in the future:

High End Video and Sound Editing Software

- Adobe Premiere 6.O or higher for both Windows and Mac

- Final Cut Pro v2.0 or higher exclusively for Mac users

- Cakewalk 9 or higher for music composition and sound editing

- 3D Studio Max is a Premiere 3D animation application for computers

More Basic Video Editing Software

- Ulead Video Studio 5 or Greater

- Cyberlink Power VCR II for DV to DVD Transcoding

- iMovie 2 or higher that is bundled with Mac systems

- Pinnacle System Studio V8 or higher

Additional equipment in the production of animated videos can be bought, but may also have to be constructed in a more improvisational way.

- Lights—Floodlights (fill lights) will do but they should have protective wire covers so that students will not burn themselves

- Tripod—Strong enough to support a camera and versatile for moving

- Tripods that come with horizontal extensions and which move up, down, and sideways, can make filming easier.

- Light Box—Such a box is used for placing drawings on top of each other to see how one movement relates to the next. These can be made out of Plexiglas, wood, and small fluores cent light fixtures (The actual blue prints for making a light box are in "The Shoestring Animator," by Byron Grush. A registration device can be as simple as using a three hole note book punch screwed to the top of the light box.

- Animation Stand and or Gimbal Box——One can make a home made stand by using plywood, two-by-fours, and Plexiglass. At least two or more layers could be created, so that background imagery could be simultaneously animated with closer imagery creating more depth.

- Rigid Table—As student animate, tables need to be solid for 3-D animation for stability of the diorama objects positioned and for non-jerky stop motion photography work.

**A Model Video Production Curriculum:
Bloomfield Hills Schools, Michigan**

2

Introduction

What is video production if not storytelling? Some would approach the medium as another form of print, as though it were merely a different device for delivering information. Many training programs across the country approach video production courses this way. They focus heavily on converting the printed word to the screen. And this, I believe, is a mistake.

Truly, most of what is on screen is news, drama, or entertainment, however the delivery of moving images must be approached with right brain input that isn't required in the construction of the printed word. Much like children's storybooks that tell a story with symbols or pictures, the best that video has to offer has nothing to do with reciting lines from a scripted page. Rather it is with the camera composition, the angle, the movement, color, light, music, or mood that a video moment may indelibly impress us. Video also allows for multiple images and ideas to be presented simultaneously. This is a near impossibility in the more linear print medium.

The printed word has many genres from poetry to short story, obituaries to sports scores, pamphlets to advertisements, fine literature to smut, news articles to propaganda. Training and preparation to create these diverse print messages is highly differentiated.

The same may be said about video production. There is as much value in teaching broadcast television news as there is in teaching installation art. The important thing to know is— what is the mission? Video can be used for storytelling or merely beauty. Sometimes it accomplishes both and that is truly a triumphant moment for both teacher and student.

Most novice video producers make the mistake of writing a script that contains all dialogue. In other words, first the character will say this and then another will say that, and so on, ad infinitum. What they forget are the moments when nothing is said but all is revealed; the reaction shot; the silent observer; the action sequence; an introspective look at oneself in a mirror; the quiet moments in film and video that bring the aesthetic to bear. That is what makes video an art and not simply a permutation of print. In addition, it has the ability, as all great art does, to evoke powerful and physical reactions such as tears, heartache, fear, and laughter.

What helps make a great videographer? The good news is that every student will enter the classroom with many years of viewing experience. Students can recognize quality work, but they can't yet articulate why it is great. Unlike fine art or symphony music that may be unfamiliar to young people, television and film have been in their direct daily experience since the time that they were born. It is the teacher's mission to unravel the mystery of how to create moving images so that students may move beyond the role of passive viewer and actively create messages for themselves and their audiences.

It is helpful to have students who have had training in photography, lighting, computer software, or writing, but these are not necessarily predictors of success. There are students who are simply naturals, just as there are people who can play music by ear. Since video production is highly collaborative, it is useful to build on each student's individual strengths and group them together accordingly to complete a single project.

A Sample High School Program

Bloomfield Hills, Michigan is an affluent bedroom community for automotive executives and professionals in the Detroit area. The public schools are unique in that they send over 92% of their graduates on to college and also offer special programs including a fully operational farm, a nature center that rivals any private enterprise, an award-winning radio station, and a state of the art television production facility, complete with a mobile production van.

In 1986 the Bloomfield Hills Schools' Video Department was formed. The video classes are part of the high school Communications and Dramatic Arts curriculum and also part of the District Video Services Department. The school system operates its own cable access channel which carries original programming 12 hours each day, including sporting events, school presentations, talk shows, and school board meetings. The remaining 12 hours are filled by an electronic bulletin board service that provides announcements for the community related to education and school district events. The channel was named the best in the nation in 1992 by the Alliance for Community Media, who awarded the channel with its coveted Community Communications Award. The Outstanding Educational Access Programming Award by the Alliance in 1993 followed this.

The Video Services Department is comprised of a staff of three. A Video Services Manager shoots and edits all K-8 and administrative programming and oversees community relations. The Video Operations Coordinator is in charge of purchases, repairs, technical operations, and live truck shoots. The high school instructor teaches five classes each day of video courses that are offered to students from the District's three high schools.

Equipment

The studio is comprised of three cameras, a switcher, audio mixer, character generator, Chroma screen, lights, and microphones. This is very similar to most public or educational cable access studios one might find throughout the country. For years the studio was exclusively analog, using 3/4 and S-VHS tape formats, but in the past few years, the studio has been converting over to digital technology. The channel's playback operations are now accomplished via a digital server.

The post-production lab is comprised of ten Macintosh G4 workstations running iMovie3 for beginners and Final Cut Pro 4.0 for advanced students (as of the Fall of 2004). There are also 14 digital camcorders available to students on an overnight checkout basis so that they may shoot on location and after school hours. Associated accessories such as tripods, microphones, batteries, tapes, and chargers are all available to students as well.

Background

The studio's recent conversion from analog to digital has resulted in an explosion of interest in the video courses. Historically the courses had attracted male students nearly exclusively and many of them were not having success in the traditional academic arena. The hands-on nature of the course appealed to boys attending a school without the traditional outlets of woodshop or auto mechanics. While many of them succeeded in video production and even won awards, the perception of the program as strictly vocational seemed to dissuade the college-bound students or females from exploring the field.

This changed rapidly with the introduction of smaller, computer related technologies. The digital cameras are so lightweight that girls were no longer intimidated by the weight or size of the technology. The computer lab for digital video editing looks and feels familiar to students, regardless of gender or academic success and therefore has welcomed the full and diverse spectrum of students into the field of video production.

Classroom Management

Juggling the management of individual student media projects with students at different skill levels should be familiar to teachers of art. Once the initial software training is completed, the teacher can concentrate on mentoring individually. Keeping a separate folder for each student is a good idea. They can keep all their evidence of planning on-site and both of you may refer to it as necessary.

Unfortunately, in a technology-based curriculum, much of the time is devoted to troubleshooting equipment problems and checking equipment in and out. This significantly affects the amount of time one can spend with student projects. It is suggested that each student have passwords and separate hard drive space so as not to interfere with their peer projects. Even so, problems will occur, equipment will malfunction, software will crash, and tears will be shed. It is best to devise contingency plans for when these events occur. It is highly recommended that students export their works in progress or back-up their work on removable media just in case things go wrong. Lining up reliable technical support should occur before instruction begins.

Video Course Offerings in Bloomfield Hills Schools

Introductory Course· Media Issues
& Introduction to Video Production:

There are four courses available to high school students. The first or prerequisite course is titled Introduction to Media Issues and Video Production. This is a 20-week course that provides the critical foundation for each subsequent course. The students are introduced to communications theory and media literacy, including critical viewing skills, writing techniques for video, the physical workings of television, video production terminology, and the operation of studio and remote video equipment. Students learn skills in producing, directing, editing and equipment operation through crew rotations on various in-class and mobile productions.

Media Literacy: The primary focus of this first class is media literacy. This includes being able to understand as well as create messages in a variety of media. The course philosophy is that one cannot create an intelligent or sophisticated technical production without first having attended to the content. The analysis and deconstruction of professionally produced media precedes the student productions. Teaching analysis and production together is a logical approach, similar to the widely accepted approach of teaching reading with writing.

The key concepts of media literacy are defined as follows by the Center for Literacy:

1. Media Construct Reality
Media may look real but even the news is selected, edited, and manipulated in order to attract and hold viewers. The stories are someone's version of what happened, not reality itself.

2. Media Use Identifiable Techniques
Scary music, headlines, close-ups, and camera angles are among techniques that heighten audience response, attract viewers, and keep people watching, reading or listening. By identifying these techniques, individuals may begin to "deconstruct" media and analyze it.

3. Media are Businesses with Commercial Interests
Media are generally not without cost. The primary purpose of for-profit media is to sell viewers to advertisers. Almost everything the media brings us is subject to influence by a profit motive. A useful question to ask is "who is making money from this program?"

4. Media Present Ideologies and Value Messages
Who and what are important? Some people are glamorized; others are treated with contempt. Some ideas get headlines; others get left out completely. The questions to ask are "Who benefits?" or "Who loses?"

Critical Viewing Skills: Media literacy educators hope that by studying the media students will acquire critical thinking skills that include the choice to view programming selectively, examining the social roles of the media, understanding how media impacts behavior, identifying stereotypes, distinguishing between fact and fiction and sources of bias, evaluating the implications of messages for health, examining legal and ethical media issues, elevating awareness of citizens' rights and responsibilities, and mastering the techniques of media analysis and production.

Course Assignments for Introductory Video Students:

1. Directed Viewing Assignments

Students are required to observe and write about media weekly. Each week there is a different directed viewing assignment accompanied by a reflective essay. This may involve viewing programming, surfing the web, collecting pictures from magazines, or listening to music. The essays are a minimum of one typed page each, requiring more formal writing conventions. Over 20 weeks the students are exposed to a variety of genres, techniques, and concepts.

An example of a writing assignment that analyzes advertising is as follows:

Record one 30-second commercial. Watch it several times. Write down in detail every shot that occurs in order. Write down all dialogue. Write down the style of music. Write down any sound effects. Examine the graphics. Try to re-create the storyboard. Analyze how it is constructed. Does it work? Does it make sense? What doesn't make sense? How does it sell the product to the target audience? How might you sell the product differently? Write an essay and include it with your re-created storyboard.

2. Media Log Assignment

Throughout this semester all students must also keep a Media Log. One page each week is entered in the log. This is a more free writing style than the essays. The Media Log is a journal in which students record responses and reactions to various media experiences. Since it is a technology course, students are encouraged to send the journal to the instructor via e-mail. The electronic entry may then include web links, jpegs, tiffs, wav or MP3 files, QuickTime movies, or anything that would enhance the journal entry.

Many Media Log topics are acceptable but examples for students include: Watch TV, read articles or listen to songs, and then write down impressions of points, methods, or concepts that strike you. For example, why you thought a character was interesting, techniques you notice, or questions about the meaning of an image or program.

- Make lists or note lyrics of favorite songs, rock videos, TV shows or other media products, and analyze why you like them.

- Note media experiences you really like or dislike and explain why.

- Make notes about media experiences that affect you emotionally or physically. For example, some experiences invoke anger, tears, laughter, or even nausea. Try to analyze how the producer or director accomplished this.

- Collect articles and clippings that you find interesting, particularly related to media issues or new technology and then respond to them in writing.

- Cut out ads and comment on them or analyze the messages given or the techniques used.

- Write down ways that you think you are changing your media use or perceptions as a result of studying media.

- Journal about your conversations about media or observations of other people's reactions as related to media.

- List media-related subjects you might want to explore in the future.

- Write movie reviews of films you see.

- Write a letter to a newspaper, TV station, radio station, or advertiser and post a copy in your log.

3. Video Production Assignments

Small groups are formed in the introductory course and students work together on four videos during the course of the semester. These include a how-to project in the studio, a narrative project to learn how to use a camcorder, a public service announcement, and a news package.

Production Preparation: Preparation and planning are the highest priorities. Nothing should occur at random in a technological presentation. Students must prepare treatment statements that force them to analyze objectives and outcomes before shooting. They must then conduct research in person and with the help of computers. Site surveys are required for all location work. This teaches them to work with adults and within limits. Students then write scripts and storyboards, schedule crew and talent, get release forms, organize supplies, and arrange for equipment.

After the planning stage, the students execute the production. Camera operation, shot composition, computer graphics, angles, movements; all must be carefully considered for the impact it will ultimately have upon the viewer. Technical considerations are very important. Students will have to properly light, white balance, check audio levels, and do the trouble-shooting that is inevitable. They must then direct the action and talent to arrive at the proper result.

Following the shoot, students must then begin the final stage of post-production or editing. They must edit the raw footage into its final form to meet the script requirements. They must be able to operate all the necessary equipment. This might include videotape recorders, switcher, audio board, computer character generation, time base correctors, or digital editing software. All operations must be synthesized correctly at this phase for the proper results.

All the technical aspects are learned in this setting. Beyond that however, the students must grasp the visual aesthetics. There is a subtle symbiosis between art and science when it comes to video production. The student must be both artist and technologist, paying attention to many aspects of light, color, texture, picture com-

position and also to decibel readings, waveform monitors, vectorscopes, and computer settings.

Content Warning: Students will model that which they have seen and enjoyed. Since many of them watch R rated movies, violence, and action films, the material they select may not be in keeping with academic goals. This can be nipped in the bud by putting a content warning on every assignment sheet. In the Bloomfield Hills Schools video classes, every assigned project comes with a statement about the kind of material that is acceptable for a school project. The following rejoinder appears on every assignment that is handed out.

Remember that your project may appear on the air or in a competition. Do not include any material that is inappropriate or offensive. Do not include vulgar language or sexual innuendo. Do not show minors drinking, smoking, or using drugs. Any other improper material such as racism, ethnic slurs, defamation, or endangering the safety of others will not be acceptable as part of this project.

Four Introductory Video Assignments:

1. How to Assignment

Students are to prepare plans for a five-minute demonstration video to be shot live-on-tape style in the studio. Teams of five are comprised of a Director, Technical Director, Audio Operator, Character Generator Operator, and Talent. The team must recruit camera operators from other groups. Topic choices might include how to do a simple procedure, how to use a tool or appliance, how to repair something, or how to prepare food. In a high school setting, the last choice is usually the most popular because the crew can eat the results at the end of the shoot.

Each group is given about one week to write the script, build the graphics, and rehearse. Then each group has one half hour to capture a 5-minute live-on-tape show.

2. Rough Narrative Assignment

Students are required to create a 3-to 5-minute narrative. It is to be shot using in-camera editing only. The video must be shot in sequence. It should be planned well in advance. Students must use a tripod, an external microphone, and a variety of shots and angles. Pacing should be tight and interesting, attempting to hold their viewers' attention.

The point of this exercise is to compel careful planning and discussion in advance of a production. It also teaches students to shoot conservatively, so as not to waste footage or memory. Not allowing a project to be edited in post-production will force students to choose only the finest material and only shots that advance the plot.

Narratives are short stories that inform or entertain. Careful consideration should be given to the overall message or theme. What is the point of the story? Employing literary techniques such as irony, metaphors, and symbolism is highly recommended. Students are asked to keep in mind fictional short story structure from their English classes. More details about narratives are discussed later in this chapter.

3. Public Service Announcement Assignment

Public Service Announcements are short, nonprofit messages that inform, instruct, or persuade. They are commercials for an idea rather than a product. They tell a mini-story visually. Students should make sure to get the viewers' attention, build interest, create desire, and inspire action. Students create a public service announcement exactly thirty seconds long that is edited using iMovie3.

Well designed public service announcements should always begin with a hook that uses attention-getting devices to grab and hold viewer interest. These might include an unexplained or unidentifiable sound or visual, a startling or provocative statement or picture, an elaborate visual effect, a rhetorical question which involves the audience, a well-known spokesman who is respected by the audience, a piece of music which evokes emotions, or a situation that immediately involves the audience.

The body of the production that builds one main concept follows the hook. The end of the public service announcement should always have a strong and memorable slogan

that helps the viewer remember the point. Pacing should be tight, interesting, and to the point.

4. News Assignment

The news assignment means covering a factual story about an issue or event. It is a straightforward accounting of the facts, lacking in interpretation, editorializing, bias, or sensationalism. To determine whether or not a story is newsworthy have students answer the following questions:

- Is it current or timely?

- Is it relevant to the audience?

- Is it close to home?

- What is the importance of the people involved?

- What impact will the story have upon the community?

- Is there a human interest factor?

People derive two types of rewards from the news:

- Instant—a laugh, a cry, sports scores, voting tallies, or weather forecast.

- Delayed—information that will have importance later such as news on the economy, health or science.

When doing a news story the facts must be accurate and the producers must double check the accuracy. Background research must be conducted. At least two sides of the story must be presented. The producers should get people's responses to comments made about them or their connection to the story. Release forms should be secured. Editors must be on guard to slanderous comments.

The basic questions to be answered in every story are who, what, when, where, why, and how. An interesting angle will help keep the viewers involved. Supplementary shots for the narration, called B-roll, are required. Lots of B-roll is necessary to make the story more visually appealing, improve the pacing and to help the viewer understand the story.

For this assignment the students turn in 90-to 120-second news packages that are edited using iMovie3. The story should start and end with an establishing shot, usually including the street reporter. This must be a 100% factual story. It should include street reporter stand-up segments mixed with B-roll, sound bytes, voiceovers, and natural sound. No ending credits or music are to be used. Titles should accompany shots of talent and interviewees. Graphics with names and titles must be spelled properly.

Advanced Video Production Courses

Once students have completed the introductory course they may take one of three courses depending upon their area of interest. They may select from a concentration in Sports Broadcasting, Advanced Media Issues, or Advanced Video Production. For the purposes of this writing, only the Advanced Video Production course will be explored.

This course may be repeated for additional credit. Due to this, students have individual assignments depending upon their level of experience. A novice Advanced Video Production student will spend the first 8 weeks of the course learning the digital editing software Final Cut Pro 4.0 and completing a practice assignment. A repeating student begins work immediately on productions, with the teacher serving as a mentor.

The ten digital video post-production editing suites are set-up so that no more than two students per class share a computer. Each workstation is comprised of a Macintosh G4 computer, monitor, speakers, and UPS (uninterruptible power supply). A total of three cameras are available for every two workstations.

Since managing computer memory is a primary concern with multiple users, it is important to carefully assign users to particular workstations and then to limit and monitor the memory usage of individuals. In this environment, if the instructor has four courses with two users each hour per workstation, there would be eight users per computer. Each user is asked to confine his or her memory usage to 10 gigabytes. If they need to exceed this amount, then it is highly recommended that they invest in a portable firewire drive for their personal storage. This should provide ample storage space for each user. A rough guide to memory usage is that one gigabyte of memory is needed for each 5 minutes of raw footage.

Post Production Suite Details: Eight users share a digital camcorder on a first-come, first-served basis. There is a reservation sign-up sheet at each workstation. Camcorders are checked out to students from 2:30 pm when the school day ends until 7:30 am the next day. Students may check-out equipment for the weekends from Friday afternoon until Monday morning since the studio is not open on weekends. Each user must sign an equipment loan agreement accepting responsibility for loss or damage and agreeing to return the equipment and accessories on time and with batteries fully charged. Equipment may only be used for class projects. This is to prevent taxpayer provided equipment from being used for entrepreneurial endeavors such as weddings or local advertising, and it ensures that the wear and tear on the equipment is kept to a minimum.

There are eight users per workstation sharing memory, but only two people sharing per hour. This allows one partner to write scripts or shoot video while the other partner edits. This is rarely a problem except directly preceding deadlines.

For every two workstations there is a spare camcorder for heavy usage times. This means at any given point the combined 16 students have three cameras available to them. Since students may only take their specific equipment, it tends to foster a sense of ownership and peer accountability, and as a result, abuse of equipment is virtually nonexistent. Occasionally a piece of equipment will fail or suffer damage, but due to having spare cameras, this has a limited effect on the productivity of students.

Advanced Video Course Structure:

All students work as independent producers. This method has proven to be highly successful in motivating students. Group projects seem to reduce student interest and effort. Individual projects give each student total ownership of his or her projects from the scripting to the shooting to the editing. This personal relationship with their subject matter pushes most students to set high standards for their work.

Advanced Production Assignments for Novice Students:

1. Practice Assignment

After completing the 8-week instructor-led Final Cut Pro tutorial, students are allowed to have one partner for the first practice project so that they may continue in the tutorial mode, combine their ideas and test their new digital editing skills. They are assigned a 1-minute segment of a larger video, a promotional video about the school with a target audience of incoming freshmen.

This is a subject they know very well and all shooting can be done during class in school. Therefore, it lends itself well to practice. Each duo is assigned a particular aspect of school life, e.g. sports, clubs, the media center, counseling services, etc. and are required to use all of their creativity and skill to make their segment informative and exciting for their audience. It gives them an opportunity to apply their newfound skills to a real project for an actual client, in this case the high school administration. This is a perfect project logistically, technically, and even emotionally, since they are not personally invested in the content.

Once they have completed this practice assignment, they are ready to move on to their individual pieces. A first-time student in Advanced Production will be required to complete four projects within the remaining 12 weeks. This is a minimum, but it is a rare student who can do more than this.

2. Personal Essay Assignment

For their first solo assignment, the students are asked to do a one-minute personal essay. There is no right or wrong way to approach this assignment, so it is ideal for the novice. It can't destroy their self-esteem because the end result is for them to decide. The sole objective is that they capture the essence of themselves. The subject matter couldn't be better for a beginner because it is what they know the most about, it is highly personal, and since it expresses who they are, they are emotionally invested in the outcome. It also allows them to concentrate fully on the technical aspects of the project since they needn't worry about content or narrative structure.

While one minute seems brief, it accomplishes several purposes. First, it requires advanced planning that otherwise would go by the wayside. In order for students to express all that they want to say they need to storyboard in advance. Brevity results in well-composed shots and tight edits, devices such as picture in picture and symbolism to make points that would have been achieved in a much more rambling way by a beginner. A time limit for the video also conserves memory, wear and tear on camcorders and play heads, tape stock, and the amount of time wasted making decisions on-the-fly while editing.

Audio tracks might include music or musical montages, combined with poetry, quotes, narration, sound effects, or anything that is meaningful to them. Students may create visual imagery that might include still photos, moving video, old family movies, graphics, important people, places, or objects, or anything else that makes sense. There should be a color palette and style that is reflective of their personality.

3. Public Service Announcement Assignment

Typically, public service announcements run 30 seconds. Because of its brevity this is another great project for students. The projects are short, require extensive research, scripting, and storyboarding, are pro-social, generate lively debate in the classroom, and are constructed exactly like a commercial. There are many organizations that desire publicity and thus provide the students with a genuine client. The client relationship means that students will learn to pitch a script and will be subject to sign-offs, revisions, and outside evaluation that gives them true school-to-work experience. Working with a client means the students must secure release forms and copyright clearances where applicable.

Public service announcements also lend themselves to contests. Contests are an excellent motivational tool for video production students and almost every contest has a public service announcement category. Each year the instructor researches and publicizes which contests are available to students, especially where cash prizes are offered. This is an excellent way for students to build resumes, enhance college applications, and to purchase their own digital equipment.

4. Music Video Assignment

Every student seems to want to do a music video. Due to the fact that professional music videos have multimillion-dollar budgets and big-time celebrities for talent, student music videos rarely measure up. This is disappointing for the student and for any potential audience. However, if some guidelines are given, the quality of the student projects may be greatly improved.

Students are directed to find a theme for the music video in advance and to storyboard their approach. This prevents students from throwing random footage together in a haphazard manner and calling it creativity. Rather, they should be expected to present a cohesive color scheme, style, storyline, or some other device that clearly ties each shot together into a unified piece.

For this assignment students are asked to confine their musical selection to 2 1/2 to 3 minutes. If they select a longer song, it can easily be faded out at some appropriate break. This allows them to gradually manage larger amounts of material. It also focuses the student's attention upon the rhythm and pacing of a piece. Students may go through a song and mark it up with markers that indicate where cuts should logically be made. This helps students estimate the amount of footage they will need to collect, something that is often underestimated. For music videos students are reminded that images should change every one to three seconds.

5. Mock Morph Assignment

As a creative exercise, the student is asked to think about symbolism and how visuals may tell a story absent of any underlying narrative structure. Students are instructed to take a single image that will be their first and also their last shot and to build a circle of connected images that link logically until the piece evolves back to the original image. Audio is not as important for this assignment except to provide a mood. The length is brief, perhaps only one minute. For most students this would likely mean a minimum of 20 shots.

A condensed sample of such an assignment might look like this: A baby, a pregnant woman, a closer look at her abdomen with a hand resting upon it, a different woman's hand with a ring on it, a ring, a shot of earth from space, an extreme close-up of the original baby's eye which then slowly widens to reveal the entire original photo of the baby.

There would be many more images linked in an actual project, but this demonstrates how a video artist can make visual connections and use cinematic devices such as pans, zooms, dissolves, and scans to reveal those connections. When executed correctly, these student pieces can be breathtaking.

6. Parts of a Whole Assignment

An option to the Mock Morph might be to approach a singular object from various perspectives of its individual parts. A colleague uses this assignment regularly to force students to look at an ordinary object in an extraordinary way. The idea is not to reveal the object until the end. Depending upon the object's size, this project may rely on extensive use of a macro lens. Emphasis for this project is on the camera angles and composition producing a sense of tension in the viewer to try to solve the puzzle before the last reveal. This seems to work best with something complicated such as a Zamboni, rather than with things that are obvious like trees.

Advanced Production Assignments for Repeat Students:
Advanced students are required to repeat some of the novice assignments, such as a public service announcement or they may develop a piece of their own choosing after careful planning and approval of the instructor. In addition to these projects they are required to produce more complex videos as outlined below.

1. Visual Essay Assignment

The goal of this project is to utilize the screen space as an artist would a canvas. Proficient camerawork and editing skills are expected for this assignment. Students are asked to select a singular abstract or tangible concept and then to explore every aspect of it in the most creative possible way they can conceive. Examples of topic choices are light, glass, curves, hands, black and white, small, motion, or a particular number, color or shape. This project might see heavy use of a macro lens, filters, and motion techniques along with a strong awareness of color principles. The goal is to concentrate on the pure aesthetics of the camerawork, lighting, framing, hue, and texture on the screen. As with the Mock Morph, the audio for this assignment should serve in a support role to set the mood for the subject selected. This is a beautiful and popular assignment.

2. Narrative Assignment

Once the student has extensive experience with camerawork, lighting, memory management, and digital editing, they may be ready to do a longer project. Only after they have proved themselves proficient are they permitted to undertake a short story project.

In order for a student to produce a short story, they must first write a treatment statement that details the objective, the audience, the resources to be utilized, the timeline, and a brief description of the storyline. This is then pitched to the rest of the class who at that moment assumes the role of potential investors to determine whether the plan for the short story has sufficient merit or has been planned out well enough to proceed.

Students take this process very seriously. The producer is often nervous to do the pitch, as fellow students are often much harsher critics than the instructor. As a result, however, it means the entire class becomes invested in the development and outcome of the project.

Once, the pitch has been approved, the producer has approximately six weeks to shoot and edit the short story. The anticipated length is 10 to 15 minutes. High school students are rarely able to handle a longer project, unless it is a talk show or sporting event. An important point for consideration for both teacher and student is that these projects often require significantly more computer memory than other projects do and this will need to be monitored closely.

The narrative must use literary structure. All of these stories should include:

- The Exposition. This is where characters, locations, and pertinent details are established for the viewer. There must be fully developed characters, including protagonist, antagonist, and supporting roles that are appropriate. There must be an evident moral to the story. Establishing shots are required for a visual story. These establish time, place, and changes in time and place for the viewer.

- The Rising Action. Here the plot starts to escalate and a series of events reveal the course of events that will eventually lead the characters to the next phase. Remember that most drama has a main character that is the protagonist or hero of the story. This is the character with whom the viewers identify or sympathize. Sometimes the antagonist is not a person but an obstacle or event that stands in the way of the hero's progress or success. Their relationship is developed in this phase of the story.

- The Climax. Here all the events come to a head and something occurs that changes the situation or character. This might be an explosive event or simply a powerful lesson or revelation. In any case, the protagonist is changed in a profound way and that is what makes the story meaningful.

- The Falling Action. This follows up on the aftermath of the climax and shows how all the characters and situations have been affected.

- The Resolution. This is the final outcome of the story.

Oftentimes, what is delivered in the narrative assignment is a very long introductory sequence that features some dramatic opening with emotional music and an individual student's name mentioned repeatedly. Then the project tends to fall flat. Students generally are not prepared for the rigors of a lengthy assignment. Realistically, one of the obstacles they face is the lack of reliable talent. It is difficult to develop a shooting schedule around talent who gets grounded, needs to study for the big chemistry test, or has to play in state finals. It is important to reserve this type of assignment for only the most experienced, organized, self-motivated and committed students.

3. Impact Piece Assignment

For the Impact Piece, students are asked to increase their target audience's knowledge about a given subject from a specific perspective. The piece needs to be factual, researched, and also take a stand. Contrary to most news programming which takes a rather neutral approach or tells two sides of a story regardless of whether each side has equal merit, this assignment forces the producer to pick a side of an issue and make a convincing argument for or against it. This requirement bolsters their commitment to producing a solid and relevant story because it drives them to win over the audience. Since this can only be achieved through a quality presentation with substantive facts, it raises the bar for the production value.

Grading Video Productions

One of the toughest aspects of teaching a subject such as video production is how to grade the work. Letter grades are virtually worthless in this arena, yet in a school where students live and die by their grade point average, they are inescapable. Therefore, a meaningful grading system must be developed and it must involve some sort of rubrics. One of the most helpful resources available is the 1995 book Using Rubrics to Assess Media Work in the Classroom by Chris Worsnop. This book provides a comprehensive look at how to design and use rubrics for media and includes many pre-made samples.

Video Rubric Categories: The rubric topics currently included in the Bloomfield Hills Schools video project evaluations are as follows:

Evidence of Planning
- Treatment Statement
- Storyboard
- Script
- Site Survey
- Release Forms

Camerawork
- Angles
- Composition
- Lighting

Audio
- Levels
- Quality
- Mixing and/or Effects

Editing Technique
- Efficient Use of Memory
- Rhythm and Pacing
- Technical Errors
- Continuity

Objectives Met
- Met Original Intentions?
- Target Audience Served?
- Project Guidelines Followed?
- Does it Make Sense?
- Met the Deadline?

True growth as a producer occurs not from letter grades but rather from the analysis that occurs during student showcases of final works. It is here that there is a real benefit to classes that mix novice and advanced producers. During project evaluation each student is asked to present his or her work by prefacing the showing with a review of the original treatment statement. They must walk the group through the intent of the piece, the target audience, what worked, what didn't, what they learned, what the perceived weak and strong points were, what techniques were used, and any other relevant considerations. After the group views the work, a dialogue and critique ensues about whether the project met its goals and what if any revisions are possible or necessary. In reality, a lengthy conversation about what works and what doesn't has a greater long-term impact on a student than a letter grade.

Conclusion

Building the video program in Bloomfield Hills Schools was an exceptional challenge. In the mid-1980s very few public schools had video equipment at all, let alone a video production curriculum. Mentors, model programs, and ready-made lesson plans were few. Trial and error has resulted in a program that has produced highly skilled producers. The students from Bloomfield Hills Schools have won cash, awards, and scholarships and graduates are now working in video or other technological fields. Many alumni are working in the telecommunications field for companies that include CNN, ABC, FOX Sports, cable affiliates, and corporations using technology. One former graduate wrote and directed a motion picture, *Hijacking Hollywood* released in 1996 starring Henry Thomas and Scott Thompson. He also has two programs that regularly air on ESPN. Another is the founder of the Chicago Underground Film Festival. Other graduates have made use of their video training in careers such as documentary filmmakers, communications attorneys, editors, web designers, network engineers, writers, and audio engineers.

My advice to teachers who wish to integrate video production into the curriculum is as this:

- Firmly establish your mission. What messages will you teach students to create? Will it be broadcast news? Music videos? Commercials? Daily announcements? Video Art? Once a genre or curriculum is established, then appropriated training can be devised.

- Get serious technology training. While it's true that many students bring technology skills to the classroom, it is imperative that the teacher be able to create examples, troubleshoot equipment failure, answer questions, and no less importantly, evaluate the complexities of the student work.

- Keep it short and simple. Students will handle 60 seconds better than 60 minutes of video. Quality beats quantity every time.

- Keep in mind it is always a work in progress. Plan on redesigning your course regularly. The software and equipment will change and so will your assignments.

- Keep what works, but always try something new.

- Don't leave out the Media Literacy component. Teaching production without teaching viewing skills is like teaching reading without writing; it just doesn't work.

One of the yet to be conquered obstacles is the notion that photography is art, film is art, and yet somehow video is not art. Video is still often relegated to vocational education status with the implication that it is about pushing buttons rather than creating beautiful and meaningful imagery. Without a doubt this view needs to change. Moving images on a screen are art. Learning production skills is an ongoing imaginative process, much like learning how to play an instrument. Students must come to view their progress as something that can and will continually evolve, as opposed to seeking a finite, right or wrong way to produce the art of video. This creative process always has room for growth.

The advent of digital editing with its affordability, availability, and its unlimited options for ingenuity has changed the field forever. Hopefully, art programs around the country will begin to include video in courses and competitions so that video's full potential as an art medium may be reached.

3

Talking With Video Artist John Toth in Central Park

Introduction

For the past 6 years, John Toth has been working with the Aesthetic Education Program affiliated with New York's Lincoln Center. As part of this program, Toth visited major educational institutions to teach college students how to use aesthetics as a model for teaching and learning. For Toth, a leading video artist, "It is all about looking, seeing, describing, analyzing, and interpreting the world, and finding one's own voice." When Toth speaks to art teachers, he explains "it is not about art activities." Instead, he says, "If you have been teaching for a while you realize that it is about connecting with an idea; it is about being invested in the idea." According to Toth, people should have real aesthetic experiences, and video is an excellent tool to access those experiences. Toth has exhibited his art in major museums and set up video art programs for Project Zero, and the Museum of Modern Art in New York. While we walked through the park on a cold winter day, Mr. Toth spoke thoughtfully of art, video, and children.

Ilona: What fascinates me about your art is your understanding of the special qualities of video.

Toth: Art speaks to action. What other aspects of the human condition are action? What John Dewey speaks about in *Art as Experience* is action. I think that is where video really shines. It is about action among people. You cannot do video by yourself. You have to point video out there, and you immediately have something captured. When I make a painting, I feel that it is very much in my little world. When I do a video, there are people and there is other involvement. It is no longer me and my little world—it is me interacting with the world. That is just what I learned. It is interaction that makes it so powerful.

Ilona: I recall you once said that when you do a portrait of someone you don't need a consent form, but when you take a video you have to sign an agreement. How does this issue of surveillance, and the power of video, relate to children?

Toth: There is something powerful, frightening, and enabling in video, especially for kids. I think it is a wonderful way to connect, because kids really thirst for this connection with one another. Yes, they really do! With the video camera in between them, they have a little bit of power to film somebody else. I see kids who are very quiet, and once the camera comes out, they become confident. Sometimes it is negative, when they pose or make phony faces for the camera and all of that.

Ilona: It is interesting that kids instinctively pose or perform for the camera, sensing that they are standing before something significant.

Toth: I am still impressed with how we know that we are in front of a camera. There is something eternal about it on some level. You are on record. I think of Rodney King, and the video filming that guy. Powerful! Beyond words, powerful! It is the media of the generation, it is their media. That is in itself something, isn't it? I am of the Howdy Doody generation. I was pacified with electronic media and its extensions like MTV. I guess that is part of my dilemma—3 seconds and we are bored. Start doing video and you are amazed what 5 seconds is, 6 seconds. You better have something important there.

Ilona: Time is an important factor in your videos. How do you explore this with students?

Toth: Video is the cure for long productions that kids want to do. Although my new rule is 1 minute. If it is more than 1 minute, I'm sorry, it's too long! There is a special place where we sit and watch a video with students. Three minutes is almost torture. The new standards now on MTV are 3-minute productions and five second shots. Three to 5 seconds—all the new stuff, the flash stuff, I cannot watch. The early video was on a single frame animation. Thirty frames go by in a second. I took my archive, and I put them all on 1 frame at a time. I figure you can see something in one second or 2 seconds. If you know an image you can recognize something in a second. That means 30 paintings go by in a second. I went through my archives in a few seconds. The whole archive goes by. Then I do it again, 5 seconds per image, 20 seconds per image. So, I am playing with loops. The information is always repeating in video. Something is always reoccurring, and it is reoccurring at different speeds. If you are a fast reader, you get it the first time. If not, the next time it comes around it will be a little slower. I am playing a lot with timing in video and what can be comprehended in seconds. Some videos I put a warning, that if you have epilepsy don't watch this.

Ilona: Children are always on the move. They are the real action artists. Is video art well-suited to fast moving and impatient students?

Toth: Most people are walking through museums with speed. They are walking through everything with such speed. Twenty-five years ago in *Ceramics Monthly* there was a survey done on how much time people spend in front of an artwork. It was something like 2.1 seconds per artwork. I don't know what video does to aesthetics, but I have had kids for half an hour in front of my video, "Mochianos: The City Rises." Their teacher was waving for the kids to move on the whole time, but they refused to leave until they were done. They were so engaged in the video piece, asking questions, getting a conversation going. "What do you see? What makes you say that? What do you think about that?" I cannot tell you how gratifying that is. There are not too many still images of an art work that kids linger with.

Ilona: What you are doing is the exact opposite in video time. You are working with short pieces which can be seen for half an hour. I know that you have used video to interview children about art works they are experiencing. Do you use video to slow encounters between children and artworks?

Toth: I believe video is the language between media. I'm not an advocate for video, or digital, or any of this. I am an advocate for communication, and ultimately the artist's goal is to communicate. I think communication is important. In our world today, it is more important. In the classroom, I don't care if you come from the rich kid's school or the poor kid's school. The same issue comes up over and over again: it is low self-esteem. I ask kids, "What do you see?" I don't tell them what to see. There is something about asking students what they see that is empowering. Video interview is very powerful. Tape is powerful. Anything that captures human interaction is powerful. Video is the ultimate because it captures voice. The community is on our tape. Video captures everything.

Ilona: How do you view editing? Is it a significant part of the art form?

Toth: Editing is another thing, and that is where the real scare is. Forget the video—it is editing the video. Because I have 165 SVHS, 80 digital videotapes, 10,000 on my Olympus, 20,000 on my Sony tapes archived—so what? It is data. What do you do with it? Editing is where I really think the skill is. Howard Gardner's multiple levels shine in the editing. The project we did in Buffalo had kids editing their material. As you say, that is hard stuff to do because we had five schools and five districts. Every kid could not be on a computer at once.

Ilona: How do you handle the logistics of artistic editing with a whole class?

Toth: We had teams. What I suggest is to break people into teams, to have different tasks and roles and different times to share computers. There are moments in a day where they have a certain type of activity. For example, one group is archiving, one group is getting material, another group is editing, another doing the sound for the video, one does props for the video, while others are doing backdrops. You know, you are just one person. When I do workshops and labs, there is only one of me, and I always ask for another tech person who knows the equipment and does this. For children who are learning to edit, I have groups of five around one computer, with one person who knows how to do it.

Ilona: There are a lot of buttons to push. Is the teacher expected to be able to answer all the technology questions?

Toth: Time movie is so simple. We had kids who didn't know anything, and in a short time they could make a speech go backwards. Okay, we have to go into the software! The basic stuff is there. You can flip audio files in both the Mac and in the PC, in the basic sound recorders. And, in every new idea that kids have, one or both of my technical guys I work with say, "Oh gee, I don't know how to do this." It is the kind of work where there is always something to ask. When I think I know as much as you can know about this stuff, someone will ask something I don't know. There is a humbling side about technology that changes all the time.

Ilona: What training did you receive and do you encourage experimentation in learning to edit?

Toth: No one trained me in any of this. I just pushed the buttons. Kids do that. My nephew William pushes the buttons. You ask adults to do that, and they freeze not knowing what to do. They have this fear. They feel they are going to break the computer or hurt it. Great, we can reformat it and reload the software. It takes half a day, and you clean your hard drive out and you start over. Kids have an advantage. Adults are afraid of pushing buttons. At some point, I think, the whole idea is letting go, to play again. Even technology requires play.

Ilona: What are some of your most memorable accomplishments?

Toth: Because it is something I had never done—I think the whole idea of working with schools and curricula ideas like the Pan Am exhibition was satisfying. You know, the Birchfield Center in Buffalo said that show had larger attendance than anything they have done. And what it was, I realized, was that it was so much about the community. People noticed that we filmed their street, and their home, that the video was about their community. So the success of a project is to take something vital to the community and turn it into a video project.

Ilona: Do you recall other student video works you have seen and admired?

Toth: My friend, Fred, teaches in Middletown High School, in New York. He started a project 10 years ago he calls, "Gangsters, Garbage, and Greed." His students used photojournalism with video, interviewing truck drivers that were dumping in a landfill. The project lasted over 5 or 6 years. The video was supposed to go on *60 Minutes*. Fred has been using video in the classroom as a tool for getting students involved. Video is not only a way to present facts. The police let these kids into the back room where they went through all the old tickets that went to this landfill, but never had a court appearance, They were all written off. They videotaped the officers, and the infractions.

They went through a book of citations that were supposedly lost. The police said, "Oh yeah, you can look back there," and they did. They filmed this stuff. They filmed the landfill, the sludge, the toxins in it. This was a high school class. A huge project. One kid did a video interview with the truck driver who dropped off the stuff, who no longer works there. Another kid was doing this little section with the police records. They edited over several years. It took a few years before they had a tape. Then they kept articulating the tape over the next couple years, adding to it.

Ilona: That was amazing work, certainly not the one minute video segments we started to talk about. Video interviews can become powerful creative and social tools. Was it all the students' idea?

Toth: Yes. I would have been so intimidated by the idea and secondly by letting a project evolve over years. There wasn't a finished product for each group, which is an idea that curriculums weave against—to actually let something evolve in these little sections. To me, there is so much in just one little interview that they did. The fine presentation the students did. They wrote the text, the questions for the interviews: Amazing. But just to take little pieces of something and have it become a whole. That also might apply to your idea of video in the classroom where everyone has very specific little parts of the whole. This is video you can use to interview and express yourself. I find when students are doing art in most classrooms they are mostly following the teacher's ideas. A lot of art room activities are teacher based. When you are talking about video, the kids are coming up with ideas. They are very invested in them. Video is very much about what is interesting to the individual child and the group as a whole, or in the context of their society. I think this is a great thing about video that should be considered even in teaching traditional art forms.

Ilona: Students' ideas are more prevalent in video art than in a teacher-designed painting lesson. So you feel that video lessons tend to be more student driven?

Toth: I say the whole curriculum should be student driven. It basically comes with letting students pose the questions. Ask them questions. What are they interested in? Teachers come to my workshops with agendas: we want to do impressionism. I did video projects with second and third graders at Lincoln Center. I've had students come to the planning session and I would say, "What are you interested in?" One principal said, "John, we got five more days for you to come back, and I want you to have the kids do what you do."

Ilona: So how does one elicit and understand students' video ideas?

Toth: What I realized is that the activity comes out of a conversation. I keep going back to activity a lot, because I believe that action is the key to the generating of ideas. I started listening to the questions I was asking kids. Teachers do a lesson plan that says we are doing perspective and points of view. They have this whole agenda. So, I am listening to the kids while I am asking them questions about Van Gogh, and one of the kids goes, "I wonder what it would look like if I was down there looking up?" Ohhhhh! There is the activity! Then I started noticing that in all the questions I asked, open questions, I am not trying to take them anywhere. What do you see in this painting? What if they don't talk about perspective in the painting? What if they don't see our agenda? I am saying, wait a minute! We made a mistake as teachers. If that is not where they are at, then let us see where they are. I start by making activities based on what they wanted to explore.

Ilona: Then how do we get from talking to kids about their ideas to their art?

Toth: So, when a student standing before the Van Gogh painting said, "What would it be like if I were down there?"—he was asking to explore an idea that could be realized with an activity. Oh, good, let's find a place in the painting where we can review the world. We can take out the video camera, and through its many possible angles of view, kids can put themselves in the sky, looking down, be the people on Van Gogh's street or inside the building looking out his window. Conversations and the camera allow the kids to investigate. I am realizing that it is us going back to communicating as a group, asking "What do you want to explore?" and they immediately are on board. The experience becomes theirs, too. Ultimately, we were doing perspective, but it wasn't through the teacher's lens. And, I went from student to student, in one class, and literally each portfolio, one on one with them, to explore their ideas.

Ilona: So that is where your student video portfolio idea came from?

Toth: In looking at one's art portfolio with a video camera it is all visual. Great! Students see what they are focusing on when the camera is on their art. You're a form person, you're the "formalist" in the group. Yes! It becomes this whole validating process of having students find a theme in their art. I thought it what a simple thing. Boy, was I an adult. I probably couldn't have answered questions of what my theme was, what my art ideas were about, when I was in high school. To me, having them actually look at their work and see, "I do this," was rewarding too. One of my motivations for using technology is that everyone should come to school with a disk and walk away with it full. That would be a requirement so that you take everything with you. It is a wonderful way to preserve your work.

Ilona: But, in your video portfolio studies you did not stop at observation.

Toth: What was rewarding, then, was to take their artwork and manipulate it. They started to manipulate the videos and stills of their images. One guy had a painting of a boat. The boat literally crossed the lake of someone else's painting. So the artwork was conceptually layered in the video. They let each other do that. They were manipulating their own and even each other's art. It became another form, another art to see what happens when you archive your portfolio; you see it as another life in the works. Keep painting, but maybe you will want to let your rock and roll band out and do something with your artwork and the rock and roll band. Mix that media!

Ilona: This is not a new art form, but a new way to look at existing art and what can be done in finding new relationships between media.

Toth: No, this is nothing new. It was all put together in theater. Wagner did it in his *West Spielhause*, building the first intermedia space, where the music, sound, and light were all performance art. Intermedia is all the senses in Howard Gardner's sense, all validated. You know, the scientist in me validates the artist in me, the dancer in me. There is a place for all of that, the whole self, rather than the one voice. My work with MOMA was led by Harvard Project Zero. It offered a way of asking questions, opening up communication. In a very nice way, we are always asking questions. I've got this really sweet video of these students translating their three-week experience with me into a painting. They performed! They not only performed, but they took pictures of all the artworks they made. So all of a sudden, their artworks were passed in front of the video, and then they had to make sounds for it. Many of them used the images they made for the past three weeks that walked by the camera. It was reflective of the process and the final product was this video.

Ilona: It is hard for me to describe your own video art. Could you talk about it?

Toth: It is video being projected into these fabric panels. They are not rectangles; they are odd shaped so some of the videos would miss one screen and fall into a back screen. For me, the little box, the frame of video is the problem. In my work, I am breaking the frame and making video be less blocked in a TV and more about the experience I am immersed in. Images are all around us. One spot is the weakness of video—it's glued to the TV.

Toth: It is so nice the equipment now. It's so accessible. The past couple of video years have been a whole new thing. Digital, you just bring it to schools, and the video looks good 90 percent of the time. CD-ROMs are smaller framed, cheaper, and everyone can take home their movies on a disk. Its a whole new world.

Recollections of Moving Image History

The trade was my tonsils for *Furfangos Kepes Konyv*, which translated from Hungarian means *The Magical Picture Book*. I consented to the dreaded tonsil operation because my parents offered to purchase my dream book of Hungarian children's rhymes, illustrated by strips of changeable pictures behind a cellophane screen. On my favorite page appeared an innocent artist ready to paint in a field. In the hidden second frame the artist is surprised by a destructive bull protecting his territory, and you can picture the results. I still have the book, worn from countless tugs on its delicate frame-changing mechanism. And I remember *Journey to Mars*, in English, my first pop-up book from the famous Jolly Jump-Ups series, which I received in a Care Package sent to Hungary. The moving imagery in these volumes made a lasting impression.

Arriving to this country as a child and not speaking English, I had many great American art forms shape my video life. I found fantastic action in the sequenced images of comic books, which I could follow without great difficulty. Saturday mornings I could feel like any other American boy enjoying the richness of playful imagery in the handsomely drawn early Warner Brothers and Disney cartoons. I suspect that these moving images were also an introduction and source of inspiration for many creative video artists today.

I don't remember exactly how or where I got my first Viewmaster® viewer, but I do recall the fun of building a collection of story carousels of the Lone Ranger, Roy Rogers, and other western heroes. My Viewmaster days ended when Fisher-Price introduced their Play Movie Camera that could flip images to simulate the feel of a moving picture. I loved the Fisher-Price camera and enjoyed building an extensive library of story cartridges. On vacations with my parents, I searched the souvenir stands, where, instead of postcards, I collected miniature cameras and TVs. Looking through peep holes, one could click to see pictures of mighty Niagara Falls or different views of the Grand Canyon—all captured in the little dark box. Among my favorite childhood objects, which fortunately remains from this period, was the windup Hop-Along Cassidy™ TV. The Bakelite television has a painted tin revolving story spool inside, rotating against a moiré patterned screen, simulating real movement. Fortunately I was careful with my toys and most managed to survive intact. I use them now in my art classes to illustrate my talks of the history of moving images.

I grew up loving the movies and dreamed of owning my own movie theater. One of the toys I wish I still had was a very primitive Soviet made filmstrip projector. I used to set it up in our living room, behind rows of chairs, facing the largest white tablecloths I could borrow from my mother. I offered snacks to friends willing to attend my film festivals and sit through a carefully sequenced series of filmstrips, with the family radio tuned on for background music. Having one's own projector was an exciting neighborhood attraction, and when I came to America, I found an unusual variety of hand held filmstrip projectors at fleamarkets, featuring Spiderman and Buck Rogers. My favorite toy was the Ideal toy company's, Drive-in Movie Theater, complete with cars, concession stand, and a working mini-projection booth. When I show my projector classics in school my students can't wait to play movie theater with me. We make our own tickets and movie posters and draw our own films on blank film strips—or paint over existing vintage film strips I find on eBay.

We did not have television in Hungary, but I heard of its invention and dreamed about what unusual moving pictures in a box would look like. I saw my first television set in Vienna, in 1958, in a department store window. My parents couldn't pull me away from the magic cabinet on the street. Since it was unusual for people to have a TV set in their homes, I spent many evenings with my family standing, along with others, in front of the store window. When we arrived in New York, television sets were large pieces of furniture with expensive price tags. My first TV was an old Dumont, found on the street, and carried up to our apartment with my friend Stephen. It had a large cherry cabinet, with heavy doors that opened up to reveal a goldframed glass screen. Unfortunately, the inner workings of the TV had been removed, but we were happy to move inside the cabinet to provide the action. This was my first screen acting job, creating characters, voices, sound effects, and backdrops for shows which began by opening the ceremonial curtain of the television cabinet doors. Our westerns and game shows were assisted by toy figures as extras and sounds we recorded from the radio. In art classes, to recapture the magic of television as I first experienced it, I still cut openings into large boxes or fold sheets of insulation boards so my art students can create their own TV shows inside. With a video camera on a tripod, I tape from the front of the television each show. As I grew up learning about and admiring the many forms of books and toys with moving images, television entered my life. It all became an exciting story to share in school.

Growing Up in a Media World

I was preparing to give a presentation entitled "Roger Rabbit at the Movies," at a convention of art teachers assembled in Washington, DC. The hotel elevator was equipped with a security video camera and monitor on which everyone on the elevator could see themselves. It became delightful entertainment for my young children, who pointed, posed, made faces, and made us miss our floor in the excitement. The odd camera angle and the closely defined space provided a moving artwork for the first-time video artists. What is your memory of the first time you saw yourself on a television screen? Prompted by the experience on the elevator, I decided to look for our first video camera. The children prepared for the important family purchase by bringing along their most significant others, toys and stuffed creatures for screen testing. I felt the instant attraction between kids and video when I witnessed how fast the children learned to use the store camera and how seriously they investigated its possibilities with the aid of the store monitor set up for viewing.

I ended up purchasing a Panasonic 440, which was one of the earliest portable home video systems. It consisted of two separate shiny metal cases that, to carry, required me to be a weight lifter. One case held the recorder and the other a separate playback system. The recorder was designed for shoulder wear, to be attached with a cord to the bulky camera. The pair took all of an adult's balance and strength to handle, but our children learned to team up to make many exciting episodes, converting their room into a television studio. My children grew up in a television world very different from my early Dumont days. They were born into a world with color TVs and raised in homes with multiple sets and ballooning screen sizes. They did not share my wonder about the magic of television. Their first memorable moments derived from being on television. My children were of the generation that first saw themselves moving on the screen, in the beginning playfully creating their own shows, and later, as teens, learning how to refine and edit their products on the computer.

At the store where I purchased the Panasonic, I looked at manuals for video equipment and discussed technical data with the salesperson. Meanwhile the children were busy playing with the camera. Even the youngest children quickly learn the basics of the media. Watch an adult use a remote control, versus a child navigating complex on-screen instructions with ease and confidence. Fearless and playful masters of technology, children are well prepared to be video makers. For young children, playing has become an on screen act. I used to build my dreams in sand, or on the floor with Legos and playing cards. But today's children envision their Lego™ fantasies and Sim Cities™ on computer screens. Plastic video cameras are found in Barbie™ toy boxes, used by future Cecil B. DeMilles to direct and film a cast of thousands from the toy box.

Video During the Early Teaching Years

When I first started teaching, I read about a video camera being ceremonially donated to our school. Its mysterious whereabouts was a closely guarded secret. The camera was only brought out for special occasions and closely guarded by our principal. Eventually video equipment came to be housed in our school library, where we had more orderly access to its use. I occasionally borrowed the camera and noticed that even its appearance spread a wave of excitement through my art class. Just seeing the camera on the teacher's desk started creative talk about its use. The children all had wonderful ideas about how they would use the camera, creative thoughts worth listening to. Even today when I start my lessons with the appearance of a camera, I solicit ideas about how the students would use it.

It was during my third year of teaching that I received a donation from Tyco™ of 12, light plastic, black-and-white video cameras in pouches, which had to be attached to individual VCRs. Having 12, virtually accident proof, easy to use cameras in the art room changed everything. Cameras became a regular classroom art supply, even available for occasional home loan. Still I found it valuable to begin using the cameras by deferring to kids' ideas, before I rushed to dream up video art projects for students. My best clues to developing a video art program came from viewing film gems from home: narrated tours of kids'

rooms, new toy setups, show-and-tell of new finds and collection displays, or a film study of the videomaker's garage sale. As children became independent filmmakers, they used the camera to record dramatized episodes of playing house, store, school, running a Barbie® aerobics class, or attending a teddy bear's birthday party. Other films offered wonderful introductions to important people from children's home lives. There were unique outdoor studies, especially the bike tour of the neighborhood with the camera attached to the handlebars. As the video revolution progressed during my teaching life, I developed a comprehensive elementary video art program to support my traditional media instruction.

Video and Art Teaching

Children looking at their artworks and themselves on our classroom monitor cheer. They simply love to see themselves on television. Video coverage makes an art lesson into an event. Videotaping a child's art is like presenting the artist with a prize, it is like a special gallery show.

When a child plays restaurant, it involves the rearrangement of home furnishings, the setup of play figures, drawing menus, signs, receipts, and creating make believe foods on a suitable table setting. Words, action sequences, and creations in home media are all part of the art, which can be recorded in its entirety on video. While adults preserve their art on slides, the playful marks and gestures kids perform in home chores and active playing have to be filmed. The photographer Cartier Bresson talks about capturing a decisive moment. Still cameras record a moment and a final product. Video has the ability to follow the art process unfolding. As an art teacher when I suggest a project to children, it is received as a challenge, explored as an adventure, tried on and changed a dozen times. If not for video, a unique record of children working through their art would be lost.

Video is a wonderful tool for capturing art in other media. Children look through the LCD screen to study their art, check its progress. They contemplate completed pieces and gather ideas for new works. Children interview each other, taking turns being the video-interviewer and the artist talking about their completed works. Before the camera, children become thoughtful speakers reflecting on their work, the plans they had, and the paths a work may have taken. In videotaped debriefings, children clarify their vision of the work, which may not yet be visible in the completed art. Adult comments and criticism of a child's work can completely miss the mark without knowing the young artist's intention and vision for it.

The message for children is clear—you are doing something important if your art is being recorded on video. Planning for a shoot requires dissecting the idea, visualizing steps, and breaking down a concept into scenes. As the steps for the shoot are built, so are deeper understandings of the art. Fresh ideas continue to surface when students play before a camera. In art classes, children are often asked to write about their art. For young artists, writing about their art work tends to be more perplexing than talking about it and having it reflected back on video.

The following examples of student videos were filmed in our elementary artrooms and others made by children who checked out classroom cameras to follow up on an art class experience at home. One of the valuable aspects of video is the ability to reach beyond the class, to take art ideas home and practice art as a full-time activity.

Student Videos: Drawing

Children's drawings are made by action, by active tool animators and tool movers. Video can illustrate a child's line making art. After class viewing of the *Life of Lines*, my animation of the property of lines, students film their own videos of line making including asking drawing tools to dance, casting fishing lines, and choreographing a chorus line of pencils. Students go for line rides with the camera, videotaping behind other artists's drawing tools, capturing their moves across a paper.

Scene 1: With music in the background a drawing tool starts to dance, leaving a trail of rhythmic marks on paper.

Scene 2: A tiny button, mounted as a steering wheel on a

pencil, is used to steer a drawing over hills and curves on an interstate map suspended between tables.

Scene 3: An elephant thumbs a ride. The hefty play figure hops on top of a marker, shifting its balance and drawing moves. The elephant's careful transport to the circus creates a distinct drawing.

Scene 4: In this scene the drawing tool saves the circus, by subbing for an absentee clown. Both the artist and the marker wear clown hats, demonstrating that even old tools have plenty of new moves, able to leave funny marks. Applause!!!!

Perspective and shading do not have to be learned as art formulas. With a video camera, art concepts can be modeled and set up to experience as fresh views. Simple sets can be constructed to film any art concept. In the following video, a student sets the stage for filming the changing views of objects in the distance and the changes of form bathed in different directions of light. The video is a study of how space and light can be depicted on a flat surface. The video shows different shots of a toy moving into the distance, then returning close to where the camera is positioned.

Scene 1: A yellow motorcycle rides along a painted highway, moving away from the camera and into deep space. Along the road, a city is laid out from play blocks on a long table. The changing views are narrated by the filmmaker.

Scene 2: At the farthest point in the distance, the cyclist turns and moves back toward the camera.

Scene 3: Several turns are made by the toy cyclist. By repositioning flashlights, the light over the play block city is changed for each trip. As the action is replayed on a television monitor, students record, through drawings, the drama of light changing on the play blocks and the shadows on the cyclist.

In the following scenes, students invent working models of new drawing tools and test their handling and line-making capabilities. Students shop for parts to extend the grip and handling of ordinary tools. The test track for their inventions is a white paper runway, rolled out in the center of the art room floor. Along the paper runway, a shopping site is set up, including a trunk full of objects such as horseshoes, skate wheels, pot covers, sprinkling system parts, old TV antennas, and assorted hoses. Velcro segments, unusual clips, clamps, fasteners, and tapes rest in tackle boxes, waiting to be connect to new drawing tools. Art is invention, and the video camera is a witness to the labor of young inventors.

Scene 1: An old-fashioned expandable TV antenna is outfitted with drawing tool attachments. Like a sleek silver bird, the antenna's wings are opened and retracted in the flight of a test drawing.

Scene 2: A worn umbrella with a long black tip gets a new pair of markers duct-taped to its point.

Scene 3: Spinning like a winged top, the open umbrella is announced on the ice as a figure skater in competition. It circles the ice, marking where it has been with elegant spirals.

Scene 4: A remote-controlled toy car hosts a row of black markers on its bumper. The remote controlled drawing tool is followed by a video camera on a skateboard.

Scene 5: In a group shot, children explain their inventions and proudly hold them up to the camera.

A generous gift from Panasonic Corporation has allowed my students to have video cameras in class. Classroom videos frequently inspire filmmaking at home. Students are trained to become careful and experienced equipment handlers for our home-loan program. The next homemade video captures what happened when a parent bought a bale of hay to use as a protective blanket over new seedlings. After an art lesson about drawing with real objects in school, the bright yellow straw pieces over the black asphalt driveway instantly revealed themselves as a natural drawing media. The camera started rolling to record the detailed straw drawings children made at home.

Scene 1: starts with straws being pulled from accidental piles, separated and re-arranged in to individual drawings.

Scene 2: shows a child framing a picture with straw.

Scene 3: includes dad coming along with a rake prepared to spread the straw. The child scrambles to save the straw formations by tracing around them with sidewalk chalk, while directing his sisters in video close-ups.

Convinced that the most interesting drawings can be found and don't have to be made, a student borrows the video camera to find undiscovered drawings on neighborhood canvases. We meet our line detective as she prepares her tool belt on which hang a flashlight, magnifier, brush, and note pad.

Scene 1: The videographer inspects outdoor floors for interesting cracks. She follows large-scale rubbings of sidewalk cracks, filming the most interesting line segments.

Scene 2: The camera moves around a wooden street pole with a wealth of graffiti carvings.

Scene 3: Like a pressure cuff around the big log, a roll of paper is fastened around the pole carvings to prepare for a rubbing.

Scene 4: The video ends with a large, graffiti portrait of a male face, spray painted along the lines of a cracked wall of an old factory building.

Everything in two-dimensional art takes place within a frame. A camera cuts away a framed segment of life; it is a fine tool to explore the challenges of framing which relate to other 2D media. The video camera frames a moving environment and keeps it in a frame of motion. Framing life's images in a video or a drawing is a creative act of making choices, selecting points of view, and focusing on meanings. To learn about framing, students explore the world through a viewfinder. From the viewfinder we move to the LCD screen, a more dramatic way to experience cuts, the framing edge, or the same setting from different angles. Children who played with the LCD screen have a significantly altered view of drawing.

Student Videos: Painting

In another video, a student uses a blender to make color shakes, highlighting the excitement of color discovery in painting. The art teacher's aging fleamarket blender is washed, decorated with stickers and nail polish designs, and set on a black, cloth covered pedestal. On a white paper tablecloth around the blender, clear cups are displayed on dark trays. Classroom seats are arranged in the round, like a theater lab. As the film begins, we witness the first batch of colors placed into the blender.

Scene 1: Mixing artists pour colors and after each pairing of colors the blender roars, mixes, and grinds to a halt.

Scene 2: Students add new colors to the mixture. Each color added is noted on the chalkboard.

Scene 3: The audience applauds the final mix and samples are poured into cups. Volunteers paint with the newly-created mixes on the tablecloth.

Scene 4: The artists even wash out the blender before a new round of mixing begins.

In the art class, we discussed alternatives to brush painting and how many designed objects are dipped in color and not painted with a brush. We researched the season's fashion colors in designed objects and tried mixing fashionable hues in plastic bowls, inspired from sample swatches of car colors. Someone suggested making a color meal by dipping make-believe food objects in our colors and filming it as a dinner party. To set the scene, students draped tables with white table cloths and arranged settings of white plastic utensils around white plates, white napkins—all placed over white placemats. Everyone shopped for food items, and as the guests were preparing to dip, filming began.

Scene 1: As the camera pans over a classy white table setting, trays with color-dipped objects (foods) start arriving.

Scene 2: Still wet and drippy, servers use photo tray tongs to arrange color-soaked erasers, rubber bands, and pencil shavings on plates.

Scene 3: A shot to the back counter shows students wearing paper chefs' hats, preparing foods by dipping them into colors.

Scene 4: As guests sit down to dinner, colors are brought to the table in which to dip utensils and table settings in building the crescendo of a color meal.

In our art class, we pay attention to all aspects of painting—the joy of mixing and discovering colors, the flow of live paint, and lively paint moving. Students constantly import new brush ideas and canvases they find, including suitcases, phones, and lamp shades. We speak of painting as an act of discovery, and students have created fantastic videos to illustrate their fantasies about the future of painting. The following home video made by two students who discovered a new brush and painting surface perhaps most eloquently illustrates this fresh thinking about painting.

Scene 1: We are inside a car, watching colors draining down the wide screen of a windshield.

Scene 2: After several drips of different colors, the windshield wiper is turned on to mix the colors together.

Scene 3: We cut to a child on his stomach on the top of the car, holding cups of colors, dispersing them with an eye dropper onto the windshield.

Scene 4: After the windshield is filled with brightly painted areas, both artists use the leftover colors to paint different parts of the car's body.

Scene 5: The final shot is through a window at the car wash as the painted canvas passes brushes and sprayers.

Student Videos: Sculpture

Before video, a great deal of children's sculpture making was undocumented and, therefore, unheralded. Children masterfully decorating their room, setting up displays of their many collections, animating play figures in complex settings— all this was considered just playing, having little relationship to real art or adult languages of artmaking. As more videos of children's playing and home inventions began to be made, many by kids themselves, the richness of children's sculptural invention finally gained appreciation. The children's videos described below are examples of the many unofficial sculpture activities of children. Just like authentic children's playing, each art room, or home setup of sculpture includes performing with objects, constructing and animating figures, and creating well-placed sound effects. Videotaping records it all, as a total artwork, as children give spirited performances before the camera.

Video captures sculpture projects, such as a classroom presentation entitled, "Derby Day." To prepare for the video, students construct festive tents by linking umbrellas over a grandstand made from pink insulation material and soda crates. They patiently pose a large cast of action figures on the viewing stand. Classroom tables are repositioned to simulate an oval racetrack. A well-appointed Lego tower looks over the field for the press and announcers of racing action. A parade is the lead scene.

Scene 1: Ladies parade their bonnets for the Derby Day fashion event.

Scene 2: Haircurler horses parade on the track, mounted by paper clip riders.

Scene 3: Students announce attending celebrities as horses move into a toast holder (the starting gate pulled in position by a mechanical cart, re-configured from old appliance parts).

Scene 4: The race is called, and players simulate action around the track.

Scene 5: Only horses are interviewed at this winner's circle, as animators and their voices are videotaped.

Video encourages young sculptors to play with all objects at hand. Sculptors can work creatively posing figures, trying out, and trying on, all kinds of sculptural forms. For example, following a lesson on ancient tribal masks, students search for examples of contemporary masks. A student's video films the results of customizing hockey masks, catchers' masks, surgical masks, and diving masks, all modeled by participants in a contemporary mask show. The video provides a visual album of a sculptural event.

Scene 1: A red potato sack is tried as head gear, with a fast-food cup holder as face mask. The camera looks into the mirror with the designer who adjusts and shapes the sack with red rubber bands.

Scene 2: Peep holes are drilled into a large foil party platter, as students try on the foil mask before a mirror.

Scene 3: A designer wraps scarves around an old bee-keeper's mask, to decorate it and hold it tight for wearing.

Scene 4: To enliven their entrance, guests shop inside an old doll trunk for play instruments, vintage noisemakers and flashlights.

Art is always a continuous process of taking apart and rebuilding. Video opens up our understanding of the art process, enabling us to see new forms emanating from the destruction or taking apart of old ones. Screwdriver-wielding sculptors take apart all kinds of things. While performing surgery on objects, students discover fantastic sculptural forms and new ways forms can be structured or assembled. Students taking apart mechanical and electronic forms, sort, save, trade, mount on pedestals and, of course, build incredible technological sculpture pieces. Before the camera starts rolling, the students dress in paper operating room gowns, masks, and surgical gloves.

Scene 1: The mechanical patients are wheeled in on a white, sheet-covered art room cart.

Scene 2: An assistant brings surgical instruments on cafeteria trays in sterile foil wrap.

Scene 3: The patients, alarm clocks, toasters, tape recorders, and phones, are prepped and disassembled with different screwdrivers.

Scene 4: Surgeons sort "organs" into a nearby parts box, and then the rebuilding phase begins.

Videos record children's playful hands and interests in handling all kinds of objects. The magic of form handlers is elevated when we see it on video, as children play with every form in their hands. They playfully manipulate forms, see all sides and all possibilities in them. While growing up, children learn not to touch, to keep their hands to themselves. This is even taught in school. Being videotaped and admired for active and investigative sculptural hands and handling, young artists learn to look for sculptural possibilities everywhere. In the following video, students empty their pockets and lunch boxes to build with lunchtime leftovers. Young artists demonstrate their appreciation for a wealth of environmental building supplies and find them in school supplies, classroom furnishings, and books.

Scene 1: Erasers of all kinds are pooled on a variety of revolving trays, boxes, and other bases. We watch as soft cities emerge.

Scene 2: Students slightly pull apart art room tables, creating a ravine, or river beneath them. Rulers and pencils join forces in the construction of elegant bridges for safe crossings.

Scene 3: Book builders stack small paperbacks on top of larger textbooks and encyclopedias, as we see fantastic architectural innovations. Architects stand by their model and are interviewed by a curious media.

Adult outdoor sculpture has had a great upsurge of interest during recent years. It took videos made by children to set the record straight as to who the first important outdoor sculptors are. They are the creators of exciting achievements. Capturing children's outdoor sculptures and play on video brings to the screen large samplings of important outdoor play and sculptural constructions using all types of outdoor media. Examples of children's outdoor art include building water tunnels and castles on the beach. Outdoor art includes rock gardens built from rocks collected by a stream or creating an outdoor restaurant with twig utensils and pine cone desserts. The next video was taken at a poolside by a child who recognized the importance of his art and felt a need to preserve it and share it with the art class.

Scene 1: Someone has an idea at the pool and takes inventory of building supplies; beach toys, floats, swim rings, and beach balls.

Scene 2: The construction of cabanas starts with an assembling of beach chairs.

Scene 3: Vaulted beach umbrellas cover the spacing of chairs, while colorful beach towels become wrap-around walls. Inflatable crocodiles guard the gate.

Scene 4: Interior comfort is provided by soft blow-up floats. Coolers become tables for food service. Builders talk on camera about their design and plans for expanding it.

Student Videos: Printmaking

One can always spot an exciting art mark; you can hear its sounds and feel its rhythm. When students print in our art room, it is anything but quiet. Jazz improvisations can warm up printing spirits; with stampers in hand we drum in the air and on the table. To see and hear connections between movement, sound, and stamped marks, we film lively printing events. In a video called, "The Printing Rhythm Band," passionate students perform with stampers as a musical group. With a variety of stampers, each band makes exhilarating sounds and leaves incredible marks on papers.

Scene 1: Students in straw hats dance, clap, and hit the surface of papers stretched over trash cans.

Scene 2: A band member rotates rubber toilet plungers in and out of large stamp pads, leaving rings of fiery marks on a paper-covered floor.

Scene 3: Print musicians test different sink stoppers for their sound-making talents. Using several different sink stoppers, students stamp marks over and around each other.

Scene 4: Revolving racks of old postal stampers spin into action, picking up the lead line of sounds and joining larger stamping instruments in a jam session.

Everyone produces prints by just walking. Prints are constantly being made by the pressure of our feet. We learn to appreciate the printed marks of intricate rubber soles of contemporary sneakers or the rubber tires of vehicles moving across environmental surfaces. To make the following video, our students actually built a road across the art room to experience walking over textures and taking prints of road surfaces. The video documents hard hats shopping in the classroom for roadworthy materials and laying down the textured highway. Video helps students see the uniqueness of an art process and how to generalize it to life experiences. In turn then the process can be presented it in interesting ways to other viewers. To make a video requires one to go beyond the understanding of a specific printing process to a broad awareness of textures and how they are part of daily events. Investigating art processes in a way that they can be visualized by an audience becomes a memorable learning experience for the young artist.

Scene 1: Students pretend to steamroll over a section of screening to lay it flat on the textured highway.

Scene 2: Builders assemble sections of brick for a stretch of the road, followed by alternating sections of textured sink liners, placemats and unusual doormats.

Scene 3: Patterned fluorescent light grilles are duct-taped to the floor, succeeded by squares of cork. As the road winds its way across the room, students already have their shoes off prepared to walk the textured mile.

Scene 4: On long rolls of paper, students create rubbings from the textured highway with crayon squares, wood, and leather marking tools.

In videos, the art teacher can observe how a lesson may influence students' thinking beyond the class. Video homework can invite students to follow up on an art concept, further explore it, and apply it to their interests at home. In the next video, a student deputizes his sister as a member of the camera crew, and they set out to capture his favorite rolling printers in action. The home video illustrates the process of art shopping, in this case looking for familiar objects to be drafted as printers. There is no question about the influence of the art lesson that officially designated everything as a possible printing tool and challenged students to look for printing tools everywhere. Videos are satisfying when showing how students apply classroom ideas at home. The video begins on the set of a kitchen table. The artist spreads a big peach-colored paper tablecloth over the table.

Scene 1: The student brings his Hot Wheels® carrying case to the table and unpacks its interior baskets packed with older race car models. He explains on the video that the older cars have rubber tires and better traction to serve as tabletop printers.

Scene 2: He shows the camera the different colored ink pads his art teacher allowed him to borrow for the experiment.

Scene 3: The student begins to line up his cars, makes a unique roaring sound for each, as he simulates race conditions across the paper tablecloth, including stamp pad pit stops.

Scene 4: The final shot frames his sister bragging about how she used to print without a stamp pad, just by riding her bike across puddles and printing tire marks on the driveway.

This upcoming video shows an act of dressing up or draping objects for printing. Perhaps in the same spirit as kids who love to dress up in towels, costumes, and masks, kids can also express interest in dressing up objects and landscapes. School printmaking, like most art in school, is in school scale. Outdoor printing demonstrates new freedoms in scale and requires a video camera to keep up with, to keep a record. In this video entitled, "Dressed for

Printing," we go behind a home to capture the fun of discovering art in patterns of nature and designed objects. Video is able to capture the dramatic performance of art making, what happens as Cristo wraps an island or kids wrap a tree.

Scene 1: A student is holding a step-stool, another is holding a long sheet of paper, and someone else is holding tape. Who is holding the camera? We see paper being wrapped around an oak tree with a handsome chest of bark.

Scene 2: As the "mummy wrap" is applied, all the students drop what they were doing—(happily not the camera man) wanting to rub the tree bark. Graphite squares render a detailed, black impression of each point touched.

Scene 3: "Lets do dad's car next," someone shouts, as the action shifts to another wrap.

Scene 4: Sparkly crayons are used to print from the old Ford logo on the hub cap and the letters on the license plate. The artists switch to graphite to rub prints of the body chrome and the surface ridges over the tail lights.

Scene 5: The artists give viewers a parting shot of the giant rubbings which are hung out on mom's laundry line.

Student Videos: Art Appreciation

From childhood visits to the Met, the artworks I most vividly recall are those I had discovered through hands-on interaction. I remember remodeling my toy guitar with cardboard overlays, designed to strum along with Picasso's *Painted Metal Guitar* of 1914. I hand video cameras to children as a tool for active involvement, leading to the appreciation of art works. To allow students a more relaxed place to practice their playing with art, the following videos were recorded at our university's Center for Contemporary Art.

The films are made by students not only for the purpose of keeping examples from the collection they can later go back to, but also to recall the experience they had with a particular piece of art. "Air Painters" is the title of the first video we will look at, depicting children in active and playful states of viewing art. The video explores a simple principle of examining art by remaking it, in this case children painting their art views in the air.

Scene 1: A child imitates the brush strokes of a painting. She examines the work intently, taking cues from it. She paints with a brush (a prop the teacher brought along) on a make believe canvas near the original painting.

Scene 2: Students are challenged to estimate the speed of the brush strokes and feel their intensity, as the artist may have made them. They try to make marks in sync with his original gestures. Students paint in the air, feeling the mood of the artist as a rhythmic brush mover.

Scene 3: With just a cushion of air between two artists, students imagine themselves dipping into the artist's original colors, one at a time, making believe the paint is still fresh.

Scene 4: In the final frames of the video, students move brushes across the original art and try to reach the painter's color spots, as they may have been laid out in different parts of the work.

A second video starts with a make believe sale of hand viewers. It is entitled, "Do You Want to Try a Hand Viewer?" In this video students teach each other different ways of using their hands and arms to assist their eyes in seeing a painting. Art works are looked at in detail, in segments, and sequences, with a variety of hand framing. Hands provide many possibilities for playing with different views of an artwork. Everyone in class searches to invent new ways to see art and demonstrates their discoveries before the camera.

Scene 1: Placing his index finger under his chin, the child's head rotates, as if it were sitting on a socket. Animated by the "finger tri-pod" we see students looking at artworks in gentle sweeps and in slow motion, up and down. They describe what they see in their individual sequences.

Scene 2: A student invents the "finger frame" and demonstrates it to others. He joins two thumbs and pointed index fingers to make a partial enclosure. Students try this viewer and describe the artworks they framed.

Scene 3: Topping the small finger frame is a full body frame. With hands pointed in the air and bent elbows to the side, a body frame is demonstrated by another child inspired by the framing idea.

Scene 4: The specialty of another viewer is seeing art through a series of openings between interlaced fingers. The student says the art seen between his open fingers is like watching moving frames in a video.

Scene 5: Children inspect the art gallery while holding imaginary telescopes and binoculars. Walking around with cupped hands, they focus to extend their views with the longer lens of another hand.

Scene 6: In a final shot, everyone finds a moment of movie fame, demonstrating hand viewer inventions. We see blinking eyes hidden behind raised fingers and hands used as blinking semaphores and frames to view art.

In another video entitled, "Body Sculptors," we see a series of large figurative sculptures in the gallery. As students sense the implied moves of the sculpture, they spontaneously take sympathetic poses. The video explores the relationship between the sculpture and the viewer, as the children wonder into sculptural space and try out active viewing modes. Students take turns working the camera as a way to investigate the sculpture, move with it, and enter its material and space.

Scene 1: Children sneak up behind a sculpture, posing as its double.

Scene 2: A student who is lying on the floor slowly rises to become the shape of a standing sculpture. Once erect, another student uses a flashlight to project well-defined shadows of both forms on the floor.

Scene 3: Playing Twister, one student creates flashlight shadows of a piece, while another tries to fit into the shadow.

Scene 4: As if sculpting with clay, a child gently moves the hands and arms of another child, molding, positioning, and turning him into the sculpture appearing before them.

Scene 5: A student is chiseling a sculpture with paint stirrers, scooping out openings, rounding edges, and learning about the form. The chiseling moves are inspired by the textures and openings of the sculpture at which he is looking.

A video camera is a playful viewer, helping students to see art works in new and exciting ways. Videotaping breaks the silence in viewing art and invites participation. Students will say amazing things about art for a video. The following is a video scrapbook, a student edited recording of conversations about art by young artists. Prompted by different role playing situations, the video illustrates a free flowing of student ideas and opinions about the art in the gallery. We learn about art by talking about it, expressing our feelings and opinions to the camera.

Scene 1: A student says that the piece of sculpture in the room has a nervous effect, like it would fall apart and its debris would cover everything. A shaky camera recording of the piece, along with the comment, recreates the feel of the sculptures crackling art surface.

Scene 2: Conversations about how a painting would look if it were hung in a different way clues the camera holder to film the piece upside down and even try different angles of viewing the piece.

Scene 3: Finding that students are having a difficult time responding to a conceptual piece of art, the camera person decides to turn the scene into a roaming interview. For a collage of opinions, students become interviewers, asking everyone in the gallery, including visitors, the guard, and the custodian on duty, for input.

Scene 4: In the final cut, the camera person provides his interpretive creative views of the show. Every control of the camera is exercised to create blurred frames, slow close-ups, and views of works in black and white, and sepia. The video is recorded with a blank sound track, and everyone back in class is invited to narrate his/her descriptions of the show.

The final video was made by a child while visiting the University of Kentucky Art Museum with her parents. Besides the video camera, she took along simple objects she compiled that kids can easily pocket and take with them to a museum. They are part of her kit, designed to make museum trips more memorable. Thanks to her parents who assisted with props and filming.

Scene 1: Taking out different sized funnels from her painted Art Viewing Bag, she walks the floor, narrating what she sees through funnel viewers.

Scene 2: A key chain flashlight is used as a pointer following the graceful lines of a painting. The camera follows the flashlights journey. With the light pointer in hand, our guide points out all the unusual things she can find in the painting.

Scene 3: The student uses a Garfield™ magnifier from her Art Viewing Bag to look at details in art works. Her finds and narrations are recorded on video tape.

Scene 4: Finally, we are shown how a piece of bendable wire can help interpret a drawing. The student bends the wire to follow the lines seen in an art work. She says the bended wire will be saved and made into jewelry.

Scene 5: In the final scene, we see a demonstration in using the new museum wrist-sketch pad, a Velcroed Post-it™ pad attached to her watch.

Television Watching as Video Homework

When my daughter Ana was nine, I came into the living room to find her testing her new tub crayons on the family television set. She made sketching look easy, as she effortlessly followed the action of her favorite character, studying the movements on screen by drawing along. Ana never met John Nagy, the famous childrens' show host in the 1950s who made TV screen drawing famous. Nagy prompted his many young fans to draw on their television sets over a layer of plastic specially ordered for the show. Television is said to keep children from doing homework, suspending young viewers in mindless states, so it is unusual for our video classes to be regularly assigned television homework.

Yet there are important video concepts students can observe and practice by watching television in active and participatory ways. I assign television homework to encourage young video makers to build their perceptions and ideas behind the camera by watching the works of camera artists. Many filmmaking concepts that are difficult to talk about can be experienced in daily television viewing. While it is easy to be swept into mindless watching, our studies have specific goals and tasks. After each video class, we practice an idea by doing television homework, making use of time when kids will tune into television anyway. The following is a sampling of assignments for television homework.

Goal: Learn about script writing, specifically how a film is divided into specific scenes, each with its own characteristics.

Task: Watch an evening television show as if you were preparing a script for it. Divide the show into scenes, numbering the scenes and noting when they change. Note and mark changes in lighting, sound, mood, and action.

Goal: Study the variety of camera shots a filmmaker uses in moving around a figure inside a rectangular frame.

Task: Take a stack of paper and sketch the head shots of a TV news anchor. See and draw how the anchor's image is moved around the screen by different camera shots over one 5-minute segment. Do the same with two people engaged in conversation on a talk show.

Goal: Record details of action sequences and determine unique qualities of filming fast-paced action scenes.

Task: Prepare several pages of small, rectangular television style boxes in which to draw or use what is called a television pad. Follow the action of a fast-paced police show, drawing continuous sequences of action and the quick changes of "models." Start and end your assignment with a commercial. Sketch in special light changes you notice in a scene.

Goal: Students are encouraged to bring home a camera to get used to playing with its controls. One way to do this is to follow live television sequences with the camera. Trying to parallel the camera work in television sequences with the video camera following live action, including close-ups and wide angled shots, allows students to get used to operating the camera's controls through an entire scene. Having the video camera mirror filmed scenes provides a new way for students to view television.

Task: With your video camera facing the screen reshoot two minute segments of a favorite television show. Replay and analyze your recording in the LCD screen of the camera. Write down as many visual ideas the camera person used in each scene as you can observe.

Goal: "Critics Corner," is a general challenge for students to become aware of the visual qualities, the beauty of a scene, and to be able to take notes on these qualities for future inspiration and reference.

Task: Watch and criticize how a show is filmed. Keep a notebook where you sketch and write down the unique visual qualities in scenes you admire. Be aware of the camera person as an artist and note how she/he paints a scene.

Goal: Recognize how a soundtrack is a significant contributor to a scene's effectiveness.

Task: Record 2-minute segments of an action TV show with your video camera. Replay the scene with your sound turned off. Add your own sound track with a tape recorder or synthesizer.

Many homes today have a video projector instead of a slide projector. These small but incredibly sharp and powerful projectors can project on an unprecedented scale on any surface, including pillows, ceilings, socks, and buildings. In the art class and at home we need to challenge children's creativity in looking for and making new screens— and in designing screening events to show home art in school and school videos at home.

A Final Cut

Children are the original action artists. Their lively moves, investigations, and animations of toys and found objects are well-suited to the action of video. Children's home plays and inventions, their artistic approaches to home chores, are art media just gaining recognition, because they are being recorded and imported to larger audiences on video.

What cannot be scheduled for show-and-tell, important areas of kids curating and collecting, can now appear in videos. We call our art class "The Kids Television Network," where we feature a different kind of programming, built upon children's art and media experiences at home. We look at painting by revisiting children's kitchen art, sculpture by references to kids experiences with action figures and play setups. Our cooking shows revisit the time when children were great kitchen artists. Our travel show correspondents visit kids' rooms as art studios worthy of notice. Kids' versions of the "Antique Road Show" feature authentic children's collections. Birthday party videos are the frontier of new art works, as children create and film the parties they always dreamed about

Video is the perfect art media to capture the lifestyles of todays active children. Children view the world from moving cars and school buses. All day children are chauffeured to and from school, lessons, and events. Even as kids' lives speed along at an amazing pace, they have not forgotten the joys of looking down and finding interest in the cracks of a sidewalk, the wildlife of bugs in the cracks, and the found treasures in nature and the environment. Video can be used as children's magnifying glass, collection jar, and travel art bag. Art classes can prepare kids for the future by using video to make every day an adventure in seeing, every trip a safari, and every video tape a wealth of recorded finds. There is no doubt if you go to any museum that the art world has embraced video. Those involved with school art need to be more active in this area, helping children expand the palette of crayons and paint to include other ways of functioning as artists today.

Illustrations

"TV Toys" from Szekely's personal collection.

Harold Olejarz

Capturing the Moving Present

5

Digital Video in the Art Room

Introduction

The present is an ephemeral moment caught between the receding past and the imminent future. For centuries, artists have captured and preserved images of their present by drawing, painting, or sculpting what they saw. In 1889, the birth of a new technology gave rise to a new method of capturing and preserving an image of the present, the photograph. In 1859, fifty-six years later, the Frenchman Louis Lumiere invented the motion picture camera, and projected the first moving pictures. In 1951, the first video tape recorder (VTR) was used to capture live images from TV cameras and save them onto magnetic tape. Sony sold the first VCR in 1971, beginning a series of technologies that resulted in contemporary digital camcorders and video editing software which now enables everyone to produce professional quality video projects. Technology has come a long way. It has changed the possibilities of image making in the art class. This paper is about the use of video in public school art classes.

Introducing Art Concepts to Students Embarking on Video Making

Before beginning their first video project, there are standard art teacher topics to present to your students. Composition, point of view, and lighting, are three topics that art teachers often discuss with traditional media classes. In digital video, these are also very important issues.

When recording video, students have a tendency to center subjects in the camera view finder. The rule of thirds, taught to painters and photographers, should be emphasized to improve the composition of student video projects. For decades visual artists have been using point of view in traditional media to enhance the meaning of their images. Exemplars of point of view taken from paintings, prints, and drawings, could easily be used to demonstrate how point of view can be used to enhance video. Traditional media may also be used to help students understand the role of light in video. As you can see, some of the most important things art teachers teach in traditional media classes are also integral to digital video classes.

The immediate feedback of seeing an image on a TV is a fun and effective way to teach composition, point of view and lighting. I connect a DV camcorder to a TV monitor and demonstrate to students the difference between good and bad composition and how to frame a subject. Also, moving a camera from one angle to another is a great way to demonstrate point of view. Working with the available light in my room helps students see the best way to light a subject.

Just as in a traditional media class, when you begin a project using a new tool or technique you review and demonstrate how to use the tool. DV camcorders are easy to use and students quickly become comfortable with the technology. It is important to stress keeping the camera steady and remind students to avoid too much camera movement. Students should also be encouraged to use a tripod, if available. If the students are interviewing someone, they need to be reminded to get as close as possible to their subject so that the camera's microphone will get good sound quality. I often remind students that the zoom feature works great for the video but not the audio.

Advice on Managing a Video Program in an Art Room

Managing nine digital video cameras with several classes using the cameras each day has led me to develop a system of tape management. If you have one camera or several this approach should work well. In brief, each class has their own tapes and the tapes are labeled accordingly, i.e. Period 1 Tape 1, Period 1 Tape 2, Period 2 Tape 1, and so on. The nine cameras that I use with my students are also numbered. Students using Camera 1 are instructed to use Tape 1. This makes it easier to isolate tape or camera problems and keep track of equipment.

Students are encouraged to tape one day and export their video to the computer the next day. If a group has not exported their video from the DV tape to the computer by the end of a period, students are instructed to put a piece of masking tape with their names on the tape cassette box. This prevents other students from coming in the next day and taping over another group's project. I have found that it is best to have students export their video onto a computer after each period of taping. Often students notice technical shortcomings like bad lighting, poor composition and poor sound quality after their

first day of taping. It is best that these problems are caught after one day's taping rather than after they have spent a week taping. This is also a good opportunity for the teacher to keep track of how the students projects are coming along.

When students complete drawings, paintings, or graphics projects, art educators exhibit the work on bulletin boards, or in display cases. Often a completed project is held up, or put on display to generate a class discussion. Students are also encouraged to take their work home to share with friends and family. Video projects also need to be displayed, discussed and shared with friends and family.

I have found that the best way to share completed video projects with a class is to have students export completed projects to one video tape. When all class projects have been exported, that tape can be shown to the class during a class film festival. After each video project is shown, teachers can lead class discussions that reinforce learning and help students develop appropriate self-assessment and evaluation skills.

Students should be encouraged to make copies of their projects to take home. Technology is available to transfer student projects to VHS tape, DVD, and Video CD formats that students can take with them. Video projects may also be exported to formats that can be displayed on the web and/or e-mailed to others. I have posted exemplary student video projects to my school web site with proper permission from parents and district administrators. Another option to consider is to present student work on local public access cable channels. Taking advantage of all of these options will excite students about their work and help gain support for your program.

Artist Interview Project

The first project I assign my students is an interview project. This is ideal for students working in groups of three; one student is the host, the second is the guest, and the third is the camera person. When I started teaching digital video I gave students the freedom to choose a topic and interview one another about that topic. The interviews ranged from what the students did on their summer vacation to how they dealt with the transition from elementary school to middle school; some students even chose to interview teachers. Generally, the interview projects, like most of my students projects, are two to three minutes long.

In an effort to bring more art content into the students experience, I now have students select and research an artist. A student plays the selected artist and is interviewed about their work. The students are also required to download images of the selected artist's work and incorporate the images into the video. This has turned out to be a great way to have students learn art history.

Before students begin taping I instruct them on setting up camera angles for their interview. The interview begins with a shot of both the artist and the host. This is called a two-shot. In this shot the host introduces and welcomes the artist. This is followed by alternating one-shots of the host asking questions and the artist responding. The interview ends with a two-shot of the host thanking the artist.

Video editing software makes it easy to cut and paste video clips. Therefore, I have found it best to have students tape the host asking all of the questions first and then tape the artist responding to the questions. The two-shots for the introduction and closing can be taped at the start or the end of the above. Taping in this manner helps students understand that video need not be shot in the order that it is presented. It also helps students gain an understanding of the concept of non-linear editing, shooting video out of order and then assembling the clips in the proper order. Students will have an easier time assembling their clips in the proper order if they name their clips. For example, the question clips are labeled Q1, Q2, Q3, ... and the answer clips are labeled A1, A2, A3, ... Once all of the clips are identified they can then be placed in the proper sequence. When students try to tape an interview in real time with one camera, the resulting video is marred by the camera moving between the host and artist.

When the projects are completed, they are presented to the class. Occasionally, students are so impressed with their peers' projects that they applaud at the end of the video.

Following the presentation, we have a class discussion about the video. I have students begin by discussing their appreciations; what they liked about the video. We also discuss the content of the video; what the students learned from the interview. When the class is done with their appreciations, I then allow students to make suggestions for improvement. Students often focus on the technical things and point out problems with sound, lighting and/or composition. Class discussions about video projects help reinforce learning and give students insight into what makes a quality video.

In the future, I may have students play roles other than artists for an interview project. They may be collectors, critics, historians, or the people represented in a painting or drawing. It might also be interesting to have students play two artists discussing their work with one another.

Video Tapes of Art Techniques Made by Students

My former colleague, Frances Hersh, taught two sections of Digital Video to seventh-grade students. She had students create instructional videos. Her students produced videos on everything from how to cook certain dishes, to how to tie your shoes, and unlock a locker. The instructional format is an exciting way for students to combine traditional art materials with new media. Students may create instructional videos that explain art techniques like working with watercolor, or pastels, or how to build an armature, or make a linoleum block print. In one case, a group of eighth-grade students in a class we team taught created an instructional video on origami. An art educator teaching a class with one video camera may select a group of students to create an instructional video on the traditional media project their class is working on. For example, if the class assignment involves printmaking, a group of students may tape the teachers' demonstrations and produce an instructional video on printmaking that may also include interviews with students about the process and their resulting prints. Over the course of a semester, a teacher may have different groups of students document different projects. This approach could yield an invaluable resource of student produced instructional videos.

Student Documentaries

Students can also take a documentary approach to digital video projects. They may research an art movement, or artist, and create a documentary on that artist or movement. This can easily be done by downloading still images from the internet, or scanning images from books. The still images may be imported into i-Movie or other video editing programs. Voice overs and additional video footage may be added to create a documentary in the style of Ken Burns. The documentary approach can also include living artists. Students can interview and tape professional artists, comparing their styles of working. Students can use the video studies to analyze how artists are affected by environment, culture, resources, history, and politics. Digital images of the artists' works may be used the video. Once the students have completed editing the videos, they may combine them and create a DVD.

Student Videos from Poetry

When I began using poetry in my digital video classes, I realized that poems provide a wonderful structure for digital video projects. The results approach Performance Art, the poem, being the script for the performance. Incorporating poetry also adds an interdisciplinary aspect to the project.

The poetry project begins when groups of two to four students are asked to find a poem they would like to dramatize. Once the poem has been approved, the group must find a way to dramatize each line of the poem. Students may also use still images downloaded from the internet to illustrate lines of their poem or better yet create images of their own in traditional, or digital media. Once the students have completed taping their dramatizations and finding suitable images, they construct their video. The students must add the text of each line of the poem to their video clip, or still image. If they did not speak the line of the poem when taping, they may record the line as a voice over. The resulting project is a true multimedia interpretation of a poem that includes images, sounds, and text. Getting the advice of language arts teachers for suitable poems for your students will make this a successful project for any grade level.

Student Commercials

Digital video can also be used for the ultimate commercial art project, a TV commercial. Students can take on the challenge of using 30 or 60 seconds to communicate a message and sell a product in an entertaining way. Also, this project can easily incorporate traditional media if students are required to create a package design and then use the package in their commercial.

The TV commercial project may be started by a class discussion of favorite commercials, and why they are successful. Teachers can easily tape some commercials and have students analyze how the commercials sell the product and use the media effectively. Once a set of criteria for a good commercial has been established by the class, groups of students can then decide on the product or service their commercial will promote. Each group should gather or create props, write a script and tape and edit the commercial. Limiting students to 30 or 60 seconds helps students learn to be clear and concise. This project may also be modified so that students are asked to create a Public Service Announcement, PSA, or a commercial for a school club or activity.

Utilizing Closed Circuit and Local Public Access Cable Broadcasts - Star Students

Television production offers another way to incorporate video into an art curriculum. Some schools now have the opportunity to broadcast closed circuit television shows within their school or over a local cable public access channel. For the past 3 years, I have been producing a daily morning show that is broadcast live throughout our school. In 2003, we began broadcasting to our community on our local cable system. In developing this show, I realized the powerful educational opportunities of video and broadcast TV and developed a program called Star Students.

Star Students is an innovative program that realizes the school morning television shows' mission—to present the learning, activities, interests and creativity, of all members of the school community. The school TV show empowers students as TV show producers, and also enables students to become school stars as performers and technical support personnel. Star Students helps students and the school community realize the full potential of video and television as an artistic medium and educational tool.

Students shine in front of the cameras and behind the scenes. Students host the TV show, read announcements, interview guests, and run the cameras, computers and other equipment used to produce the daily show that is broadcast throughout the school and on our local cable channel.

Most importantly, students produce and present features that highlight the artistic talent and outstanding achievements of students. The school morning shows feature students interviewing student government officers, dancers, artists, team captains, school club members, students involved in community service projects, teachers, administrators and community leaders. The outstanding achievements of students from all grade levels, faculty and community members are presented to and shared with the entire school and our local community every morning.

Prerecorded student-produced features focusing on students and the community as a whole are also an integral part of the show. In these features, students from all grade levels have dramatized poetry, combined music, dance and drama, discussed their art projects and demonstrated their ability to use digital video and imaging to present compelling narratives.

This sharing of outstanding achievements and exemplary work helps the school communicate high standards to all its students and encourages a dialog among the school community that focuses on the creative work of students. In addition, the value of the acknowledgment students receive from their peers after a school TV appearance is priceless.

Star Students builds students visual communication, performance, language, technology, interpersonal and planning skills. Star Students also encourages students to work cooperatively and seek out and document the talents of their peers. The program instills a sense of professionalism in students and gives students an opportunity to use technology in a practical manner. The program also creates a dialog among the members of the school community that focuses on the achievements of students by using TV as a school-wide multimedia experience that goes beyond simple announcements or written acknowledgments. Televison has a tremendous impact on our culture and our school's daily morning show continues to have a tremendous impact on the culture of the school.

Summary

For centuries, artists have used the tools and techniques of their time to create visual images in a variety of media ranging from drawings scratched on a cave wall to images displayed on the latest flat screen monitor. Teaching students to use traditional media such as drawing, painting, printmaking, sculpture, and photography has given art educators a firm foundation in the visual communication skills that are essential to creating outstanding video projects and producing visually engaging TV programs. Developments in digital video and video editing software have given teachers and students the ability to produce professional video projects in their art classrooms. It is only natural that art educators now use their knowledge of visual communication to take full advantage of the possibilities of digital video.

In this essay, I have offered several ways for art educators to use video. One way is to create instructional videos that teach students a process or skill, how to create a linoleum print or shade a sphere, for example. Digital video may also be used to engage students in art history. The artist interview project discussed earlier is one example of how art educators may use a video project as an alternative to a written report. Students may also create their own documentary video on an art movement. Imagine showing your students a documentary on impressionism created by their peers.

Video may also be treated as an art medium in and of itself. Students may work on short films that they develop from story-boards. The work of video artists such as Bill Viola and Nam June Paik may also be presented to mature students, who may then be assigned to develop their own video art.

Over the centuries, advances in technologies have given artists new opportunities to create images that reflect their times. Art educators can now give students the opportunities and training that will prepare them for our media rich, technology driven environment, by incorporating video into their art programs. In 1895, a little over one-hundred years ago, Luis Lumiere used a suitcase-sized machine to film, process, and project the first motion pictures. Lumiere's suitcase has now shrunk to the size of a DV camcorder and laptop or desktop computer that can easily fit into any art room.

Digital Video Assignment Sheet & Evaluation Rubric

Student(s): _____ _____ Period: _____

Description of Project: _____

_____

Approved by: _____ Start Date: _____ Completion Date: _____

Interview Project

Appropriateness: Pass_____ Fail_____

· The feelings of others are respected; people are treated with dignity; language, music, and visuals are appropriate for a middle school audience; the subject is appropriate for a middle school audience.

Evaluation Rubric

(Excellent)...5...4...3...2...1...(Poor)

Subject

· is interesting	5...4...3...2...1	
· is educational	5...4...3...2...1	
· is relevant to middle school audience	5...4...3...2...1	
· provides insight into person or topic	5...4...3...2...1	Concept Score _____ out of 30
· is discussed thoroughly	5...4...3...2...1	
· is entertaining	5...4...3...2...1	

Content

· presents interesting information and/or reactions	5...4...3...2...1	
· presents guest and host well	5...4...3...2...1	
· language is used properly and effectively	5...4...3...2...1	
· images and/or graphics relate well to content	5...4...3...2...1	Content Score _____ out of 30
· student(s) behave professionally on camera	5...4...3...2...1	
· student(s) demonstrate thoughtful approach to subject	5...4...3...2...1	

Technical Aspects

· camera is stable, smooth movements and pans	5...4...3...2...1	
· subject is framed well, images are well composed	5...4...3...2...1	
· subject is lit and clearly visible	5...4...3...2...1	
· sound is clear and understandable	5...4...3...2...1	Technical Score _____ out of 40
· video is edited effectively, flows well	5...4...3...2...1	
· titles are used effectively	5...4...3...2...1	
· transitions are used effectively	5...4...3...2...1	
· project was completed in a timely manner	5...4...3...2...1	

Total Score _____ Project Grade _____

A+=100-96, A=95-91, A-=90-86, B+=85-81, B=80-76, B-=75-71, C+=70-66, C=65-61, C-=60-56, F=55 or below and/or failure of appropriateness.

DV Poem Assignment Sheet & Evaluation Rubric

Student(s): _____ Period: _____

Title of Poem: _____

_____

Author of Poem: _____

_____

Approved by: _____ Start Date: _____ Completion Date: _____

Poem Project

Appropriateness: Pass_____ Fail_____

· The feelings of others are respected; people are treated with dignity; language, music, and visuals are appropriate for a middle school audience; the subject is appropriate for a middle school audience.

Evaluation Rubric

(Excellent)...5...4...3...2...1...(Poor)

Poem Presentation

· lines are spoken clearly	5...4...3...2...1	
· props are used effectively	5...4...3...2...1	
· is relevant to middle school audience	5...4...3...2...1	
· provides insight into poem	5...4...3...2...1	Concept Score _____ out of 30
· language is used properly and effectively	5...4...3...2...1	
· is entertaining	5...4...3...2...1	

Visual Content

· scene backgrounds are appropriate	5...4...3...2...1	
· props are visually interesting	5...4...3...2...1	
· actions are clear and understandable	5...4...3...2...1	
· images and/or graphics relate to content	5...4...3...2...1	Content Score _____ out of 30
· student(s) behave professionally on camera	5...4...3...2...1	
· student(s) demonstrate thoughtful approach to subject	5...4...3...2...1	

Technical Aspects

· camera is stable, smooth movements and pans	5...4...3...2...1	
· subject is framed well, images are well composed	5...4...3...2...1	
· subject is lit and clearly visible	5...4...3...2...1	
· sound is clear and understandable	5...4...3...2...1	Technical Score _____ out of 40
· video is edited effectively, flows well	5...4...3...2...1	
· titles are used effectively	5...4...3...2...1	
· transitions are used effectively	5...4...3...2...1	
· project was completed in a timely manner	5...4...3...2...1	

Total Score _____ Project Grade _____

A+=100-96, A=95-91, A-=90-86, B+=85-81, B=80-76, B-=75-71, C+=70-66, C=65-61, C-=60-56, F=55 or below and/or failure of appropriateness.

Erin Tapley

Does Video Art Have to be the Green Eggs 'n Ham for Students?

Background

Art specialists and art educators who train them often struggle with the addition of another medium or issue to address in the curriculum. With attentions pulled in directions such as integrated learning, assessment, aesthetics and design education; for many art teachers the classroom is already too complex to clutter with more equipment and the relatively unknown genre of video art. Nonetheless this is the media of the future. In reality, the general public is more likely to recognize what they see on TV than what might be displayed in any art museum. Video art is also an expressive medium where design, sound and time are integrated to create attention-getting results. Training in the foundational arts certainly begets better video results, but training in the technological medium of video also produces students who are better trained for the future of human expression. This chapter discusses video artists and ways of using video art with pre-service art teachers.

Introduction

A versatile medium of representation, video permitted artists to transform communication and distribution systems and promised a potentially unlimited viewing audience. While artists created works for television, art video often differed from commercial television because of artists' unorthodox use of the equipment and intent to subvert the codes of commercial networks. (Stiles & Selz, 1996)

I had always thought video art was for other people until my state of Wisconsin issued a requirement of technological competency to be demonstrated by all preservice educators, which of course sent many supervisors like myself into a panic. In many cases our student teachers were in schools, which had little computer equipment or expertise to rig a technologically based art lesson. But as "how to?" questions went back and forth between my student teachers, the administration and their teaching placements, we came to understand a widespread definition for technology. In fact, I was almost right in quelling my students' worries about completing this assignment by saying, "Find something with a plug, use it and write about it–that's all we can do at this point." I don't recount this remark as a stellar teaching moment, but because I was so subsequently dissatisfied with my posturing, I soon took on the technology quest myself beginning with video.

In time, I began to teach "Video Art and the Art of Making Videos" as a unit in my Elementary Arts Methods courses. I expected to have my students question the application of this to real-life elementary classrooms, but the use of camcorders and digital cameras is widespread among youth today, and their dearth in the classroom is more a matter of economics than competency. Additionally, with each passing generation, the number of jobs involving electronic image production increases significantly. Thus it is the duty of art educators to enable students to use the expressive and technological tool of video, which also benefits teachers both professionally and personally.

How I Define Video

I believe there are two types of videos, one records what happens, the other manipulates the abilities and limits of the equipment in the name of creating an audio-visual art form. It is this category, which I stress to my students. Knowledge of video tools begets special effects, which ultimately summons new tools and artistry and so on. It is important to also remember that video equipment has only been available to the public for about 20 years. Prior to this, expensive film equipment was available and some artists experimented with this medium and thus I see early artistic "films" as synonymous with art videos in terms of aesthetic intent. Today a fundamental difference between the full-length filmmaker and the video artist is primarily equipment, audience and length of production. Although the average length of an art video is about fifteen minutes and the content is generally more abstract than that presented in a film produced for mass entertainment, both genres strive for sensory stimulus, suspended belief of the audience and eye-catching visualization. For educators, availability of video art may seem another distinction between "movies" and artistic films or videos. The challenge for many of us is that we're familiar with video art in art museums, but historical chronology, who's who in video art and accessibility of video art for classroom use is unclear. Gathering a sampler of video art to my students entailed digging and defining.

Where does video art live?
Who does it?

The video artists I presented to my students were selected based on factors of interest and easy access of their work from libraries or video rental outlets. I rejected videos,

which were recordings of live performance art. While there are countless performance artists whose work is visually compelling, I needed to highlight videos where the filming was conscientious and embellished by manipulation of the camera and other production devices. Finally, while there are compilation works about video artists, I found these cost prohibitive, and many of the featured videos would not be appropriate for elementary audiences.

What can you do
with a video camera?

Aside from enduring my video art unit, all of my art education students must also videotape themselves several times teaching (while student teaching) and therefore with these purposes, the video camera can seem like an invasive syringe on a tripod. I'm not claiming that previous use of the camera alleviates this pressure, but using it as expressive tool may also be applied to the analysis and presentation of their teaching video. I once had a student who used editing equipment to complete her "written" analysis of her teaching on tape and while she didn't exclude any portions of the original tape she did categorize them into strengths and weaknesses, which she introduced with hilarious text. I felt the video was almost marketable as a teaching tool for future educators and I think the task of breaking down and rearranging moments of her teaching was valuable for her and for all of us.

What techniques and
equipment may be used for
the beginning school videographer?

After my class reviewed the parts of the video camera, we listed what can be done with it given our shooting and editing parameters. Although equipment and technological support varies in each school; usually a modicum of video and editing equipment is available. This may be as simple as two VCRs from which edited portions of an initial tape may be extracted and background sound enhanced. Some students have even found that intermittently including aspects of everyday television or films to be a good enhancement to their videos. On the more elaborate scale, some schools have purchased software programs such as IMovie from MacIntosh which enable videos on CD's to be manipulated with greater nuances from computer programs. Since all of this stuff was Greek to me a while back I recommend involving the media specialist in your school or going to inquire and/or play at stores selling electronic equipment to become better informed.

Even if such equipment is not there, there is still a lot of artistry to consider with just a camcorder that records what is in front of it. For example, filters in actual lighting or in front of the lense can alter color schemes and mood. The zoom mechanism should be practiced and not overused or used too quickly as this leads to viewer malaise. Students should learn to define the setting by panning or zooming in on definitive objects within it. Varying the type of camera shot also makes for good variety as is essential in any two dimensional art. Long and wide shots, tilted angled shots, aerial shots, and cutaways have to be thoughtfully planned to allow the viewer different perspectives but also continuity of theme or narrative. Many video handbooks recommend seeing a video without the sound to focus on these visual tricks. Likewise, closing one's eyes and listening to the sound of the video before viewing it for the first time provides a good opportunity to focus on the typologies and uses of good audio effects. Homemade devices for sound as well as shaped lens blocks can be fun to employ as well as yielding original results. Basically, seeing the camera as an eye, conjures a number of banal activities, which can be done to it, or at least in front of it, which affect the video. One student for example simply tickled the lens, which was a good mottled and funny interlude between the scenes of his video. To reinforce the organization of planning and executing a video, categories such as preparation, idea, shot planning, scripts, production and post production may help. Finally, division of labor is essential and many of my camera shy students turn out to be the most insightful camera people.

Logistics

I can imagine many different ways to present and inspire the art of video among students. Assigned themes, required techniques, a class-wide video shot over a long-time period could also provide thoughtful direction. As a short unit of my class however, four small groups are usually formed and students sketch out a quick storyboard and begin work immediately. Of crucial importance is deciding where to shoot the video, how to use the camera and how long to spend on creating the scenes versus how long to spend editing them. Once the video is "done" it is hardly perfect as the result of this rapid lesson but the videos are fresh in their spontaneity and my students are usually happy to critique their work given such shortchanging of time.

No Video Is Created Similarly

When I taught elementary school art, one of my mantras was that if there were 25 students in the room, I wanted to see 25 different responses to the assignment. Video art has never let me down in this quest. I have done the video-making unit for three semesters and no group responds the same way. I've had a group make Powaquatsi-like video using strange sounds and images made from close-ups of moving objects in an art building. Another group took an almost Dada approach and moved through daily locomotive tasks backwards. They interjected very short clips from television, which made the piece less performance, more cinematography. A more traditionally minded group in my class used tricks of puppetry and object stills to create a narrative about the day in the life of a Kleenex. A fourth group painstakingly made a claymation video including six characters, dialogue and paper scenery all filmed on a small box-sized platform. What I've elicited from my students' experiences is how freeing this medium can be, how it promotes collaboration and ice-breaking activities within the class and how easily students can carry over ideas from their traditional fine art training (such as value, composition, rhythm, etc.) into the moving image.

How Preservice Art
Educators Perceived the Exercise

The first time I taught this unit to my art education majors I did so out of the need to familiarize them and myself with some technological interaction, but the subsequent times I taught it came with added conviction that this was a useful activity—constructive also for adaptation in any K-12 art room. Student feedback bolstered my opinion. At the end of each unit I took a brief survey of student perceptions and was pleased that they noted that they saw themselves more interested in experimenting with video even to make homegrown but creative videos about favorite artists so that they could play these for students rather than gathering materials for each time they taught the lesson. Another student noted that even if the school had but one camcorder, the material planning of a video through storyboarding would be useful and could lead to an entire class constructing a video including prop-making, acting, lighting, sound-making and editing. Finally, one student constructively criticized that artistic techniques would really have to be emphasized as she thought that making videos was becoming a common assignment in classes such as social studies or science.

Extended Uses for Video
Art Across the Curriculum

As with everything daunting, once we confront it and work with it, such intimidation fades. Seeing its artistically inspiring potential also tends to ameliorate frustration or fear of technically challenging tasks. I think if approached as art, video art can be made and appreciated as such. As per its use in other classes, I believe its use as an artistic medium could only enhance such expression. The difference between a silly and clever or funny TV commercial for example is usually the creativity of the designer. Video art was said to be born from the brain-numbing quality of television. "A versatile medium of representation, video permitted artists to transform communication and distribution systems and promised a potentially unlimited viewing audience. While artists created works for television, art video often differed from commercial television because of the artist's unorthodox use of the equipment and intent to subvert the code of commercial networks." (Stiles & Selz 1996, p. 390). This is a fundamental mission of any art classroom. While crayons may be used for coloring in the general elementary classroom, many more permutations of this medium are explored in the artroom. The making of art videos requires paying attention to the nuances of life as well as the capacities of the camera and then manipulating both. Every artist thrives with this commitment to play.

Illustrations

Scene from "Noise"—from preservice art educator video unit.

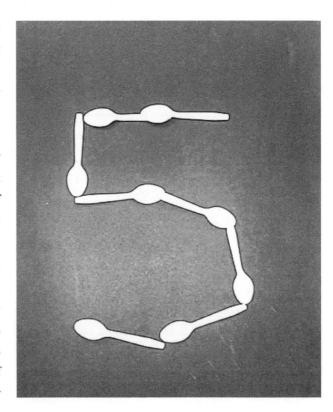

A handmade number serves as a transition shot before video #5.

Scene from "Tissue Away"— from preservice art educator video unit.

Claymation set up—scene from pre-service art educator video unit.

References

Battcock, G. (1978). *New artists video: a critical anthology.* New York: Dutton.

McEvoy, S. (2000). *windows movie maker handbook.* Redington, WA: Microsoft.

Broughton, D. (2002). Art education and visual culture *NAEA Advisory* Spring, Reston, VA: NAEA.

Cameron, E. (1994). *Sex, lies, and lawn grass, notes for video art.* Toronto: Art Metropole, Inc.

Cubitt, S. (1990). *Timeshift: On video culture.* New York: Routledge, Inc.

Decker, P., Edith. (1998). *Paik video.* New York: Barrytown, Ltd.

Fifer, S. (1990). *An essential guide to video art.* San Francisco: Aperture-Bay Area Video Coalition.

Hanhardt, J. (1986). *Video culture: a critical investigation.* New York: Visual Studies Workshop Press.

Hedgecoe, J. (1992). *John Hedgecoe's complete guide to video.* New York: Sterling Publications.

Morgan. R. (2000). *Gary Hill.* Baltimore: Johns Hopkins University Press.

Paik, N. (1993). *Nam June Paik: Video time, video space.* New York: H.N. Abrams.

Rush, M. (1999). *New media in late 20th-century art.* Michael New York: Thames and Hudson.

Schlossberg, E. (1998) *Interactive excellence: Defining and developing new standards for the twenty-first century.* New York: Ballantine Publishing.

Stiles, M. (1996). *"Art and technology" in theories and documents of contemporary art.* Berkeley, CA: University of California Press.

Syring, M.L. (1994). *Bill Viola unseen images.* Catalog Dusseldorf: Statdtische Kunsthalle.

Viola, B. (1986). *Selected works.* New York: Voyager Press. (VHS)

Viola, B. (1997). *A world of art. Works in progress. Bill Viola.* Burlington, VT: Annenburg/CPB Collection.

Wayne, M. (1997). *Theorising video practice.* London: Lawrence and Wishart, Ltd.

Wegman, W. (1998). *Wegman's world.* New York. Video Data Bank. (VHS)

Zippay, L. (1991). *Artists' video: An international guide.* New York: Cross River Press.

Websites:

Gary Hill
http://www.djdesign.com/artists/ghavi.html
http://www.donaldyoung.com/hill/hill_1c.ht

Video Chronologies
http:.//www.wdb.org

Early Videos
www.eai.org (Electronic Arts Intermix)

Curriculum development for media arts
http.www.childrensmediaproject.org/

Addendum

Videos I have shown in class
to inspire student-made videos

Hans Richter: Early Video — While looking at parts of *Citizen Kane* or even *Birth of a Nation* gives an indication of how early film creatively used lighting, editing, textual interjection and other techniques to enhance storytelling, classically-trained visual artists of this era also used film as expressively as paint. In 1941 Hans Richter immigrated to the United States and produced many prize winning short films in conjunction with the spirit of the Dada group to which he belonged. For me, Richter's short films, combine tricks available in most photo labs with existential absurdity. Most of his films are under 5 minutes and are silently narrated with simple and descriptive text (in French). Richter coordinated movement in his films with music overlays and his most famous, award-winning work *Before Breakfast* features many serendipitous scenes of every day life with a twist. In this film, hats come to life and people nonchalantly bicycle backwards on busy streets. Richter manipulated film much like a cartoonist and spliced in negative shots and even made some early attempts at time-lapse photography, in an era where most homemade films were sped-up because of irregulated reels and expense.

Charles and Ray Eames: Here is an American couple and artistic duo who will probably go down in history more for their contributions to post WWII furniture design than film-video art, but to see some of their educational films or even multiple image slide shows is to appreciate what can be done with little training and a lot of imagination. The Eames' most popular and highly accessible film, *Powers of Ten* seeks to visually demonstrate the concept of exponents however it also features microscopic photography and some interesting sound effects. For the purpose of demonstrating artistic videography (note that the Eames' films have been moved to video format now), *Toccata for Toy Trains* is probably their best film for this purpose. It is purely entertaining and fosters appreciation for the homologies between natural and human-made shapes. The Eames' design-trained eyes take full advantage of convex reflections, close-up shots and super-speed splicing. The Eames headquarters and website now under the direction of their grandson features many interesting and forthcoming projects for exposing youth to their films.

Nam June Paik: Korean born Nam Jun Paik is almost synonymous with televisions in the art world and many college students become familiar with his work, if only through pictures in art history books. But the strength of Paik's work is not that he sculpturally uses the shell and icon of television set, but that he also creates the guts of the TV–through video art. Paik's videos often feature non-objective and kaleidoscope-like displays, which are eye candy for some and irritating yet colorful "interference" for others. Yet, Paik has also made pseudo-documentary, biographical pieces such as *Alan and Allen's Complaint* (about Allen Ginsberg's and Alan Kaprows' paternal relationships), which embodies videography as a collage process. Nonetheless, Paik is most famous for his activated television installations. His video art fosters an appreciation for the television screen as lens, which can highlight visually interesting effects such as interference, reflexive images and rewound sequences.

Animation Art: Cartoons may be debatable as video art, but the many short films or videos of internationally-competitive animation artists count in my book as video art. These films often use expressive drawings or sculpture as their matrices, and now computer manipulation animates and extends their dynamics. Students can also stop and pause video cameras for easy animated effects. Compilations of animation videos (such as those from annual international festivals) are readily available at many libraries or even K-12 art video distributors. A noteworthy artist to mention from this genre is William Kentridge whosecyclical additive and reductive drawings are cleverly morphed into narrative whose transitional effects also involved drawing and obscuring. Kentridge's work centers on human injustice and suffering as a South African. Like many artists who may not be as well known as Paik in the video genre, I accessed his work by tracking his recent shows where I purchased a copy from the exhibiting museum.

Guillermo-Gomez Pena and Coco-Fusco: Both of these artists are classified as performance or conceptual artists but one collaborative work, *Couple in a Cage* is a thoughtful drama about the demeaning treatment of exotic people throughout history. The artists' central performance consists of their dressing and acting as indigenous people from an unknown Pacific island who are bribed into touring developed countries as live anthropological specimens. But the video is not simply a reporting of this activity. The video is successfully interjected with selections from historical films and glimpses of actual eugenic experimentation and freak show personalities. Note that some parts will be inappropriate for young elementary students but it can be carefully cued so that either the techniques or the subject matter can generate discussion. It is a good example of video as persuasive essay.

Laurie Anderson: With many glimpses of her work now available on "meet the artist" type of videos aimed at art appreciation classes, the often-live work of performance artist Laurie Anderson is fairly accessible. The video series *PBS Art: 21* features a 5-minute introductory segment on Anderson and shows portions of her recent work as does an inexpensive video, *Art as Video*. I consider Anderson a video artist because she manipulates her performances with invented sound makers and other technological nuances such as light and dance. She and her assistants also manipulate the recordings post-filming. Compilations of Anderson's and other performance-oriented video artists can be found in videos *Two Moon July* that was made at the Kitchen — a New York City venue for performance and contemporary art. At the time of this chapter's publication this video was out-of-print, but various ebay sites were offering it.

William Wegman: William Wegman will always be associated with his dogs, which he has used as manikins and subjects for the last thirty years. While many people see Wegmen as a photographer, his early work relied on video art. Glimpses of these and his recent videos for children (using his alphabet forming dogs) can be seen in a new biographical video about Wegman, *Wegman's World* that is commercially available through educational distributors. Wegman's video work is a strong model for students who want to create a video for child audiences using creatively-posed, human subjects.

Gary Hill: American artist Gary Hill brings a poetic sense of perception and language into his work, which is almost exclusively shown as video art. Admittedly because I was once able to briefly meet Gary Hill, I became interested in his work enough to purchase the video, *Video Art: Gary Hill* available through select distributors. This intensive, interview format film about Hill explains his work which is often seen as obscure and esoteric. Hill should also be noted as the US representative at the 2001 Venice Biennial with his video entitled: *Wall Piece*. This video featuring Hill throwing himself against a wall with his quintessential sounds indicative of the undulations of all languages. Not all of Hill's work contains such aggression, but this black and white piece made use of still frame cutting which makes his movement seems digital and frenetic. It is also fun to tell students about Hill's youth as a California surfing teenager and art school dropout. Like many artists of his generation, video art was not a part of their early artistic education but rather they found it auspiciously in wanting to create sensory experience through direct means. Another viewing option I exercised with Hill's and other video artists' work was Internet sites containing video clips. Of course, this might not always be possible or appropriate to assign to elementary students, but drawing attention to this recent capability of websites emphasizes another use of videography within cyber commercials.

Women Make Movies: This is a New York City based program that assists in the production, promotion and distribution of independent films and videotapes by women.

The subject matter is often pursuant to women's issues as the group was established in 1972 to address the under-representation and misrepresentation of women in the media industry. Today the organization provides over 400 films, about 12 of which are classified as video art. However, for my purposes the documentaries made by some of these film artists were beautifully done and available from the university library because they addressed topics of eating disorders and dance. One of the most interesting tapes, I watched was *Mirror, Mirror* directed by Nan Kravitz that cleverly dealt with women's bodily perceptions in 17 short minutes. It was a good example of how creativity and film cutting can make a simple set and candid interviews captivating.

Bill Viola: The best news about Bill Viola is that his videos can be as calming as watching a fishbowl or as compelling as watching open-heart surgery. His output is vast and various and interviews with Viola which include peeks into the production of his work are available. Also considering Viola is probably the most well-known video artist of all time and among the first video artists to have a one-person show of exclusively video art, (Whitney 1997, Art Institute of Chicago 2000) his commercially-available videos are reasonably priced. Themes for Viola's work may be described as tributes to balancing life forces in everyday occurrence. Viola is well grounded in mythology, philosophy, Tibetan Buddhism, Judeo-Christian mysticism and other thoughtful enterprises, which transport the self to sublime experience. Some people, on the other hand, find his videos slow moving and anticlimactic. My favorite video to show the students is *Ancient of Days* (1979-1981), which is a 13-minute video beginning with a desk on fire transforming into strangers walking across the lawn around the Washington Monument and then ending in Asia where the movement of the city is reflected in cloud movement within a landscape painting on a wall. Here, quintessential Viola video techniques come into play, such as slow motion, reflections in minute objects, long length film shots, and meditative white noise. One of the things which makes Viola exemplary for beginning video makers is that although quite technologically enhanced now, his subject matter is quite simple, he capitalizes on the spirituality of noticing sensual aspects in everyday life. A series of artist interviews made by the Annenburg CPB Collection features Viola's work for the 1995 Venice Biennale where he depicted the Virgin Mary greeting her sister Elizabeth — a biblical scene often depicted in 16th-century European art. Viola however focuses on the universality of meeting and greeting and the mammoth efforts needed to produce this moment in the video are well explained.

S u s a n   L e h m a n

If I can, you can!

7

Me—Teach Video?

Having inherited one period of media production along with four periods of art when my predecessor retired last year, I reluctantly came to teaching video. Actually I came shaking in my boots, kicking and screaming. I'm the person who on the second day of computer class was downstairs in the bathroom in tears because I couldn't remember how to turn my computer on. I still don't really know how to program my VCR at home. I've always felt that I was "technically challenged." But having been an art teacher for years, I approached teaching video the only way I could and that was from the point of view of an artist. Video is indeed a visual medium, add to that a little audio and there you go!

Fortunately, Panasonic Kid Witness News Program has generously sponsored our school for the past dozen years, providing student booklets, video equipment, tapes, and repairs. Through a grant written by the former instructor, we were able to build a studio set modeled after a TV newsroom where our KWN team produced an early Wednesday morning news program dedicated to interviews with the principal and vice-principals. They invited teachers to send their own representatives with the latest goings-on in their own classrooms. This program was taped by the 7th and 8th grade students using the studio equipment, edited minimally by the instructor and broadcast throughout the rest of the school. Part of our VAPA grant funding had been used to wire most of the classrooms for co-axial cable. This had been going on pretty much the same way for the last 12 years.

In anticipation of taking over this video class set-up, I contacted our local Sacramento Access television station where they train people to use their studio equipment. Part of their course included video editing and movie making, using iMovie on iMac computers. Their approach was the traditional one of beginning by writing a script. Unfortunately, it was a very cut and dry method and it took several classes of script writing and making storyboards before we ever got to see the whole process and the end result. It seemed like an improbable way to engage younger students. The best part was the editing work on the iMacs. Digital editing made sense—and it was fun! But the problem as I saw it was getting to the fun part quickly.

When our school district was giving an inservice on iMovie, I jumped at the chance. This workshop did more to build my own confidence as a teacher and my understanding of the process than anything else. It gave a direct approach to understanding the process and was geared for teachers! We met at an iMac computer lab in one of the school libraries and were paired together on digital camcorders. We began by going out and shooting video clips around the school grounds. We came back and they walked us through the editing possibilities, titles, transitions, special effects, and how to record music from CDs for our soundtracks. We created our first mini-video in one afternoon! This approach I could see working with students. I truly believed if I could show students what was involved in editing, then their camera work could improve. Their concepts for their projects would expand and become more complex. This really opened up more possibilities for creativity!

Back at school—in our studio full of obsolete equipment that was purchased over a decade before, there was only one editing system that worked similarly to iMovie—the Avio Casablanca. Along with that we had two hand-held camcorders—a digital 8 and the Panasonic mini DV. We also had a mini DV VCR for downloading our footage to the Avio—that was also provided by Panasonic—and a regular VHS VCR. I could transfer the enthusiasm that I had felt at the teachers' workshop to my teaching of video! Teachers starting out today with just a video camera, a computer, and digital editing software similar to iMovie would probably have an easier time since today's technology is more advanced.

There are three things that have made the most difference in my teaching of video:

1. Learning digital editing in the iMac workshop.

2. Teaching and letting children edit their own work.

3. Inservicing three students in editing and using them as teacher assistants to train the other students. In my class these were three video students who were continuing as 8th graders in Media and TV Production.

Why teach video editing to students?

First of all, it frees up the teacher to become a facilitator. If you are editing your students' work, you will always have work to edit! Children get a camera in their hands and they tape everything without regard to the steadiness of the shots, the composition of each frame, or the noise distractions that are being recorded. When they are doing the editing, they learn to do better camera work. They start seeing things clearer through the camera's eye. They plan better. They can learn to write scripts that make sense. Their imaginations take off and their videos become more creative than you could ever envision.

Editing isn't something you start out with. You'd introduce it after general lessons on the camera, tripod, shot angles, composition, and endless taping, re-taping, and experimenting. To teach digital editing—simplify! Get down to the very minimum variables to deal with. With each project, increase the variables, adding movement, varying the length of shots, and finally by adding edited sound. Here are my first three editing projects.

Editing Project #1

All work is done by students in groups of 2-4.

1. Select 8-10 art prints representing a "theme" (landscapes, people, faces, seascapes, flowers, boats, birds, etc.) These could be photos in a book or some other posters.

2. Shoot 10 seconds of each picture, pausing the camera in between pictures. They need to be on an easel or on the wall. The camera should be on a tripod. Record with audio off.

3. Download the footage to either iMovie or a digital editor like Avio Casablanca—each picture or poster in a separate clip. This way they can be manipulated individually.

4. Trim each shot to 8 seconds. Add to the movie track in the order desired. Create 10 seconds of black before and after the movie for titles.

5. Create titles on the black clips.

6. Make transitions between each scene. Experiment with all of the different transitions available for the system you're using.

7. Record music from a CD that goes with your theme. Jazz and instrumentals work really well. Record enough sound to match the length of your video footage.

8. Trim and fade in/out on the audio clip and insert to the audio track.

9. Depending on the system you're using, finish appropriately and download to either VHS or DVD.

This project has had insightful results. One student whose mother was no longer in his life, used prints of mothers and their children paired with rap songs honoring mothers.

Because some students didn't have their CDs available on the days they were to record their audio, they listened to my jazz collection and learned to appreciate a different style of music. The jazz they chose actually enriched their projects. Because they could choose art prints that appealed to them, they didn't have to worry about what to shoot. The choices were limited. They also didn't have to worry about shaky camerawork—we used a tripod and 10 seconds of each shot. They did learn to reposition and refocus for each print so that the white margins didn't show. The finished projects were looped and shown at Open House. They could be used at any grade level as inspirations for art lessons.

Editing Project #2
1. Record 10-second shots of plants, trees, or buildings around school—no moving people, no sounds.

2. Edit using the same process as in project #1.

3. Record music for the audio and after editing, insert as before.

4. Record to VHS or DVD.

"Spring" was used for a theme. "Trees," "Things Around School," and "Cars" were also used. This project helped make the transition to taping the students' own footage. By eliminating the sound and any movement, they were essentially taping "stills" just like their art prints. The editing process was the same. These projects were also aired to the rest of the school building the students confidence and also their recognition as film students.

Editing Project #3
1. Shoot moving video footage this time—no audio these cuts can be of varied length (8-20 seconds each).

2. Edit as before; trim cuts to various lengths; add transitions and titles.

3. Choose and record music for audio; you can also at this point use several different sound clips and experiment with fading them into each other.

4. Finish as before and transfer to VHS or DVD.

Some of the most original themes came up with this project. One group of Hmong students taped girls around school that they admired. They put it all together, entitling it "Asian Girls," adding an Asian song as their soundtrack. I asked them if they knew what the song lyrics meant and they told me that it was a Korean song that one of their brothers had and no one understood it—that they just thought it fit their theme!

Another group was attempting to videotape people in the class, but they kept ducking down or turning or covering their faces when the camera was in sight. The group edited these shots all together and entitled it "Shy People." My favorite was one that was shot on a rainy spring day, entitled, of course, "Rain" but including a soundtrack from a relaxation tape of rain sounds that they had found.

You can continue teaching moviemaking in this way, adding more variables until students begin thinking of the things they might want to attempt. Their imaginations work in quantum leaps and bounds at this point. On the Avio

Casablanca as well as on the iMovie, you can add voice-overs and vary the decibel levels of the audio tracks. Students really get inventive and sophisticated in planning out their projects once they are empowered with editing skills. I found that my students actually understood the process much better than I did and actually could vary the sound tracks beyond anything that I could imagine. Remember—they have grown up in a technological age!

What kind of projects work best in order to explore the medium of video?

After spending the first week having my three teaching assistants introduce our different camera set-ups (two hand-helds plus the TV studio), we sent small student groups out to interview other students or adults on campus. We also conducted interviews of each other in class after practicing writing interview questions. I always ask students to include the question "What is one thing about you that we would be surprised to know?" We recorded each interview, watching as we went, looking at what we needed to do to improve. Interviews help both the interviewer and the interviewee by developing an on-camera presence and by building self-confidence.

A news program format can be either broadcast live if you have the capabilities or can be recorded and sent around from classroom to classroom. These can include sports commentaries and footage as well as interviews with the principal and news of upcoming events. We had three groups interviewing staff about the new food in the cafeteria, sports that are available through different programs on campus, and the services available in the library including our new computers.

Another favorite among students is the TV commercial parody. I always begin by recording a few dozen real commercials. We watch for products, slogans, songs, and filming or editing techniques. The students then create their own product, a slogan, and write a script. We include varying camera shots and zoom in for close-ups. Hair gel, sham-poo, basketball shoes, dieting products, and sodas are past products. If you give children something to hold while they are being filmed, they aren't as nervous.

However, the video project that is the very top favorite among my middle-school students and the one that truly recognizes their love of music is the "Music Video." They can choose to rap their own raps, lip-synch to a song or rap, or for those brave enough, they can sing on camera. The students get involved in choreographing, costuming, and designing props. The teacher just needs to set the parameters for appropriateness. Dress codes and language come to mind.

Our big project every year is the Panasonic KWN Video Competition. The categories include Public Service Announcement, Fiction—Drama and Comedy, Commercial, Documentary, and all have different guidelines set down by Panasonic. Panasonic helps prepare the students for what is expected by sending support materials including a video of the previous year's winner in each category. The maximum number of videos submitted is two per year. The deadline is midyear. If your school is being sponsored, you are required to submit at least one per year. There are so many schools hoping for sponsorship; Panasonic needs to know that you are using the camera and materials to actively teach video. You can contact Panasonic, but I understand there is a waiting list for sponsorship. They update their requirements each year and ask for a list of your students with their video release forms signed by parents. A video release form or some sort of parent permission letter is a good idea for all teachers teaching video. Most school districts have addressed this and have one available.

Our current project is being taped completely in one shot from start to finish. It is the "How to…" video. This is a demonstration of how to do just about anything, showing all the steps. This is the only project that I have taught that starts with script writing. I have designed a page that is divided into two columns—the one on the left is "What You See" and the one on the right is "What You Hear".

Included under "What You See" are the camera shots—close-ups, medium shots, or wide angle shots. Because there is no editing at all, a script ensures that all aspects of the video are thought out.

The video footage begins with a poster showing the title and the names of the talent. The students on camera introduce the concept and the materials needed and then proceed through the steps involved. They can use an additional poster with a recipe or the steps displayed. Because this is a non-edited project, students who are in line waiting to edit one of their other projects can complete this video in the meantime. I usually have one or two of the teaching assistants helping in the editing room while another can assist with this project. The steps for this are pretty simple and do not involve a lot of teacher supervision; however, a demonstration at the beginning is helpful. Some of the "How to..." concepts we're working on include arranging flowers, cooking different ethnic foods, lowering the front end of a toy car, different hair styles using gel, and where to find a boyfriend.

Our last video project this year will be what I call a "Service Video." These videos will follow an outline indicating the dozen of areas on campus that a new student would need to know—the front office, the attendance office, the gym, the cafeteria, etc. Each group of students will then find someone either in their group or on campus who will, on camera, tell about each place, welcoming the new student or family in their own language, explaining about our campus. Our school is over 60% English Language Learners. We have over a dozen different languages spoken on our campus. In just my video class alone, we speak at least six. This is our gift to the school for the resource library.

Inspirations?

Looking, critically looking, at videos just jump-starts the imagination! I actually begin the school year by showing the videos that the students from the year before completed. We also look at the Panasonic winners from years past. Whenever I find video footage that pertains to or illustrates a project I'm introducing, I bring it in. Even taping

footage from television, pointing out editing, transitions, and camera shots helps increase what the students can see all around them in this video-enriched world.

Guest speakers from local news stations have volunteered time to explain some of what is involved with their jobs. Our community is lucky enough to have two or three independent film festivals every year—one including student work. Our local Community Access television station offers free digital classes to teenagers after school and during the summer. Our local newspaper carries great reviews about movies and articles where movie directors talk about their work. I reproduce these and discuss them with students. We're also fortunate to have a local director who hit it big with his second locally filmed movie!

A "Film Appreciation" segment can include viewing and discussing film classics and film styles, such as the film noir genre. "SunDance" Award winners on DVD can be viewed with the director's commentaries. These insights into the filmmaker's process can be translated to some of our more creative projects.

Don't overwhelm your students with too much too soon. Start with the fun part of just shooting endless footage, rewinding and shooting again! Introduce them to being in front of the camera as well as behind it. Introduce the editing after the interviewing practice and other confidence building lessons. Then step back and watch where they can take video.

How Do Art Skills Relate?

The California Art Standards for my middle school students include self expression through multimedia processes including photography, computers, and video. Having taught the elements of art and the principles of design using color, texture, line, and balance, I could see a correlation to creating individual frames or shots in video. At one of the workshops and subsequently in video books, I learned that in video there is a 1/3 rule of proportion. You divide the frame into thirds both vertically and horizontally, so that nothing is right in the center. Using variety in your shots—close-ups, medium shots, and long shots—adds to the visual interest of the footage. These can all be written into a script if you are using one. Composition and balance are important concepts in all visual mediums.

In my art classes, I am assigning a small video project designed after a Polish filmmaker who entitles his videos with a color name—"Blue," "White," and "Red." Each small group is assigned a color—yellow, green, red, etc. They brainstorm things, places, or situations that correlate to their color. This can be either a non-edited or edited project with 10 seconds shot of each situation, beginning with a title card. For example: a title card showing the word "YELLOW" followed by 10 seconds each of a bunch of bananas, a bowl of lemons, a student dressed all in yellow, a yellow wall, a yellow chair, ending with a yellow card with the students' names. This should probably be taped with the audio turned off. If you are capable of adding a sound track, maybe a song that relates to the color could be used. In the case of the color yellow, "The Yellow Submarine!"

Success Stories?

Teaching video has definitely changed my life and the students around me. I know there is another Spike Lee or Robert Altman in the making in these classes. Video is a medium with few limitations. A student from last year, who asked for the chance to learn technical direction, ended up running the TV studio this year, displaying leadership qualities that had before gone unchallenged. He experimented with equipment and was doing editing that no one else had thought of doing. He had such success using video that it was written into his Individualized Educational Program as a positive learning strategy to include in other classes where he was struggling.

Students who cannot concentrate on reading and writing can often focus better on the visual and audio stimulus of a video screen. Hyperkinetic learners can get involved in the challenges that come on both sides of the camera. One of my best editors had been diagnosed as being hyperactive and having Attention Deficit Disorder. The children

in my classes are largely children of poverty—often coming from homes and situations that challenge their abilities to learn and to get involved in school. Video offers them a way to express the things they see around them, as well as the things they dream for themselves for their futures. It gives them a future!

Video has helped me gain insight into the lives of my students. It has taught me tolerance and appreciation for their likes and dislikes—especially when it comes to their music. As they have grown in self-confidence, so have I as I've designed lessons to meet the challenges of what needs to be taught next. I've watched as students begging for attention through misbehavior have found their voice in a medium that sparks their storytelling imagination. Give children a means to express themselves and they will amaze you. My predecessor left me one thought that says it all—"Video is the process, not the product. The experience is all."

So, Can You Do It?

You've already started to build your own confidence by reading this book! You're searching out information. That's the first step. Sign up for a workshop. If you're anything like me—you learn by being shown. The iMovie Video workshop given in my school district changed my attitude about teaching video. Ask a colleague who teaches video to walk you through it.

Technology is so advanced these days—check out at your local computer or camera store. You might have some of what you need already. Basically that's a video camera, a computer, and movie editing software. That also needs to include the connecting cables that usually come with a video camera, so that you can input information into your computer. A technology salesperson should be able to advise you what will work with any components you already have. Some school districts have a technician who can advise you what equipment they can work on or what will work with what you have. Most video suffers from too much background noise and camera work that is too wobbly.

Additional equipment might include a separate microphone and a tripod. Explore grant writing options and donations for getting your equipment.

Get started! Devise some simple lessons. You already know how to teach—how to break things down into little easy steps! Video is no different than teaching reading and probably even easier. You must have had some idea how you wanted to use video in your classroom when you started exploring this process. Look at movies, at advertisements, at the news! Video ideas are all around us. Watch the difference video makes in your students and the level of enthusiasm in your classroom. The doors are open to a world of possibilities.

PART TWO

Video Art Projects in the Schools

An Interview with Video Artist-Teacher, Renee Shaw

8

Ilona: I have watched the many video artworks you've made with children. I also attended screenings of your own video art. I appreciate the opportunity to speak with you about video art in the classroom. How did you start doing video animation?

Shaw: There is a photo of me when I was 3 years old. I was squatting down next to a dairy farmer's cat named Boots. I am holding a Howard Johnson's purse filled with rocks I collected. I have the purse in one hand and a rock in the other, showing it to Boots. Actually the rocks were talking to Boots. The rocks were my friends. Each had its own life, personality, and things to say. They especially needed to say things to the cat. I thought Boots was really happy about what the rocks had to say, because as they talked from my hand, Boots would talk in loud purrs back to the rock, rubbing himself against my hand. The cat really liked my rocks a lot.

This photo serves as a memory of one of the earliest animations that I created and a testament to children's early development as animators. The ability to animate starts at an early age with an understanding of what it means to have an inner life. It is not uncommon for children to animate trucks, Barbies®, or household objects. Children are fascinated with the world of animation and exercise their abilities to bring out the inner life of inanimate objects. Children learn about the world they live in by animating everything around them. Animation, perhaps, is one of the most natural types of play that children do.

Ilona: You have spent a lot of time assisting children in the animation process.

Shaw: I have been helping children to animate their drawings for almost 5 years. It is a natural progression from children play-animating objects to animating their drawings. I act as their technical support, helping to bring drawing adventures that exist in a child's mind to life. I work at an elementary school, grades K-5, as the video arts instructor. Every child in my class innately understands the value of giving life to drawings, and they know exactly how their characters should move and in what environments and circumstances they will be involved. Animation is my children's art media. It is their voice.

Ilona: Working with young animators is a way to bring their dreams to life.

Shaw: I am not a dream maker, or a Willy Wonka figure, but simply a technical helper to the students and their ideas. I let them know that in animations anything is possible.

There is life in everything. Anything and everything can be given a life. If we pay attention to an object, it will tell us about its life—it will tell us about its dreams. Through animation we make imagination visible in time and space. Animators can create a time and space that is not possible in our physical world but can exist in an animated universe. Through their animation, children can move outside the things they are told are true into a world where imagination and creation of life is held in high esteem. For my students, animation is a stress-free world without test scores or notions of stereotypical "smartness," where knowing school facts does not matter. In animated worlds, anything is possible and dreams can come true.

Ilona: The children I watched you work with appeared to be deeply involved in an artistic state.

Shaw: The other day, one of my students brought a tiny pair of socks to class to wear with a specific pair of shoes that she adopted. She said it had a sweet little soul. She dreamt of making a special home for the socks and shoes. She talks to the shoes and socks and she dreams up adventures for them. Student animators journey through object fantasies, experiencing deep artistic states. Animators young and old who play with the inner life of objects understand each other and appreciate their extraordinary abilities. I teach students to listen to what inanimate objects have to say. We learn what an object's voice sounds like, and we learn about ourselves though the object. Students ask questions—"How does the chair feel when I sit on her?" "Is my coffee cup as happy as I am when I drink out of it?" We learn to listen to our artworks. I joke with my students saying, it really doesn't matter if you like a piece of art, but you can ask a piece of art if it likes you. Artworks are brutally honest. They will tell you. They hold nothing back. An artwork will tell you what it is thinking. I ask students to listen to the artwork's criticism, what it says about how we look at it, interact with it, and relate to it. It is often hard to listen to an artwork's brutal honesty towards its maker. But if we are interested in the things the artwork has to say, it will tell us more. If you listen with a disinterested ear, an artwork will not say much, it will not reveal itself to you.

Ilona: I heard you giving interesting advice to young animators. What is essential to get across to young video artists?

Shaw: Be present with the artwork. Be aware of the moment. Observe the community of time and community of space in which you and the artwork share. Be aware of the artwork having an inner consciousness. Be aware of art making as a shared experience—of growing older together. Be aware of the intimate relationship you create in making an artwork. Tap into the vein that runs in-between you and the artwork. Step outside your own stream of consciousness and share a common artery of consciousness. Focus some moments not on each other but the in-between—the shape or space that you cocreate. The greater the awareness of the relationship between the artist and the art, the more we lose our ego and are transformed by the true relationship between a piece of art and ourselves.

Ilona: While talking to one of your fifth graders about why he thinks animation is important he said, "Kid animators know the subject best. We definitely know ourselves better than adults. We know what we want to say better than adults—we know the issues that are important to us."

Shaw: In helping with student animators, I found that they do know the issues that concern them best, and it is more meaningful when their projects animate their own issues. Animation has the ability to transform student lives, by working out issues through a different sort of life, a life outside the artist, existing independently from the artist. The life students give to animated drawings take them outside of themselves. As artists, students are amazed to see their drawings transformed and living what seems to be another life. A student once told me that it is hard to imagine separating herself from the artwork, to give up her art after all she has put into it. Through animation, students learn that art exists on its own. It has its own time and space, and it will exist in the minds of other viewers. My students learn the power of their art by watching it on the screen— how their art lives on its own. They created it, but it becomes forever different from what they have created. It takes on a life of its own. A life outside of the artist.

Ilona: The beauty of children's drawings and the stories they tell in animation are unique. They speak of the beauty of things imperfect, impermanent, and incomplete. It is a beauty of things modest and humble. It is a beauty of things unconventional. I find in your students' animation that many of the more emphatic, anti-aesthetics that invariably spring from the young, modern, creative soul: beat, punk, grunge, or whatever it's called next, is displayed in their animated videos.

Shaw: My students' animated drawings are primitive and raw. They are unashamed of disproportionate body parts; they are unafraid of imperfect straight lines and not embarrassed about the use of unrealistic color. The back view of their characters looks completely different from the side—and how beautiful that is. Children's drawings and ideas are unusual and creative and proudly stand as one-of-a-kind animations. Unlike mass-produced cartoons from the big industries that dictate form, content, and aesthetic look like Pixar, or Disney studios, my students' raw characters look different from scene to scene. Their drawings are not polished. They are not perfect, but they are uninhibited by what an ideal, industry drawing should look like. The students' stories are comfortable with ambiguity and contradiction. They are not neat, clean, predictable—and like Disney cartoons—perfectly tied up. A kindergartner wrote a story for an animation called, "Free Willy Is a Nice Whale." A nice whale is captured, put into a tank, and his friends come and they have a sushi party for Willy in the tank. Giving life to life-affirming, beautiful images comes natural to children's animation. It is not hard to see that life. Look into the soul of a child's drawing, and it will tell you that it is already living. The spirit that lives inside children's drawings calls out to be animated.

Ilona: In your program, it is easy to see animation as an art form children connect with. Animation is perhaps the earliest art form children experience in our culture. Your animation classes appear as an effective tool to take charge of the animated art forms children watch on television.

Shaw: We produce videos that the children take home on a CD, or videotape, using home TVs or computers as home art galleries. Children take home videos as traveling art shows to their parents and to show friends and relatives.

Ilona: I was amazed to enter your video portable, to see that you have a fantastic professional quality video studio parked as a trailer next to a public school. What is the story behind your unusual program?

Shaw: In 1996 Ronda Clevenson introduced a video program to the Arlington public schools. It was called Project Interaction, which started as a television studio emphasizing the importance of communication. So it was a part of a big communication push between the school community and the community at large. As part of communication, we still send videotapes back and forth to keep parents informed of school issues and activities.

Ilona: Was it a specific program designed for Barrett Elementary?

Shaw: Arlington County funds special projects for every school. We were one of the pilot programs. We were also the first elementary school with a complete TV studio. Arlington County is very supportive of our program and provides complete technical support. I guess this is pretty unique, because as good as our county support is, they try and standardize everything. We are all supposed to look the same, yet this studio is very different. Our focus is on animation. I came in with an art background and approached the work of this studio differently then my predecessors. I renamed the "TV studio" to "Video Art Studio."

Ilona: So the approach video takes in a school has a lot to do with the interest and background of the teacher. It is very exciting to see the stills you have on display. What are some of the creative projects that your students are currently working on?

Shaw: I do lots of drawing with the kids. I teach special video art classes where kids will come in to work during recess or other hours during their school day. In addition, I consult with the teachers and see how I can coordinate with their lessons. The first-grade teacher Mrs. Bowman is great. I am basically a center for her first graders who will just come in, sit down, and start drawing. I draw with them so that they feel their ideas are welcome here. Even the youngest child is treated as an artist as we draw as a way to come up with characters. In the drawings, the children discover their characters and the stories and scenes they are in. As we draw characters and scenes, we scan them and finish coloring on the computer. Most animation we do starts with the drawing process.

Ilona: So some of your work with the children is driven by their drawing ideas, while other projects are suggested by their academic work?

Shaw: Yes, there are projects totally driven by the kids and their stories, and I encourage them to come up with their own characters. But, the teachers will want to tie into our standards, like retelling the story of Molly Banake which you see on the wall. There is room for art even in the teacher driven projects, since animation is so open to artistic interpretation. As images start to move, even academic content becomes very kid like, and their drawings become things other than themselves. It is amazing to see the kids when they watch their work on the screen, because it is almost like they have been given a life outside of themselves. Even though the kids create them—their stuff—it is amazing to them. There is something magical about the whole process that turns the academic projects into something more creative, more life affirming than just videotaping a book report.

Ilona: Is all your work animation, versus children shooting straight video?

Shaw: I started a program where kids could check out a video camera. Students come in and take a test to see how well they know the camera. They show that they know how to load, zoom in, zoom out, and understand all recording basics. After they pass the test, they can check out a video camera for a few days. Kids feel responsible for

the camera when they are trusted to work with it. If you are only allowed to use the equipment in class for specific things, you are not really learning about the camera. You have to put a camera on a tripod and just learn to shoot. I feel that students get a handle on the camera by using it independently. The students come back and we watch the footage they shot. They come up with great things. It is because they are able to take the camera out of the school and do it on their own, reflect on their own experiences, and feel free to use video as an art tool.

Ilona: Do they come back to school to edit?

Shaw: We just create short films, little movies about their bedrooms, and funny things about their parents. When we did these films, we did not have time to edit them, but it is a possibility using iMovie. We started with open projects, like filming something to do with your room. The children then expanded it with their own ideas. It was inspiring, actually. Before, they were not paying attention to what the camera could really do. They were more interested in being able to take the equipment home. I am not sure how easy that is for every school, but regular video cameras are inexpensive, and it is an extremely important experience. By the way, I make them and their parents sign a release that they are responsible if anything happens to the camera.

Ilona: I know you work with the art teacher at your school. Is that an important relationship?

Shaw: I do work with the art teacher. We do a lot of the drawing together, and we collaborate on many mixed media projects which are later turned into videos. She does not teach video art, and I am sure that is in part because I am here, but the collaboration contributes to a more comprehensive art experience for the children. Video is just another art media. It is just like painting and drawing, and it should be incorporated into the regular art room.

Ilona: I know art teachers feel that it is hard to incorporate video in their art program because of expensive equipment and the demands of many other media to teach.

What kinds of things can an art teacher do to make video more accessible?

Shaw: There is a spectrum of video art. Video art can be done even without the video camera, just using stills from a digital still camera, and doing stop motion animation. Just using Kid Picks, which is an animation program on most school computers, wonderful video art can be made. There are definitely things art teachers can do without the camera. I have taught large classes by introducing iMovie, using a single video camera. Even editing can be done with a small group of students after school and then slowly building a core group of kids who know what they are doing, teaching their skills to others. I show a small group of kids the video camera, and then slowly build towards larger groups, and they become responsible for teaching more kids. Children have great computer savvy and they catch on very quickly. If you introduce a concept to a few kids pretty soon it will blossom. It is a part of their world already. There are definitely projects that every art class can do. There are simple things to do with Kid Picks, or digital stills, or photo elements, especially when combined with iMovie.

Ilona: Does it make sense to have separate video art from art classes?

Shaw: It is separate in my elementary school, but that is not the ideal. Video art classes can be a part of an art class or, in secondary school, part of other art offerings. Many schools that operate a video program are not doing video as art. Often art teachers are not teaching the video classes, and instead of art-related projects, kids videotape the morning news or school's sports events. There is a difference between teaching video art and teaching kids how to use the video camera to tape school events. Art teachers are very independent people. If they realize how important and enjoyable this media is for students, they can easily make up for the lack of formal training. I always say start slowly, exposing yourself to the many resources on the Internet. Video files are easy and accessible to download. The technical issues are easily accessed.

Ilona: Do you ever show examples of video art to inspire your students?

Shaw: I think it is important to show examples of my own work and that of others. It is also great to show student videos. Good examples are accessible on the Web. Children are so familiar with television that it is hard to separate video from it. Children feel they know video because they watch television everyday. Video art is another language. It is read differently from painting, drawing. It has its own art history. Video is read differently from television which children are used to seeing. It is a more demanding viewing. It is important to learn the vocabulary and see it as an art form, to see how it functions differently than television. When you say animation, children automatically think of cartoons. Cartoons are a great art form, but students need to learn why video art is different and what is its special language. What I find difficult is the lack of video art history available to children. Video art books only have stills, and it is very expensive to get copies of original video works. Students cannot understand the art of Pippolty Risk by seeing a still frame from her video. With time-based art, it is very hard to introduce students to great pieces of video art in class. Therefore museum experiences are important for young video artists to see original video works.

Ilona: How much can be done with the camera itself? How important is it to play with the camera, to shake it?

Shaw: I try and get students to think about what they are doing. I think experimenting is important. There is a time to do that, and yet there is a vocabulary. It is not about handheld, or a tripod, or shaking versus not shaking. Video is a tool that allows you to be poetic with your ideas. The question is always what are you trying to express? Maybe your poetry is telling you to shake the camera, and you want to communicate that to the viewer. There is a time to do unusual experiments to shoot from the floor, from the ceiling, or upside down. At a point, however, you want to start thinking about what does it mean—sure it may look really fun—but what does it mean for the viewer to watch it: I see art teachers teaching the poetry in art and using video as one of their tools. Different tools say things differently. Our job is to provide tools and enough knowledge about the poetics of art, and of course the more you are aware of the intrinsic nature of video maybe the better you are able to pass that along through the inner excitement of the video camera. We can pass on the tools and expose our students to tools that express visual poetics.

Ilona: So shaking the camera can be a step toward developing a vocabulary of video art.

Shaw: I have done a Yoko Ono poem on how to find yourself as a video artist by making a list of steps, like shaking the video camera and turning it upside down. Students can make a list of silly things that can be done with the video camera and feel comfortable doing this. But then students develop their own vocabulary of the camera and what it can do. Students need to look for meaning in the different shots. OK, that looks interesting, but what could that mean, and where are we going with this? Definitely students need to play and experiment to know that the camera can do more then just sit on a tripod. You could say it is easy for me, because I have extra cameras. A lot of teachers are fearful of children spinning around and dropping their only digital video camera. I think there are alternatives like very inexpensive surveillance video cameras that hook into a VCR and allow students to experiment using their TVs as monitors—even videotaping the results.

Ilona: I think that is true with any media. I would not just hand a child clay and say make a bowl. I would have them take a piece of clay to experiment with first, to understand its possibilities. How do you think we can encourage school video programs, like the morning school news, to be a work of art?

Shaw: We incorporate our video animations into the morning news. We use a blue screen, which allows us to make different backgrounds. Instead of just featuring morning school announcements, we include art that kids drew, and we include improvised performances with the news from the video class prop box. With iMovie, we can change location for the news, incorporating unusual backgrounds

and environments and making even the titles fun. We reported the news from a tree, from the teachers' rest room. Improvising with student reporters can be very innovative each day and changed on a daily basis to keep it exciting. It does not have to be just a camera on a tripod.

Ilona: What would some of your final thoughts and recommendations be?

Shaw: I feel strongly about the importance of taking video in college, as part of the art education degree. Teachers should study video art along with other art media. I know more colleges are doing it, and I think it has to start at the university level. The ideal is to start at the core of your education. There are a lot of grants out there. There are many sources for getting public funding. I just attended an international children's video art festival in Italy. In many countries such South Africa, Denmark, Spain, Portugal, and Canada, video art is sponsored in after school programs. In America, we have many public schools with video offerings. The next phase I think would be to strengthen video art instruction at the college level and to insure that enthusiastic and well-trained art teachers will take on leadership roles, participating in school media programs that are often separated from art. It is hopeful that more video artists are becoming public school artists in residence and that their special short-term projects will inspire everyone in the public schools, from art teachers to students, to pick up from where the resident left off.

Ilona: That is a nice way to get started, a resident video artist who works with the children while educating art teachers. I want to thank you for the many ideas you shared and the time you spent in answering these questions.

Lights! Camera! Action!

9

Changing Places Through Filmmaking

Background

The environment described in this article is that of an elementary school situated in a Midwest suburban school district. The school building, while located on the fringe of the school district, is actually within the corporation limit of a large neighboring city. The school serves approximately 830 Kindergarten through fourth grade students and is the workplace for 89 faculty members and two administrators. The student population has doubled since the school opened its doors in 1996. I am the visual art specialist in the school and project director for *Changing Places*, a school-wide arts-inspired integrated curriculum that employed filmmaking as a process for exploring community issues.

For the purpose of this chapter, the term *integration* is aligned with Beane (1997), who states that curriculum integration *Centers the curriculum on life itself rather than on the mastery of fragmented information within the boundaries of subject areas. It works off a view of learning as the continuous integration of new knowledge and experience so as to deepen and broaden our understanding of ourselves and our world. Its focus is on life as it is lived now rather than on preparation for some later life or level of schooling. It serves the young people for whom the curriculum is intended rather than the specialized interests of adults. It concerns the active analysis and construction of meanings rather than merely assuming the validity of others' meanings. And it brings the idea of democracy to life through its participatory framing.*

Changing Places: An Integrated Curriculum

Prefaced with the concern that today's transient society promotes an apathetic existence, this elementary school community has been actively involved in developing *Changing Places*, an ongoing school-wide initiative that looks to the past, present, and future with hopes of affecting responsible change in creating a sustainable planet. *Changing Places* is an integrated curriculum that encourages students to understand that as people set foot on a place they leave their mark, no matter how much time they spend in a place. The school program supports the concept that, it is by those marks and records that are left behind that we will be judged for the contributions that we have made while in a given place at a given time. Through collaborative planning, the faculty facilitates situations that empower students to confidently share their ideas and direct responsible action.

The goals of the "Changing Places" curriculum are:

- To make learning student centered

- To pose problems of emerging relevance to our students

- To structure learning around community issues

- To seek and value students' points of view

- To adapt existing curriculum to address students' suppositions

- To assess student learning in the context of teaching

- To challenge faculty to facilitate opportunities for students to actively affect change

- To initiate community partnerships to accomplish our goals

The *Changing Places* curriculum began in a most creative way—all art driven, or at least driven by the desire to reflect upon discovery through imagery and written composition. It was originally designed to take a historic look at regional landscape painting, portrait painting, photography, crafts, architecture, and artifacts to see how art captures a place in time to reflect and sometimes influence how we change our place (Sheridan & Zollinger-Sweney, 1998). The curriculum evolved through activities that encouraged action-oriented inquiry, a cyclical process and life-long endeavor that include direct experience, observation and reflection, critical thinking and taking action (Krug, 1997).

Changing Places is based on the belief that our students' education is greater when it can be webbed in school to outside of school into the text of the students and teachers lives (Wilson, 2001). How can teachers create an evolving curriculum that would provide students, both individually and as a school culture, with a sense of their importance in the scheme of both the local and global community? When the staff adopted *Changing Places* as a school-wide initiative in September 1997, a number of issues related to our initial experiences as a school culture were identified. This approach advocates life-centered learning, encouraging planned instruction that looks

beyond the program goals to "issues that provide depth and a variety of perspectives that help students develop significant understanding" (Perrone, 1994, p.12). The design of *Changing Places* endeavors to promote an "understanding of life-centered issues through meaningful educational experiences" (Krug & Cohen-Evron, 2000, p. 258).

Partnerships with Professional Artists

During the past 6 years, many artist residency experiences were designed to broaden the *Changing Places* curriculum. Professional artists were invited to collaborate with the students and faculty in order to challenge all learners in the school to practice alternative means of communication in response to experiences. The professional artists include authors (poets, environmentalists, playwrights), visual artists (ceramicists, metal workers, quilt makers, and muralists), and performing artists (musicians, storytellers, dancers, and puppeteers).

The most extensive collaboration was with Steve Bognar, an independent filmmaker. Bognar collaborated with students and teachers throughout a 3-year filmmaking residency. Early exploration piqued the curiosity of many of the faculty, who had been given classroom equipment (computers, cameras, software, etc.) through state-funded technology programs and were being pressured to use what they were given but had no idea as to how. The first of three annual filmmaking residencies with Bognar provided a peek at the possibilities. It gave us the courage to admit that we didn't have all of the answers and the confidence to ask more questions. It introduced us to a brand new world!

Throughout all of the residency experiences, the faculty discovered that the value of working with professional artists is that they intuitively saw creative potential where we were sometimes blocked by order and routine. The artists brought knowledge of materials and equipment that they have had the time to experiment with, suggesting the most efficient, the best suited, and the surest route to a successful experience. They came to us with a unique perspective that resulted in the potential to concentrate solely on the task at hand, capitalizing on the moments of inspiration and epiphany that occur from the experiences of the participants. And, most importantly, by sharing their own work, the professional artists who came to the school shared a part of their souls. We learned some of their language, heard their words of encouragement, and felt supported by their commitment to our journey.

Filmmaking:
A Transformative Practice

Bognar collaborated with the faculty and students at the school through three annual eight-week residencies during three consecutive school years beginning in 1998. The early activities that were developed for *Changing Places* had introduced the idea of marking time through portrait painting and, as technology evolved, through photography. Filmmaking seemed like a natural extension of the lessons that had been previously introduced. In light of emerging technology, the faculty felt that filmmaking was affordable and would provide the potential to tell stories about personal journeys through the language of the moving image. Current literature supports this supposition: *The DV format and FireWire interface have transformed video production, dramatically lowering the price and hardware requirements for creating professional-quality video – thus making it easier for the rest of us to tap our creative juices, preserve our family memories, promote our businesses and organizations, or just play Hollywood. (Heid, 2000)*

Bognar provided exposure to methods that employed technological advances of the past decade, including a variety of filmmaking formats (16mm, VHS, and digital technology). He indicated that the concept of working in conjunction with the community issues being investigated through the larger *Changing Places* curriculum sounded "very solid and intriguing. The theme of people changing places and places changing people has real potential" (Sheridan, 2002). He also agreed that a professional development component would be beneficial so that the teachers could experiment and learn about the filmmaking process along with the students by developing ideas for using the filmmaking process in their classrooms.

Grant proposals were prepared by the faculty, resulting in initial grant awards of $4,000 from the Ohio Arts Council and $50,000 from the Ohio Environmental Education Fund, a fund that was established by the Ohio Environmental Protection Agency through penalties that are assessed to companies and individuals who have not been kind to the earth. Over the 3 years, the Parent Teacher Organization at the school committed over $20,000 toward the filmmaking project. This funding enabled the faculty to purchase equipment and to pay Bognar's salary.

It is important to understand that Bognar was not hired by the school district. His partnership was with the school faculty, the result of collaborative planning to enhance the activities of the *Changing Places* curriculum. For each of the three years, he was paid for 40 days in a schedule that usually spread out over many months.

The residency schedule was developed to include *core group*[1] sessions and *peripheral group* sessions. The core groups are considered the *brain cell* of the residency. The participants in the *core group* are responsible for developing the concept behind the film. They conceive the story, write the screenplay, storyboard the shots, and audition for the starring roles in the script. Core groups were generally comprised of 12 to 18 students. The core group supervises the filming and does the editing of the raw footage.

Different core groups were assembled for each of the films. Children were selected for a variety of reasons that were as much related to their social wellbeing as to their academic ability to stay successful in the classroom during the course of the residency. A conscious effort was given to selecting a student core group that represented diversity through considerations of academic ability, cultures, ethnicity, gender, learning styles, modes of expression, and so on. Choices made for residency core groups, evidenced by the process of and considerations for selection, illustrated that the diversity of this school community was celebrated as a source of strength and possibility (Beane, 1997).

Teacher core groups consisted of the faculty from the school district who signed up for the professional development workshops associated with the residency. Throughout all of the artist residencies, faculty members were offered an opportunity to learn along with the students. Over the course of 3 years, 47 teachers participated in the filmmaking workshops. Teachers were offered the option to apply for graduate credit from a local university. During these workshops, we encouraged debate about issues affecting our work. As a staff, we created and sustained productive dialogue through self-reflection, collegial dialogue and ongoing critique.

Film production relied heavily on the work of many other people typically referred to as *peripheral groups. Peripheral groups* were usually comprised of anywhere from 100 to 150 students and adults. They became extras when additional characters were required for shots, created scenery and props when the storyline called for them, and assisted with technical tasks including filming, sound, musical accompaniment, and the tedious processes of animation.

During the first residency, three film projects were completed. Two *student* films were created using 16mm technology and one *faculty* film was shot with a VHS camera.

The first film is an animated narrative story in which a giant trash monster named *The Big Cheese* threatens to take over the school because people quit caring. When the trash monster takes control of the school, the students discover that they have the capacity to shrink him and take back the control by changing their attitudes and cleaning up their school.

The second film, *Picture Day*, is a collection of half-second vignettes of each of the students at the school. Picture day in an elementary school, in any school, is a very important day. On that day, students are adding to their public record. That public record will provide evidence that they were in a given place at a given time. This film was inspired by a discussion with Bognar as a way to involve more students in the filmmaking process. All 601 students included in the film both acted and were the cinematographers for the film. This lively, animated and energetic portrait captures the images for posterity, all the while entertaining the viewer. The film also includes audio clips from interviews of kids by kids about why pictures are important.

That first year, the faculty produced a film using VHS technology that is based upon students' ideas about what teachers do after the school day is over is. *What Teachers Do When Kids Go Home* provides a whimsical look at how teachers are viewed by their students.

After all three films were *in the can,* Bognar suggested the idea of contacting the local movie theater to see if they would let us have the use of one of the theaters as a screening rooms for one evening. He reasoned that it set up a win-win situation for both parties involved. From the school's perspective, it provided a professional venue to showcase some admirable work. From the theater management's perspective, it served as a show of community support. We were also confident that the theater would sell a lot of popcorn!

The theater graciously agreed to host the world premiere of the films. We held four separate screenings throughout one evening and during each session we had a full house! We invited the students' families, school board members, school district administrators, and representatives from our funding sources. Over 1,000 people attended the world premiere of the films. The filmmakers, both students and faculty, were called to the front of the theater to answer questions about their projects and take well-deserved bows. This public forum provided the opportunity to thank the community of students, parents, teachers, administrators, local businesses, community agencies, and especially Bognar, for the part each played in making meaningful and memorable experiences for all involved.

As a follow-up, we solicited help from local businesses to create a video collection of all three films: A local filmmaking company dubbed over 200 copies of the films for the cost of the video tape; a high school student who worked for a local printer designed the cover of the video; a local printer produced color copies of the cover free of charge; and, the parents in the school bought the films, generating funds for future projects. So began a relationship with community residents and businesses that lasted throughout the three years of filmmaking.

During the second filmmaking exploration, the availability of digital video format, FireWire[2] interface, and iMovie software made it possible to create professional-quality films using an emerging technology that was relatively affordable, integrated computers, and incorporated hands-on in-house control of the process from beginning to completion (Heid, 2000). Those factors contributed to the development of newly defined partnerships within the school district and a shift in relationships of the planners, instructors, and participants, resulting in the decision to have a second filmmaking residency. Planning for a second residency began midway through the first filmmaking experience. Likewise, planning for the third residency began midway through the second residency.

The potential to explore a variety of filmmaking processes contributed to the sustained interest of the staff. The opportunity to process the information over time contributed to the increased involvement of a large number of students, both child and adult, who voluntarily joined in the learning activities at varying paces and to varying degrees. Ultimately, students and faculty created 19 films during the 3 years, all related to the integrated curriculum *Changing Places*. The films that were created fall into three distinct categories:

- Films that investigate community issues related to change and sound

- Films that document student activities related to the *Changing Places* curriculum

- Films that teach about the process of filmmaking

A few of the 19 films that were produced during the three-year filmmaking course have won acclaim both locally and globally. *The Trash That Came From The Can* appeared on *Zoom*, a national public broadcasting systems television show for children. *Picture Day* was selected as one of 60 films from a field of over 2000 for screening at the Sundance Film Festival in 2000. It has been screened at over 35 film festivals across the United States and around the world. It won *Best Short Documentary* at the Florida Film Festival in 2000, and was screened at the Guggenheim Museum, New York City, on April 14, 2001. The Academy of Motion Picture Arts and Sciences named it one of the *Outstanding Documentaries of 2000*, ranking in the top 20% in contention for an Oscar in 2000.

While I am very pleased with their success, I am most proud of the fact that they leave an archival record of a community's journey within an educational environment that encouraged introspective investigation of personal, social, and technical knowledge, placing significant emphasis on democratic values, respect for human dignity, and celebration of diversity (Beane, 1997). The nature of filmmaking exploration is central to the development of an open dialogue that promoted collaboration, cooperation, and compromise between the director, producer, cinematographers, actors, prop/costume/set designers, distribution agents and audience/critics. The development of ideas and the technical production that ultimately resulted in the creation of the films relied on a mutual respect for all participants. In this environment, humor, openness, and energy were instructional tools used to promote positive and productive relationships between people. Filmmaking provides an opportunity to work together in a manner that is both productive and playful. The nature of the process alleviated isolation and fostered a spirit of collegiality and collaboration. It is this environment that continues to restore my enthusiasm for teaching.

The success that we experienced relied on a variety of factors that included administrative support at the building level, administrative support at the district level, solicitation of support and partnership from funding organizations, open meetings with stakeholders, planning meetings with partners, and collaborative problem solving between the faculty, the filmmaker, and the students. In many schools, there is a definite distinction between administration, faculty, and students. Traditional definitions place each individual in roles that are clearly defined. Administrators manage, teachers teach, and students learn. Those traditions were not standard in this school's environment.

One of the most positive aspects of what occurred during the implementation of the filmmaking curriculum was a shift in relationships between the people in the school community. Bognar was welcomed as a member of the faculty, students directed, and principals acted. But beyond the obvious, with each endeavor, attitudes changed, power structures shifted, and relationships of the participants (students, teachers, administrators, parents, and community partners) were differently defined. The integrated filmmaking curriculum resulted in the development of more positive relationships.

There have been ample opportunities to witness the honest openness, sharing, and trust that are distinctive of the relationships of people working together. They include watching a principal take time out of his busy day running an elementary school building that houses over 800 students to patiently run through multiple takes of a scene that he is acting in until a student/director judges it worthy; or a mother, who takes off time from her job to answer a casting call when an adult is needed to play a role in a script; or a father who trusts the instincts of his child's teacher when she assuages his concerns about the time outside of class that his son will be required to spend through a listing of attributes that are gained by being involved in a core group collaborating on a film project.

The (Re) Integration of Knowledge

Why offer filmmaking to children? Davies (1997) notes "media education is different from other education and virtually unique as a subject area because many of the pupils are likely to have more direct experience as consumers of the products under review than have their teachers" (p. 140). Throughout the *Changing Places* activities, especially during the filmmaking exploration, there have been countless opportunities to witness students' "performing knowledge" (Beane, 1997, p. 61), those times when students (adult and young person) put their knowledge to

use for the group's further understanding rather than just accumulating it for themselves.

Consider the example of the two fourth-grade students who created a camera shot that hadn't been completed on an offsite shoot, a filming opportunity that couldn't be re-created: I came upon two fourth-grade students who were working at an editing station outside their classroom. They were having a serious discussion, the intensity of which caught my attention. They seemed perplexed and when I asked them what they were talking about, one of them told me that they had discovered the fact that they had not completed an important shot for their film project.

They had looked through the raw footage a couple of times, trying to find a shot that showed a time machine disappearing from view (as it was supposedly transporting the actors back to the future). Both of the students remembered filming the shot when the time machine arrived in the past (accomplished by filming the space where the time machine would supposedly land, then placing the time machine in that space and re-shooting the scene), but neither one could remember reversing the order so that the time machine would appear to be disappearing from the scene.

When I asked them if they had any idea how they would remedy the situation, one of them told me that they were considering a couple of solutions. Since they didn't ask me for any suggestions, I simply stood back and listened to them work through a couple of ideas. Through a series of suppositions, which resulted in experimental tests, the students were able to solve their problem. I watched them create the missing clip by reversing the order of the frames for the shots where the time machine appeared to be entering the scene. When they reversed the clips, they had to experiment with a couple of timing adjustments to make the clip work. When they were satisfied with the results, they turned to each other and gave a high five, celebrating their success.

Tales of their technical understanding of the software's capabilities and their reasoning ability to adapt the raw footage that they had to produce what they needed left many of the adult filmmakers marveling at their higher-order thinking. The story of this pair's experimentation and ultimate success stymied many of the faculty members who admitted that they would have had no idea how to solve the dilemma.

And consider the first grader who, through a re-integration of knowledge of the camera and editing software capabilities garnered through his involvement in the first and second grade core group during the third residency, solved a teacher's dilemma by having the confidence to suggest that he could fix a problem: Nathan was working in his first grade classroom on the Friday before Mother's Day. His teacher was on the other side of the room fretting to a new student about not having a picture of the student to put on a project that had been made as a gift for the student's mother. The teacher was using the extra photographs that teachers get after the annual picture day at the school. But she didn't have one for this particular student because the student had enrolled in the school after the annual picture day. She was unhappy because, had she realized the problem sooner, she could have taken a picture and had it developed.

Nathan went over to his teacher and told her that he could take care of the problem. He asked permission to come to my room to get a video camera. He asked me for a camera, telling me that he needed to do something for his teacher, and went back to his classroom. He returned after a couple of minutes to tell me that he needed to download the clip from the camera to the computer so that he could save a frame from the clip in order to get a picture for his teacher. He explained what the picture was for. I sent him into my office to do the necessary steps that resulted in saving a frame as a jpeg on the computer and then I helped him to resize the photograph to the measurement that he indicated by the fingers on his hands using Adobe Photoshop, a program that had not been used in his filmmaking core group. I sent the image to the printer; Nathan retrieved the copy, and then took it to his teacher. The entire transaction took approximately ten minutes. But the story of the feat lasts and lasts.

Nathan's teacher was surprised and somewhat embarrassed. She had taken two of the faculty workshops but she admitted that the solution to her dilemma, the one that Nathan had devised by using the video camera, would never have occurred to her.

I think that it important to note that Nathan's decision to act was supported by the assumption that his teacher would let him try to help her and that, when he asked for the equipment, I would hand him a $1,200 camera simply because he *needed* it. That factor was in direct relation to the shift in relationships between teacher and student that was established during the residencies. This child not only saw a need, but he was also confident enough to assume a responsible role, achievable because the classroom teacher and I respected his considerable dignity!

Conclusion

As educators, we look specifically for work that illustrates enhanced self-concept in our students, their parents and faculty members We always try to document examples of the transfer of experiential learning to other contexts, thereby increasing understanding and application, ultimately promoting and improving future exploration.

One example of a component of the filmmaking experience that resulted in enhanced self-concept is easily described: The audience response at premiere screenings. This is the final assessment for whether a film project is successful. All three years, filmmakers (both young and mature) have felt the pressure of having to complete a film project that will be screened in a public venue with critical review. Community screenings at the local theater provided an opportunity to take students through to a completion in the public domain, a rarity in most educational venues.

That the films have gained worldwide exposure is a testimony to the fact that the assessment standards were set high and not lowered based on the age of the students. Expectations were high and all of the filmmakers took the challenge and met with considerable success!

The filmmaking curriculum offered alternative ways for children (and adults) to express understanding and to explore their own inner language. The school faculty advocated for situations in which students felt self-worth through the freedom of artistic license and through the chance to express themselves, their feelings, and their beliefs. The practice of making films provided a means to activate their senses, their imaginations, their emotions, and all of their life experiences, encouraging learners to make connections between their world and the world society.

The faculty of the school heartily supports the belief that an integration of the arts throughout the curriculum accelerates and facilitates the learning process. We encourage development of learning experiences that offer flexibility and informality in order to provide an opportunity for our students to experiment with materials and processes, experience new situations, generate ideas, and develop communication processes that will stay with them throughout their lives.

Endnotes

[1] The term *core group* is used to describe the participants who worked consistently with the filmmaker, on a daily basis when the schedule was consistent, but for at least one and one-half hours per day when Bognar was at the school. There were primarily two kinds of core groups, those that consisted of student participants and one or two faculty aide/supervisors, and those that were made up of faculty participants alone.

[2] FireWire is a cross-platform implementation of the high-speed serial data bus—defined by IEEE Standard 1394-1995—that can move large amounts of data between computers and peripheral devices. It features simplified cabling, hot swapping, and transfer speeds of up to 400 megabits per second. FireWire speeds up the movement of multimedia data and large files and enables easy connection of digital consumer products—including digital camcorders, digital videotapes, digital videodisks, set-top boxes, and music systems—directly to a personal computer. (http://developer.apple.com/hardware/FireWire/)

Illustrations

Process-Oriented Concept/Filmmaking

This Example illustrates the process and organization related to making two films during the second year of the filmmaking curriculum implementation. The first film is a narrative story about a school play that goes awry, during which second grade students investigated the concept of teamwork through issues of collaboration, responsibility, and compromise. The second film is a documentary that features second grade students talking about issues related to their first day of editing with iMovie software. This film has been used as an advocacy tool to promote the use of filmmaking as a curriculum methodology.

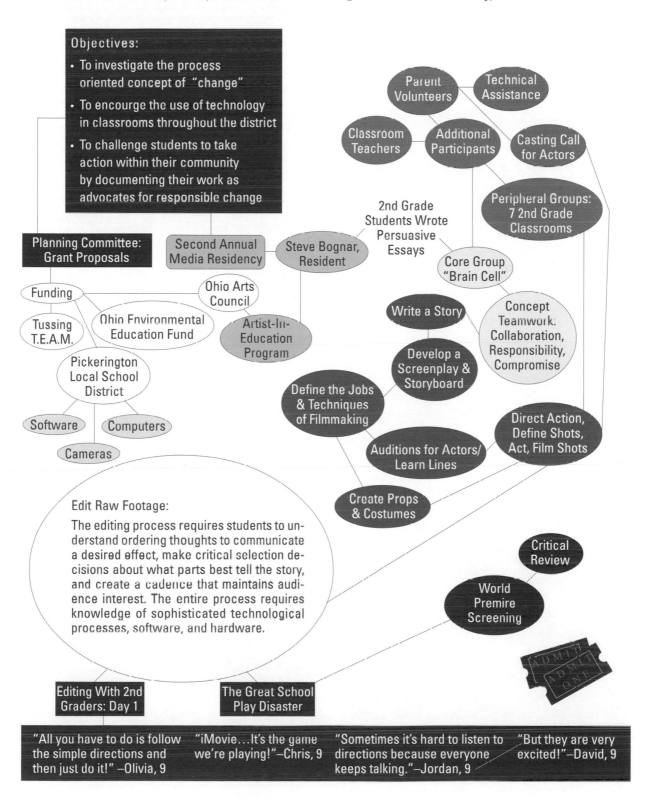

Objectives:
- To investigate the process oriented concept of "change"
- To encourge the use of technology in classrooms throughout the district
- To challenge students to take action within their community by documenting their work as advocates for responsible change

Planning Committee: Grant Proposals

Funding

Tussing T.E.A.M.

Ohio Arts Council

Ohio Environmental Education Fund

Pickerington Local School District

Software

Computers

Cameras

Second Annual Media Residency

Steve Bognar, Resident

Artist-In-Education Program

2nd Grade Students Wrote Persuasive Essays

Parent Volunteers

Technical Assistance

Classroom Teachers

Additional Participants

Casting Call for Actors

Peripheral Groups: 7 2nd Grade Classrooms

Core Group "Brain Cell"

Concept Teamwork: Collaboration, Responsibility, Compromise

Write a Story

Develop a Screenplay & Storyboard

Define the Jobs & Techniques of Filmmaking

Auditions for Actors/ Learn Lines

Direct Action, Define Shots, Act, Film Shots

Create Props & Costumes

Edit Raw Footage:
The editing process requires students to understand ordering thoughts to communicate a desired effect, make critical selection decisions about what parts best tell the story, and create a cadence that maintains audience interest. The entire process requires knowledge of sophisticated technological processes, software, and hardware.

Critical Review

World Premiere Screening

Editing With 2nd Graders: Day 1

The Great School Play Disaster

"All you have to do is follow the simple directions and then just do it!" –Olivia, 9

"iMovie...It's the game we're playing!"–Chris, 9

"Sometimes it's hard to listen to directions because everyone keeps talking."–Jordan, 9

"But they are very excited!"–David, 9

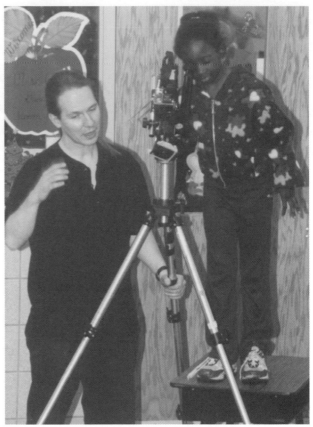

Editing

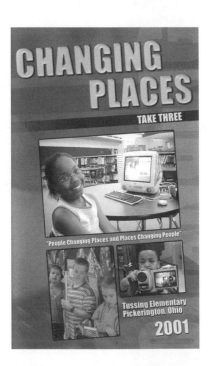

References

Beane, J. (1997). *Curriculum integration: Designing the core of democratic education.* New York and London: Teachers College Press.

Davies, M. (1997). *Fake, fact, and fantasy: Children's interpretations of television reality.* Mahwah, NJ: Lawrence Erlbaum Associates.

Heid, J. (2000). Home-movie magic. *Macworld.* April, p. 74-79.

Krug, D. (1997). Action-oriented inquiry strategies. *Art & ecology* [On-line]. Available: http://www.artsednet.getty.edu/ArtsEdNet/Resources/Ecology/Curric/action.html.

Krug, D. & Cohen-Evron, N. (2000). Curriculum integration positions and practices in art education. *Studies in Art Education, 41*(3), 258-275.

Perrone, V. (1994). How to engage students in learning. *Educational Leadership.* 51(5), 11-13.

Sheridan, M. (2002). *A descriptive analysis of a case study: integrated curriculum through filmmaking,* (Doctoral dissertation, Ohio State University). Dissertation Abstracts International, 3072926.

Sheridan, M. & Zollinger-Sweney, B. (1998). Changing places: An interdisciplinary elementary curriculum. *Voices: A USSEA Newsletter Insert on Teaching Practices, 22*(1), 3-4.

Wilson, B. (2001). *Shifting (In)sights: A dialog on the emergence of visual culture.* Slide Talk: NAEA Visual Culture Panel. New York City, New York.

Joanna Black

In conjunction with students:
Justin Yu, Priscilla Li, Amanda Ielsma, Chrisitine Mercier, and Nancy Vuoung—ages 16-17

From the Still to the Moving Image:

10

How to Create an Award-Winning Video

The video, *The Lost Dynasty,* won first place in the grade 10-12 category at "Sprockets," The Toronto International Film Festival for Children, the same organization which runs the famous Toronto International Film Festival. Priscilla, who was part of the video crew, wrote about her experience: It "was the result of hundreds of hours of planning, scripting, shooting, and post production editing. I think that's what probably won us the Sprockets award...the genuine idea, this historical period piece set in China, of all places, is created by this group of kids." Nancy sums it up, "It was a lot of work to prepare for this movie and it paid off in the end... my experience in creating *The Lost Dynasty* was great. I was able to learn many new things and have fun creating it." In this chapter I will discuss this project in detail: the teaching of narrative film; the integration of Visual Arts into this project; the production of digital stills and their connection to the video, as well as the creation of the final video product.

First and foremost, this experience would not have happened without my students. So, as well as my point of view as a teacher being expressed, I have also included those opinions of my pupils involved.

As a teacher, I have always integrated Visual Arts with videography. This is my eleventh year teaching video production at the high school level and my students have won many awards internationally, nationally, and locally. They are hardworking, talented individuals. Last year my program included teaching video production to senior high school students. During this course I created a different way of approaching narrative video in which there was an integration of digital photography ideas utilized by Cindy Sherman. I will outline this innovative approach in which narrative video was taught by having the still image be the impetus for the moving one.

The Structure of the Curriculum: Preproduction

Before the video curriculum began, students learned and had already been taught animation and part of this was learning pixilation. The group members involved in the making of *The Lost Dynasty* were Justin, Priscilla, Amanda, Christine, and Nancy. In the course they gained a working knowledge of basic video shots, camera angles, camera movements and framing/composition. The next step was learning how to write a script and film narrative productions which I believe are two of the most complicated tasks when teaching video at the high school level because it involves creating story lines and directing actors.

This entire project entailed that three products be made: a digital still image, a video, and desktop-published VHS covers or CD covers. Utilizing visual arts skills was part of all three works. I began by showing the film by the American independent director, John Sayles, called *Matewan*. This introduced students to an accomplished American director, and the significance of Sayles who is an independent director working outside of the major Hollywood studios. We analyzed his untraditional, pacifistic protagonist, who, as Sayles himself writes, would likely never have been accepted as a hero in mainstream American film. We then read parts of his book, *Thinking in Pictures*, in which he outlines the process involved in making his film. Students learned about the importance to Sayles of visual images, the framing of shots, and the manner in which he approached the screenplay. They discussed notions of racism and socioeconomic class structures in the screenplay and they became aware of the concrete day-to-day realities Sayles and his film crew confronted in terms of financing his film, writing the script, casting, location scouting, "shooting" and editing.

After this, students formed groups in which they decided upon the basics of what their film would consist: era, culture, and genre. We examined Cindy Sherman's photographic portraits from 1977 to 1990. "Untitled Film Stills," was Sherman's early black and white body of photography in which the central idea is the depiction of heroines reminiscent of 1950s films. We proceeded to look at her series on "Rear Screen Projections" from the early 1980s: In this body of work Sherman created color photographs in which the settings are reminiscent of the 1960s and 1970s. She projected the settings onto herself using overhead projectors and then took the photograph. After this, we examined Sherman's series entitled "Centerfolds," "Pink Robes" and "Fashion" and finished with her "History Portraits" works. I wanted to particularly stress to the students a few key areas: firstly, Sherman's chameleon like capabilities to fit into the surroundings she creates; second, her ability to self transform given each new photo-graphic context in which she places herself; third, her superb compositions in which her facial expression, her pose, the manner in which she is placed in her environs, is not only visually superb but is suggestive of the subjects' psychology; and last, I wanted students to be aware of Sherman's manipulation of the female image and her exploration of the impact of image representation. I found the series "Untitled Stills" particularly pertinent to video/film as Sherman constructs herself as a familiar archetypal film heroine around which the viewer is invited to build a narrative.

After studying Sherman's body of work, students were then told that they, like Sherman, must transform themselves into new characters and document this via digital photography, paying particular attention to their setting, costume, make-up, positioning, lighting, props, and pose. Thus, before writing their own character in a screenplay, all pupils had to visually depict themselves in a pose, which describes their character's personality. I asked the students to make certain that their digital images would appear in the film; how they decided to do this would be their decision. The movie, *Butch Casssidy and the Sundance Kid* is an ideal example of how to do this: throughout this movie there are many shots in which a still image transforms into a moving one extremely effectively. Along with the digital photographs, students wrote a character sheet depicting the character's personality, past experiences, present situation, and motivations. This character sheet is a brief synopsis. The character study used for the digital photograph was later used to develop a character in the film. Hence, students would work out characterization before the plot was written.

The digital photographs produced by the film crew were the foundation for the screenplay. Using these pictures, students wrote film treatments, then drew the storyboard, and finally wrote the shooting script. Again we turned to John Sayles's book, *Thinking in Pictures*, for in it he has included the full version of the shooting script, *Matewan*, which students used as a model for professional scriptwriting. They were expected to write the script in the same manner using fonts, proper capitalization, spacing, and proper script text format. Finally students created call sheets, crew lists, location drawings, and storyboards of scenes that needed prior visual depictions.

Before actually getting involved in the production process, students were taught the difference between acting for film and acting for the theatre. Michael Caine's video, *The Acting in Film: An Actor's Take on Movie Making,* offers a superb description of the way in which one acts for films. Any prior acting experience students had was in theater. We ended up doing some improvisation to differentiate between the two acting styles. During improvisation, it was pointed out to students that it is not only what they say that is of significance but how they say it. Slight body movements, minute facial expressions and expressive poses are equally as important as the spoken word.

Overall, the process of preproduction for the students was lengthy. I kept hearing the question over and over again: "When are we going to start filming?" Students had to create their photographs, write a screenplay, draw storyboards, create crew sheets, location plans, plan their costumes and their make-up, and coordinate their filming schedule. What I have outlined above is the preproduction stage of video making and it took them easily three weeks. Nancy reflects upon this process, "I now understand the basic method of creating a movie, which was the purpose of this assignment. It's not just coming up with a story line and then filming right away, but the preproduction is very important also. It makes things a lot easier when filming the actual movie because the setting, scenes and shots are already decided. Knowing what to film and framing the exact shots—it helped us when putting the movie together." Amanda comments on the concrete day-to-day concerns the group had: " …we realized there were a lot of things that go into making a movie that people overlook and this was especially true for the type of movie we were making which was an historical one. For one, there was finding a setting that was authentic: Nancy got into contact with a lady from the Japanese Cultural Center; we also used sections of Priscilla's building, as well as a section of the Japanese Cultural Center. Now that we had sets we needed costumes and during the time when our movie

took place men had long hair and women did not have blond hair." To this end they bought elaborate wigs which they wore everyday of the shooting phase. Justin recounts his perception of the planning stage: *Before filming, a thorough and strenuous preproduction phase began, during which an immense amount of brainstorming and storyboarding took place. Although at the time irritating and very frustrating, this was also a crucial part in the production of the film. Proceeding through with this stage laid the foundation for our movie and the plans for the following weeks to come. There is no doubt that preproduction was the most aggravating period of the whole production. …Soon after we had finished the majority of the planning and such, filming began.*

Filming: Production

The production process involved students shooting video on location. They chose a variety of sites throughout the greater Toronto area. Nothing makes for a more boring video than shooting scene after scene at a school and trying to make it seem as if each were in a different location. Permission forms were signed by parents enabling students to videotape during the school day, during and in-between classes, during the mornings and evenings, and on weekends—in short, whenever they could. Filming took the group approximately one week. About the filming process Justin writes, *Although some may think filming would be the most challenging and time consuming task, it was executed surprisingly quickly and smoothly. Since most of the preparations were already complete, all we needed to do was to go out and recreate what we had envisioned on paper. What you create in your mind and what is actually captured by the camera is a totally different story. Taking into consideration that level of product that we were to produce, it became evident after some time that hiring helicopters, clearing streets and filming from cranes would be a touch out of our reach. Thus, we had to compromise some of our more ambitious shots and eliminate some plot ideas totally. Although disappointing, problem solving and getting us out of those tough spots gives a certain feeling of satisfaction.*

For practical reasons, the group shot the film "out of continuity," meaning not in the chronological order of the script. They confronted practical problems: the fighting scenes were rather complex and, as a result, they were choreographed. Moreover, by the time the group began filming it was December in Canada. It rained (not snowed!) and it was cold and damp. Christine writes, *I can remember filming the final battle in the pouring rain and being thrown/pushed into a giant puddle of ice cold water. Including the wind that may have been the coldest I've ever been."* Priscilla provides similar observations: *"When Christine and Amanda fought in the rain outside, both of them had to lie on the ground and they were SOAKED! We would come in from the rain and grab the jackets and huddle and cry. We thought it would be a good special effect and we were so disappointed when it didn't show up on film. I guess this made us realize what hard work shooting a movie could be, with the crazy hours and the crazy weather.*

Postproduction

Editing is part of postproduction. The screenwriter of *the Shawshank Redemption*, Frank Durabont (1996) wrote about this process: "Finally there looms the editing room, where the movie is *really* made (everything else is mere preamble). It's where the editor and director write the final draft of the script, using film instead of paper. It never ceases to amaze me how a movie takes on a life of its own during cutting, making its own suggestions and demands" (pp.133-134).

Part of the editing process is the act of cutting down the film. The famous film editor, Walter Murch writes, *Many years ago my wife, Aggie, and I went back to England for our first anniversary (She is English, although we'd been married in the United States) and I met some of her childhood friends for the first time. "Well, what is it that you do?" one of them asked, and I replied that I was studying film editing. "Oh, editing," he said, "that's where you cut out the bad bits." Of course I became (politely) incensed: "It is much more than that. Editing is structure, color, dynamics, manipulation of time, all of these other things, etc. etc." What he had in mind was home movies: "Oops,*

there's a bad bit, cut it out and paste the rest back together." Actually, twenty-five years down the road, I've come to respect his unwitting wisdom. (p.10)

Although one of the primary roles of an editor is indeed to do just that—cut down a scene—I feel I must be more specific here. Editing also involves putting the film segments in a coherent order; integrating music, voiceovers, subtitles, credits; and working with spacing, timing, repetitive elements and the magic of special effects. Editing can be the most labor intensive of all the stages of filmmaking taking up huge chunks of classroom time and time outside of class. During postproduction, students worked using the following software: iMovie (if movie editing was new to them) or Final Cut Pro or Adobe Premiere. For the special effects they used 3D Studio Max and Adobe After Effects.

Editing is where the 'alchemy' of filmmaking happens. No matter how good the preproduction and production are, if students cannot edit well the final product will not be good. It is analogous to making a collage. The pre-production planning process is like making rough sketches for the collage; the production process is similar to creating the individual works of which the collage will be comprised; the postproduction is the creation of the final full visual text. It is during postproduction when those individual pieces are placed on a large canvas. The way one does this can make or break the artwork and it is the same in film. Hard work and creativity in this area is paramount.

Priscilla writes, *we had all these ongoing jokes during filming that we could just do everything in 3D studio MAX...if we'd forget makeup or a chunk of our costume, we would just tell Justin to remodel us in After Effects.* Justin, who oversaw most of the postproduction process, comments, *"I've always been taught to aim high, but when making a film this can get you into a lot of trouble! Watching those Hollywood special effects in theatres can really get a little kid's imagination stirring. Resulting was a movie filled with fireballs, magic portals, and super human powers. This alone generated almost half the work load of the post production stage; but in the end it paid off big time.*

Issues of Multiculturalism

Canada is known for its multicultural policies. Toronto is a rich, vibrant city comprised of many different cultures, and, in fact, to illustrate this point, when driving through the city one sees pockets of different ethnic groups meriting their own district. Names such as "The Greek Village" are common in which street signs are written in the native language of specific cultures that have settled there. Don Mills Collegiate Institute is reflective of this multiculturalism. In the most recent comprehensive school profile taken from a student body of just over 1,000 students, it was found that 53% of students had a primary language other than English, and that students' birthplaces were from 55 different countries. 75 percent of students and/or their parents had immigrated to Canada and there were 44 different languages represented in the school. Given this type of environment, and in addition, given a city that has numerous theaters screening foreign films, it is not surprising that the group who made *The Lost Dynasty* decided to make a "foreign language" film. The entire film was shot in Chinese, and later the students added subtitles. Amanda and Christine did not know the Cantonese or Mandarin languages so they had to memorize their lines.

Issues: Student Interaction and Lessons in Solving Group Conflicts

In a professional production, making a film requires a large cast and a large crew all of whom have different responsibilities and are working towards the same goal: the making of a successful film. The same is true of a classroom narrative film although on a smaller scale. My students worked in groups of five to six people, and every group had their own dynamics. I have had students frustrated to the point of tears, students working together extremely well (rare, but it does happen!) but in all situations they had to face and overcome many conflicts. While Priscilla, Justin, Christine, Amanda, and Nancy were working on *The Lost Dynasty*, three other groups were working on their own narrative films. Priscilla's group was the one which had to deal with the most conflicts. In filmmaking students have to work closely inside and outside of school for a long duration of time. They have to work in tandem, some shouldering more responsibility, some putting in

more hours; they must suffer the whims of perfectionists who drive them crazy, and students who time manage either well or poorly. Believe me, it is all too evident when students do not carry their weight or hinder their group. Christine reflects on this: *Soon like the weather we didn't get along. I guess if you work in large groups such as five you can't always get along and someone always gets singled out or forgotten about. Everyone except yourself forgets the little things that you do. Another problem was that of scheduling. With five people you're bound to have scheduling conflicts. Unfortunately mine were on the opposite days as everyone else and I had to sacrifice everything (yes everything) until the completion of this assignment. So unfortunately for me my personal experiences were not something pleasant or enjoyable but the end product was well worth the hard work and the years of therapy I will need (Just kidding about the therapy part, it wasn't that bad!)*

Justin also comments on this, stating, *"There was certainly no shortage of disagreements and conflicts amongst the group; whether it be concerning the story line or shooting schedule you can be sure there was never a dull moment!"*

In fact, I had to intervene more than a few times in my role as a teacher because of the mounting frustration; however, I look at this as a positive experience in which the group has to work out their problems in order to successfully complete a production. It is full of emotional challenges, personal interactions, hurt feelings, and compromises, but this is all reflective of the type of dynamics occurring on professional crew sets. Students learn that they have to work together and to find resolutions that will be satisfactory and this is a good thing. The role of the teacher in this situation is more like that of a social worker helping individuals work through their situations in order to resolve their issues.

Some Final Words

Justin comments, *"The making of* The Lost Dynasty *was in no way a 'cakewalk': it was chalk filled with huge problems and struggles. However, in the end it was more than worth it. We set an extremely high goal and we set out to* attain it, we challenged ourselves. With the creative freedom that we were given, there was nobody telling us that 'this couldn't be done' or 'this was out of reach'. With that freedom we might have gone a little overboard but what's surprising is that we actually did it."

And Amanda writes that, *"All in all, it was a great experience. The recognition we have gotten is neat, too. Don't get me wrong, but I would rather remember the fun times we had making it."* And that, in a nutshell, is what student filmmaking is all about. It is about writing a good screenplay, visualizing the shots, and creatively putting together the final visual, sound and textural compilation; it is about working within a team structure, learning and enjoying the complicated, demanding, challenging but entirely creative and rewarding process." To this end, Priscilla concludes, *"It was an amazing experience. I would do it again in a second."*

Illustrations
CD Covers

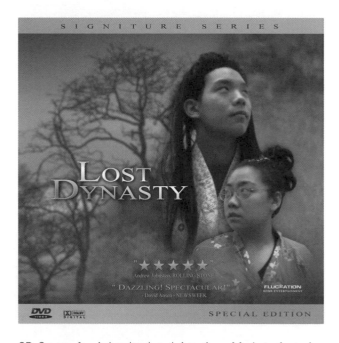

CD Covers for Asian (top) and American Markets featuring images of Justin Yu and Priscilla Li.

Amanda Jelsma in a kimono (top). Christine Mercier in an action pose.

Storyboard

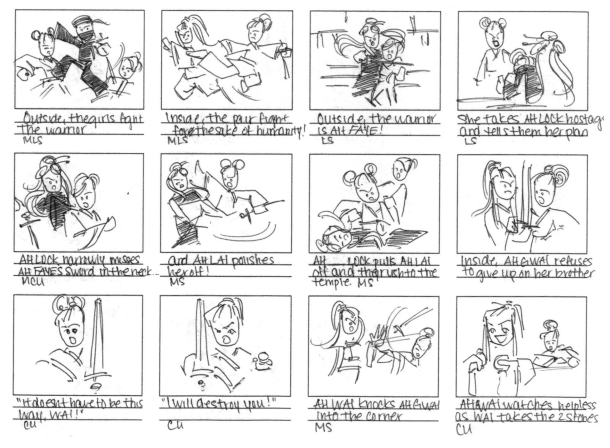

An example of the storyboard.

SCRIPT VERSION 3.01
THE LOST DYNASTY
November 2001

CAST

TZE HO	Justin Yu
AH GWAI	Priscilla Li
AH LAI	Christine Mercier
AH LOCK	Nancy Vuong
AH FAYE	Amanda Jelsma
AH WAI	Justin Yu

PROLOGUE

Thousands of years ago, a God named TZE HO fell in love with a mortal woman. Although this was strictly forbidden, they gave birth to a son and a daughter, both blessed with superhuman knowledge and strength. Knowing that his children would never be accepted into his Kingdom, TZE HO created a magical stone that held the power of eternal life, so they may one day return to his side and rule the dynasty they were once robbed of. When the Gods found out, they placed each child in separate ends of the country, believing that they would never find each other, telling TZE HO that he was forbidden to ever see them again.

Now, the story continues in the next generation with TZE HO's children, AH WAI and AH GWAI. When AH WAI discovers a legend about a lost dynasty, he believes that this was his past life, and his obsession grows so intense that he turns evil, vowing to find the keeper of the other half so he can combine them and turn into a God. Now TZE HO must find his daughter and prepare her for the ultimate to defend Earth, and everything she believes in.

SETTING

1	Guangzhou - Tea House owned by AH FAYE'S family
2	Guangzhou - Temple where AH GWAI learns Kung Fu
3	Beijing - Temple where AH WAI lives
4	Shanghai - Temple where AH WAI and AH GWAI fight

OPENING CREDITS
AH WAI narrates the prologue

1. INT - GUANGZHOU - EVENING - TEA HOUSE

Opening credits blur and fade into a plate of steaming stir-fry set on a table in a restaurant. A hand picks it up and we follow the figure as she moves through the Japanese screen doors.

CUT TO - Zoom Out - We see AH GWAI as she sets the dish on the table, where all of her friends are already seated.

> CUT TO - Group Shot - AH FAYE
> What took you so long?

> CONT'D - Group Shot - AH LAI
> She's bringing you dinner, leave her alone. What's to eat?

> CONT'D - Group Shot - AH GWAI
> This one's fried rice… the other one is fried noodles.

> CONT'D - Group Shot - AH GWAI
> It doesn't matter to me! I'm so hungry, I'll eat anything!

OFF - A noise is heard just outside door. All four girls turn.
CUT TO - A close up of the stranger's feet, tilt up to reveal TZE HO, the God disguised as a highly respected mortal Judge.
PAN TO - AH FAYE hurries out and greets her father's guest while her friends bow to him.

> CONT'D - MCU - AH FAYE
> Uncle TZE HO! I missed you!

CONT'D - TZE HO ignores her, walks right past AH FAYE, who is clearly not ex-pecting that kind of reaction. He walks over to the girls, and helps AH GWAI up.

> MCU - TZE HO (Extends his arms to her)
> You must be AH GWAI. I have been looking for you for a long time.
>
> (Looks away slightly to the other girls in the room)
> Please let us have a moment to talk privately. We have much to catch up on.

CUT TO - MCU - The girls get up and prepare to leave through the screen door.

Justin Yu in the sun (top). Amanda Jelsma with Nancy Vuong.

References

Caine, M. (1989). *Acting in film: An actor's take on movie making*. New York: British Broadcast Production.

Darabont, F. (1996). *The shawshank redemption: The shooting script.* New York: Newmarket Press.

Don Mills Collegiate Institute: *School profile*. (1998), Toronto, Canada. (Available from Don Mills Collegiate Institute or the Toronto Board of Education.)

Monash, P. (Executive Producer). (1969). *Butch Cassidy and the Sundance Kid*. USA: 20th Century Fox Corporation.

Murch, W. (1995). *In the blink of an eye*. Los Angeles: Silman-James Press.

Sayles, J. (1987). *Thinking in pictures: The making of the movie, Matewan*. Boston: Houghton Mifflin Company.

Pamela G. Taylor

Music Video in High School

11

Students in a typical high school art class have a wide range of interests, maturity, and ability levels. With these various levels come different concerns, perspectives, and expertise. The value of multiple and differing class approaches reveals many opportunities for understanding and teaching including student-initiated and directed learning that is relevantly connected to popular youth culture. One such student-initiated learning experience may include the study and criticism of music videos.

With unprecedented immediacy, music video is a medium that creates artists, invents the world it represents, and changes life as we know it while purposefully disrupting the flow of our visual landscape. New visual ideas are brought to light through the medium of music video faster than any other medium. With remote control in hand, many music video viewers watch the screen for hours as image after image is literally thrown at them faster than the speed of light. Designed to hold up to repeated viewing, successful music videos are densely textured with images and clips that are performance-driven, gothic, animated, computerized, moody dreamscapes, classic portraiture, futuristic extravaganzas, and up-close-and-personal home movies (Reiss & Feineman, 2000).

Typically high school students spend more hours in front of the television watching music videos than they do in the classroom. To date there are seven music video channels from which viewers become keenly aware of the cutting edge images, styles, and innuendoes incorporated in the video performances of their favorite music stars. In addition, programs that rate, describe, satirize as well as promote specific music video artists serve to motivate as well as inform viewers of this increasingly important form of youth culture.

The following is a story of how one music video was used in a high school art class as method and means toward developing media literacy through understanding signs, symbols, references, and art appropriation techniques. The resulting project was the creation of an interactive computer hypertext that mapped and linked the students' thoughts, ideas, and interpretations of the band Rage Against the Machine's video entitled *People of the Sun*.

Pastiche and Appropriation

The Art II class began a unit of instruction centered on artist Mark Tansey's *Innocent Eye Test* and the use of pastiche or borrowing and changing images and styles in art. After discussions of various artists who borrowed from each other including Van Gogh, Gauguin, Ringgold, and

Wood, the students began research to find works of art from which they would create their own pastiche projects. They looked for a work of art that they could change or satirize to fit their own ideas. They also deliberately searched for critical writings, artists' statements and historical or cultural influences.

Once the students chose their research, they presented their plans to the class. Typical ideas included re-facing the *Mona Lisa* with varied expressions and creating self-portraits in Grant Wood's *American Gothic*. Other ideas such as placing an image of the world in the figure of Edvard Munch's *The Scream* and manipulating Napoleon's arm to be a "scratching" form of Jacques Louis David's *Napoleon in His Study* were presented. A more interesting idea came from a student who wanted to create a colored pencil drawing of a photo of Dominique Mazeud's *The Great Cleansing of the Rio Grande* with an added grocery cart. Another student explored and challenged her own Iranian ethnicity in Rene Magritte's *Lovers* by choosing to cover the male figure only and thereby, unveiling the female. And one student who had been looking at the painting *Zapatistas* by J. C. Orozco came rushing in one day with videotape in hand.

Chris had been watching MTV (music television) one night and noticed many art works and symbols that related to his chosen work of art. He couldn't wait to share them with the class. The music video featured the rap group Rage Against the Machine's song *People of the Sun*.

The students and the teacher were completely enthralled as they watched the video in class. The students began telling/teaching the teacher about a rap group that she had never seen or heard. There was an authentic dialogue going on where the student voices were just as important as the teacher's voice.

The class discussed the video at length and with each new exciting viewing came even more ideas and inspiration. Finally, there was simply no choice. The students wanted to go further, they wanted to know what was behind the images in the video. They wanted to understand why this popular rap group was concerned with *The People of the Sun*.

Rage Against the Machine's *The People of the Sun*
Since 1516 minds attacked and overseen,
now Crawl amidst the ruins of this Empty Dream
Wit their borders and boots on top of us,
pullin' knobs on the floor of their toxic metropolis
So how you gonna get what you need ta get?
Tha gut eaters, blood drenched get offensive like Tet
When the fifth sun sets get back reclaim,
tha spirit of Cuahtemoc alive an untamed
Face tha funk now blastin' out ya
Speaker, on the one Maya, Mexica
That vulture came ta try and steal ya name but
Now you found a gun
This is for the People of the Sun
It's comin' back around again
This is for tha people of tha sun
Neva forget that tha wip snapped ya back,
ya Spine cracked for tabacco,
oh I'm the Marlboro Man
Our past blastin' on through that versers,
Bridgades of taxi cabs rollin' broadway like Hearses
Troops strippin' zoots, shots of red mist,
Sailors blood on tha deck,
Come sista resist
Tha new era of terror check this pronto lens,
tha City of angels does tha ethnic cleanse
Heads bobbin' to that funk out ya
Speaker, on tha one Maya, Mexica
That vulture came ta try an steal ya name but now
You found a gun. . . You're history
This is for the People of the Sun
It's comin' back around again
This is for the people of the sun.
(De La Rocha, Z. & Rage Against the Machine, 1996)

The video features the members of the rap band, Rage Against the Machine, performing in a brick-walled room. Shocking images of death and accusations seem to flash incessantly with each dramatic beat of the song.

Throughout their performance, the band appears to be yelling at the viewer as if they are trying to demand their attention.

The video begins with a black and white still image of a bearded man inside a four-pointed star that appears to be some type of medal or ribbon award. Over this image are the words, "In 1994—the Zapatista army rose up demanding an end to the P.R.I.— the U.S. backed Mexican dictatorship" (De La Rocha, Z. & Rage Against the Machine, 1996). The scene that follows, featuring a movie projector is reminiscent of propaganda war films shown in movie houses across the U.S. during World War II. White words are projected on a black wall of what appears to be a morgue with two partially covered bodies lying on gurneys. Projected phrases include, "Racism, dumping their own waste, tuberculosis, no decent roof over our heads, no land, no food, enough is enough."

Other images include civilian armies with black scarves partially covering their faces, graffiti-filled walls, and phrases accusing the Mexican government of electoral fraud, murder, and media control. Scenes of people climbing Mayan ruins and holding skulls introduce the viewer to historic images of young Mexican rebels dressed in white being lassoed and dragged behind sombreroed men on horses. The morgue scene follows X-ray images of broken necks, fingers, and hands again. A young child sits in front of the black wall of the morgue with projected words reflecting on his face. Scenes of military tanks and guns seemingly unloaded by U.S. soldiers follow along with U.S. helicopters filling the air. Phrases flash across the screen revealing the $64 million U.S. arms export package to the Mexican government. The projected image in the morgue appears to melt the words "People of Mexico" and "justice" as more bodies are covered with white sheets. Images of mural-like paintings of Mexican leaders are covered with such revealing text as "The P.R.I. is a 70 year-old one party dictatorship that is U.S. supported and financed. They control labor unions, television, and electoral agencies. 200 members of the opposition party have been murdered. The P.R.I. hand-picks all political candidates."

The video continues with rapidly alternating scenes of the band and other shocking images of death, coffins, burials, and skulls including what appear to be line drawings and political cartoons. The final images of the video flash and then burn the words "There Must Not Be Another Vietnam in Mexico" as the film seemingly melts away on the television screen.

Interpreting the Video

Following several viewings and discussions about research questions and ideas, the class began the formulation of a single communal hypertextual computer web[1] to aid them in their study and interpretation. The organization of the computer web included video clips, lyrics, and stills placed in the middle with the student research boxes surrounding them (See Figure 1). The students' boxes contained their own formulated research questions and ideas for discovery.

Chris began the web by placing some general information about the history of Diaz's modernization of the country. He described the resulting oppression of the poorest people of Mexico that inspired Orozco's painting. Chris explained that the painting depicts the rebels, following E. Zapata in fighting against the established government.

Now the people of Mexico are being oppressed again. Yet, just as the Zapatistas of the past rebelled against the injustice, rebels continue today. It is true history repeats itself. (The lyrics), "It's coming back around again" (are voiced over) flashbacks of the reign of Diaz, like a mirror of what takes place next door in Mexico. The parents next door are beating their kids and what do we do? We give them a hat . . . millions of dollars are sent to Mexico (from the U.S.) to fight the rebels (Chris in Ben, et al., 1996) (See Figure 2).

Chris linked the words, "There must not be a new Vietnam in Mexico," that were flashed across the screen in the video, to an image of Maya Lin's *Vietnam Memorial*. The *Vietnam Memorial* box was linked to another box containing the melting video clip of the word "justice." A dollar sign image from the video was connected to Ben's research box about special effects and personal reflections of the video's meaning and importance to young people. Matt, like many other students, was intrigued with what "EZLN" meant as it had been flashed across the screen throughout the video. "(It is the) Ejercito Zapatista de Liberacion Nacional, the new branch of Zapatistas, who are fighting against the Mexican government and the American president who sends money to Mexico to fight against the rebel movement," he writes in his Storyspace box. Matt linked this box to an image from the video that stated, "If the lie returns in the mouth of the powerful, our voice of fire will speak again. . . EZLN" (De La Rocha, Z. & Rage Against the Machine, 1996). Merrilee and Juliet were excited about the Mayan temple images they saw in the video and chose to try to understand what link this culture had to the meaning of the song (See Figure 3). In her box, Merrilee wrote, "I think this ties in with the video in that the Maya were people of the sun because one of their main gods was the sun god, for whom they sacrificed many innocent lives" (Merrilee in Ben, et al., 1996). This link revealed to Merrilee, Juliet, and the rest of the class how interconnected culture and art are to the understanding of such a heated political issue as was presented in the music video form of popular culture.

Juliet looked at Mayan architecture and grimacing sculptures, also in the video, but she went further to try and understand more about the rap group. "Rage Against the Machine is a very symbolic name for the group because their songs deal with many different issues concerning problems with the world and society. Rage means anger and the machine stands for capitalism," she wrote (Juliet in Ben, et al., 1996). This was also a very significant and insightful explanation. Juliet's class had previously studied the role of capitalism and society's resulting consumerism in our study of environmental crises. Therefore, her ability to use and connect what she had studied previously indicated her understanding that our lessons were not isolated activities, but meaningfully connected to each other.

When Merrilee said that she didn't like the music style of the video, but felt the theme was important, I challenged her to voice her criticism in the web. She responded that "We need to help those people, but not through so much

violence" (Merrilee in Ben, et al., 1996). Another student, Kim, wrote, "I think the group was trying to say that everyone tries to solve problems with guns and violence and people have forgotten where they came from. It's like we have lost our values and traditions" (Kim in Ben, et al., 1996). Such self and societal reflection became a very important aspect of this music video study experience. Many of the students commented that looking at music videos, especially controversial ones such as this, usually made them angry. However, they rarely looked to the source or reflected on the reasons for this anger. Because this project required them to research and reflect, they were beginning to understand and connect what was going on in the video with their own lives. In the process, they were beginning to question many of their old assumptions about the society in which they live as well as, the videos they watch.

Joe discovered that an image used in the video could have been a woodcut created by artist J. G. Posado who worked in the late nineteenth and early twentieth centuries. Joe included an image of Posado's *Don Quixote and Sancho Panzo* with its laughing skulls and skeletons. He linked this image to his other research of the Mexican celebration known as Los Dias de los Muertos or Days of the Dead (See Figure 4). In this box, Joe explained that the festival was full of frivolity, feasting, and fun, as families remembered and honored their dead loved ones. Joe created links to a sugar skull, an example of the many special foods such as candy, breads and buns baked in the shape of skulls for the celebration. He wrote about many "Days of the Dead" activities for the Mexican children including puppet shows and mask parades in his web box. He linked this box with the video clip of a boy and a still from the video of a hand holding a skull. Joe also discovered the skull-filled work of artists Calavera and Daumier. Joe's research was especially significant, as I had included the Mexican celebration of Los Dias de los Muertos in my classes prior to this activity. Joe's research provided more value to the lesson by virtue of his personal involvement, initiative, and investment in the structure of the curriculum of the class.

Analyzing the
Student Initiated Experience

Because this process involved the students in teaching their teacher about this music video, the students were empowered to open and design the curriculum. They became "masters of their thinking by discussing their own ideas and views of the world" (Freire, 1994, p. 105). They demonstrated how intricately connected their study of art could be with their world outside of school. They researched and made connections from the music video to other cultures and history. The teacher's original pastiche lesson only involved them in looking and changing works of art. These students went much further than that. And by doing so, Chris provided an opportunity for much more learning than the original lesson plan might have provided.

The students witnessed the pastiche technique being used in their world of popular culture through their study of this music video. They learned about another culture and critically looked at their own in the process. But, they did not only learn these things because of the art class. They actually wanted to know these things and more about the culture, issues, and ideas that resulted from our study. As part of the original project, the students were required to research and discover. However, because the focus of the study was a part of their popular youth culture and was initiated by the students themselves, they were much more interested and motivated in the process. They informed each other as they added, read, and responded to each other's research, discovered images, and ideas there on the computer screen. The students were able to see and make connections between their study and the world around them. These experiences did not stop when the computer was shut down. The students said that they wanted to find more and more connections between everything. This desire to know and make connections is the most significant aspect of this class' study of Rage Against the Machine's *People of the Sun*.

The Zapatista movement was going on in another country, far from their hometown. Reports of it, however, came nightly to the students' homes via this music video and the television news. Because of their class experience, the students were able to connect the music video with art, culture, history, and the political issues that were being addressed on television and in the newspaper. They began wondering about other music videos that they were watching. They said that the experience caused them to look more closely at how music videos might be reflecting what was going on in the world around them. Many of the students saw for the first time that many aspects of their lives outside the classroom could be linked or connected to that, often, very foreign land of school.

Conclusion

Education theorist Henry Giroux, known for his critical approach to education, calls for the questioning as well as recognition of the power associated with who and what dictates the knowledge and information associated with literacy. "Literacy means engaging the full range of what is in the library (conventional notions of reading), the art gallery (the making and interpretation of art), and the street (popular culture and student experience) (Giroux, 1992, p. 243). Giroux refers to such popular youth culture as the music video as sites of resistance. Although he believes such sites are excellent avenues toward learning he warns against an insensitive appropriation of popular youth culture in the classroom. Popular youth culture belongs to young students. It is their site for satire and parody as well as rebellion and protest. In many cases it is the only possession of young students who approach their schooling as a time of coercion and dictatorship. Therefore, when bringing such popular youth culture as the music video into the classroom, it is important to refrain from teacher-directed interpretation.[2] Like the Rage Against the Machine experience, students should be encouraged and indeed find a sense of empowerment in the fact that they are initiating and leading the learning and knowing process when bringing the music video[3] into the classroom.

The primary focus of using video technology in the Rage Against the Machine experience was as an impetus for student-initiated inquiry and a strategy for teaching aesthetics and criticism. Although the students could have created videos in response to this study, the bigger idea surrounding this experience was not directed specifically toward the media. As art educators know, teaching and learning to and from works of art may involve us in entirely different media and technique exploration than that found in the work of art. Like slides, posters, books, and overhead transparencies, video technology offers excellent presentation opportunities. More than that, however is the fact that the video apparatus is relevant and alluring. It is an active dynamic medium that mesmerizes and transports. It is important to note also that while videos about specific artists, styles, and periods are useful in art education, what is being advocated here is an approach to the video as a work of art to be studied, interpreted, and connected. In other words, Rage Against the Machine's *People of Sun* music video was the central work of art studied in this classroom. Granted, what many may refer to as mainstream music videos, viewed on music video television channels, are more appropriate for high school audiences (and even then they must be closely screened to avoid inappropriate language, etc.). Other videos that may be considered include television commercials, sitcoms, film, and animations such as Disney's *Fantasia*. Just as when choosing works of art to present for study in the classroom, care must be taken that the video is narratively complex and challenging. The video content and design should provide possibilities for connections and contain visible signs, symbols, and metaphors that are relevant to students' lives (Carpenter & Barrett, 2000). It is not necessarily important that all the students like the particular music artist or the video, just that the video is rich enough in content and design that it will promote and provoke artistic inquiry.

I see the use of video in the art classroom as just one of the many ways that technology may enhance if not completely alter the way art educators approach the study of art history/artworld, criticism and aesthetics. Gone are the days when using posters and slides is our only vehicle for introducing works of art. Computer slide presentations make it possible for us to show our students virtually anything that is capable of scanning. The Internet instantly provides us with contemporary cutting-edge images, sounds, and video. And, more importantly the world of art itself is filled with moving images, performances, and shifting/changing images. Therefore, video technology offers not only a way to teach art that is relevant to students' lives; it provides us with a way to authentically represent the contemporary art world.

Endnotes

[1] Interactive computer hypertext provides the reader and the writer (author) the ability to create, organize, and rearrange boxes that contain a variety of content including written text, images, film, journal entries, and dialogue on the computer. These boxes can be linked with each other electronically, through hyperlinks in the form of specific passages, words, images, or portions of images, as a means of exploration of a subject or subjects. Because these boxes are changeable by both the writer and the reader–who becomes a writer by adding new boxes, images, and information–hypertext provides a site for continual redirection in the cognitive processes of thinking, interpreting, and knowing. The class used the software Storyspace™ to create our web. See http://www.eastgate.com.

[2] One way of doing this is to ask students to bring in music videos for their teacher's perusal. Teachers can then capture video still images for viewing in the classroom. Music video artists also often feature still images as well as video clips on their WWW sites that are available for download or for viewing in the classroom through the use of a computer connected to a projection device. WWW sites also provide information regarding history and interpretation of television situation comedies. Challenging students to formulate questions as well as find answers encourages ownership of their educational experience as well as more critical and reflective learning and living practices (Taylor and Ballengee-Morris, 2003).

[3] Copyright issues as well as inappropriate language and content are important concerns when bringing the music video into the classroom (Aufdenspring "n.d."). As always, previewing videos before showing them in class is crucial. Communication with parents and administration is important along with the development of detailed information regarding curricular connections and rationale. Artmaking projects that result from or are connected to the study of music video can include video production as well as most any other technique or media-explicit projects if the video for study is rich enough in content to promote the exploration of ideas.

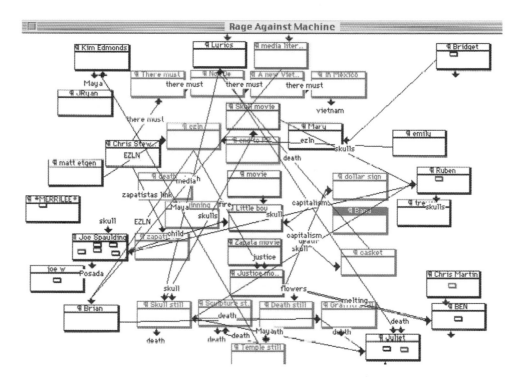

Figure 1: The organization of the computer web included video clips, lyrics, and stills placed in the middle with the student research boxes surrounding them.

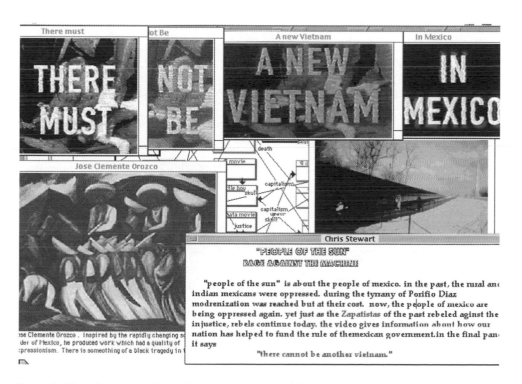

Figure 2: Chris began the Rage hypertextual web with an explanation of Orozco's painting, linked with the Vietnam Memorial, and the video stills saying "there must not be another Vietnam in Mexico."

Additional illustrations on the following page

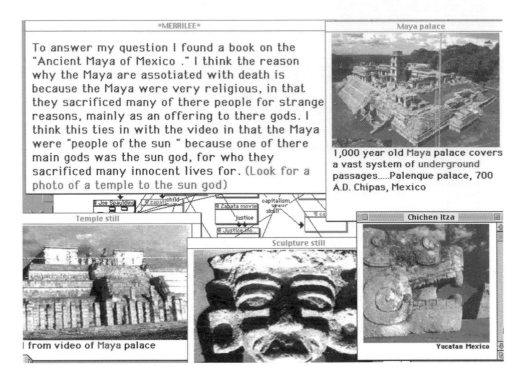

Figure 3: Merrilee and Juliet researched the Mayan art and architecture in the video.

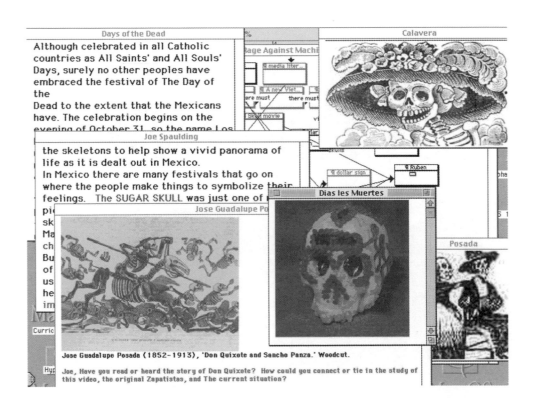

Figure 4: Joe informed the class about the Mexican cultural festival Los Dias de los Muertos.

References

Aufdenspring. D. (no date). Images of America-Analyzing music videos: Videography. Retrieved September 20, 2002 from www.aufdenspring.com/video.html.

Ben, Brian, Bridget, Chris M., Chris, Emily, Joe, Joe W., Juliet, Kim, Mark M., Matt, Rubin, & Travis K. (1996). [Rage against the machine Storyspace™ web]. Unpublished raw data.

Carpenter, B. S. & Barrett, T. (2000). Choosing works of art. Unpublished handout used at the Summer Institute. VA Beach, VA: Contemporary Art Center of Virginia.

De La Rocha, Z. & Rage Against the Machine (1996). *People of the sun*. Retrieved August 7, 1998 from www.masadsign.nl/llama/Lyrics/evilemp.html.

Freire, P. (1994). *Pedagogy of the oppressed*. New York: The Continuum Publishing Company. (Original work published in 1970.)

Giroux, H. (1992). *Border crossings: Cultural workers and the politics of education*. New York: Routledge.

Reiss, S. & Feineman, N. (2000). *Thirty frames per second: The visionary art of the music video*. New York: Harry F. Abrams, Inc.

Taylor, P. G. (2000). Madonna and hypertext: Liberatory learning in art education. *Studies in Art Education 41*(4), 376 389.

Taylor, P. G. and Ballengee-Morris, C. (2003). Using visual culture to put a contemporary "fizz" on the study of Pop Art. *Art Education, 56* (2), 20-24.

Those Smart, Tech Savvy Students:

12

How Can Teachers Keep Up?

In the last quarter of this century, video equipment, to quote a well-worn, much reviled, media advertising cliche, "has come a long way, baby!" When I first started using video technologies, circa 1970s, the carrying cases were so cumbersome I needed a mini van to transport them. Only 15 to 20 years ago did sleeker, lighter equipment appear on the market; nevertheless, by today's standards, huge, frustratingly clumsy analogue VHS cameras were still being hoisted upon the slim shoulders of film students. If fortunate enough, a teacher had sophisticated editing workstations worth perhaps $25,000 each (considered cheap at that time!) which fit into a large room. Then, along came high eight cameras—still analogue—but, a lot less cumbersome and easier to use. And finally, a few years ago, digital cameras appeared on the scene, along with the blessed firewire and an editing computer workstation one-tenth the size and price of the previous analogue models. These technological innovations made video technologies increasingly accessible to schools and subtly transformed the classroom.

Tapscott (1998) writes: Computers can be found in the home, school, factory and office and digital technologies such as cameras, video games and CD-ROMS are commonplace ...Today's kids are so bathed in bits that they think it's all part of the natural landscape. To them, the digital technology is no more intimidating than a VCR or toaster. For the first time in history, children are more comfortable, knowledgeable, and literate than their parents about an innovation central to society. And it is through the use of digital media that the N-Generation will develop and superimpose its culture on the rest of society. Boomers stand back. Already these kids are learning playing, communicating, working, and creating communities very differently than their parents. They are a force for social transformation. Moms and Dads are reeling from the challenges of raising confident, plugged-in, and digital-savvy children who know more about technology than they do. Few parents even know what their children are doing in cyberspace. School officials are grappling with the reality of students often being far smarter on cyber-issues and new ways of learning than the teachers.

To this end I will discuss the relationships between teachers and students in video production. With video technologies evolving at such an accelerated pace, teachers have had a difficult time keeping abreast of the change. Students often have more technical knowledge than their teachers who are sometimes forced to seek instruction from their pupils. Little has been written about this topsy-turvy phenomenon: an even smaller body of research has been written about it from students' perspectives. I will examine the relationships within teaching environments that employ video art technologies, studying how this new situation affects educators' relationships with their pupils and students' perceptions of their teachers.

The following information is based on case study research I had conducted at two Canadian high schools: one a multicultural, inner-city public school, the other a very wealthy, exclusive, private one. Both institutions use cutting edge technologies and have students who use these on a day-to-day basis. These technologies are integrated into the curriculum; however, in the case of videocameras, teachers and students at the two schools use the technologies for different means. The public school students use videocameras on a regular basis, particularly to create films, an area in which they have been extremely successful winning awards at film festivals citywide, provincially, nationally and internationally. The private school had used them for a television production, but found the program was too expensive and dismantled it after they had established what teachers believed to be a very successful in-school weekly TV show reporting on the life of the school. Teachers and students discussed their experiences in depth.

Topsy-turvy Relationships

It was found that a good majority of teachers have had no formal computer education (Jordan & Follman, 1993; Pelgrum & Plomp, 1993; Willis, 1985). What happens to teachers who have not been trained to handle a videocamera, who do not know anything about production or post production, and yet, are expected to teach videography? Oftentimes they panic or become frustrated. What happens to teachers—there are a few of them who are more fortunate—who have had some digital technological training during university? Perhaps the technologies they used were older obsolete systems and teachers are now confronting newer computers, and newer software? Can most teachers turn to teacher training support in the schools? Unfortunately, not—support is often inadequate.

One of the teachers I interviewed, Mr. Tyke, gives workshops internationally to teachers on how to use computers. He discusses the typical type of teacher training he has observed: *In terms of technology, a lot of people are looking at it as, "Get those computers into the classroom. Get those damn teachers in front of them and get them doing something!" That is it. That's the extent of the thinking behind it. I talk to teachers particularly in the United States all the time who say, "I'm sitting here with this thing in my classroom and nobody has told me how to use it. They've told me what they want me to do but it's so vague I can't understand how to actually do it." That's the first big struggle.*

With hectic schedules, little time, curriculum to plan, classes to teach, and administrational duties, all of which constitute the daily lives of teachers, educators have little time for training. So, how do teachers learn on the job with little support training systems in place? Some of the traditional ways are through (1) workshops, (2) on-line tutorials, (3) mentoring, (4) modeling, (5) peer coaching, and (6) use of 'help desks'. To add to this are (7) extra time provided for teachers to teach themselves, (8) additional courses taken, (9) lectures and (10) any other type of support that aids in the acquisition of technological knowledge. At both schools in which I conducted case study research, I found that none of the above ways were offered to staff for training in videography. This is not unusual.

One of the teachers, Ms. Herbiere, voices her frustration in the following words: *...there's such a lack of resources and funds for staff development. So, I feel that I'm developmentally arrested at this date at which I got hired, plus a little bit that I managed to do on my own. What I find disturbing or certainly disappointing is that they [the administration] are not there for me. I don't know any other professions that are so technologically based where there's so little upgrading for their employee base.*

Teacher support is considered a necessity in order for teachers to cope with rapid technological change (Cuban, 1997; Cummings, 1990; Goodson, Ivor, Clark, Pitman, Rutledge, Mangan, Rhea, 1990; Haycock, 1991; Klier, 1992;

Knupfer, 1993; Luke; 1996; Pearlman, 1989; Peha, 1995; Pelgrum & Plomp, 1993; Schultz, 1995; Tinson, 1996; Wei, 1992). However, in reality, little formal effort has been made to support educators who have tried to implement new technologies (Hannafin & Savenye, 1993; Schofield, 1995). Close to 15 years ago, Pearlman (1989) pointed out the sorry state of fiscal investment in teacher training for the new technologies, writing, " The historical record of investment in teacher productivity is not promising. Less capitol is invested behind teacher productivity than in any other profession ($1,000/teacher vs. $50,000/worker in all industry" (p.15). If anything, with recent cutbacks in education, the situation has regressed rather than improved (Gidney, 1999; Laino, 1994; Schofield, 1995). This results in "too many teachers having to play catch-up by trying to learn on the job" (Jordan & Follman (1993, p. 27).

How do teachers cope, confronted as they are, with their own often inadequate background knowledge yet great expectations from others to teach videography? The teachers I interviewed employ many different approaches: they advise that one should be (1) flexible, (2) design interesting, creative assignments, and (3) concentrate on the theoretical rather than the technological aspects of an assignment. Teachers should connect videography to their strengths in other areas such as the Visual Arts, which is so much a part of film and television production. If one is fortunate enough to have a teacher on staff who is knowledgeable about videography, teachers advise to (4) learn from him or her and collaborate. Moreover, teachers should (5) reach out to the community and ask questions from the experts who work at stores or who are in the film or television business. However, the most important approach teachers use was to (6) turn to the resource most at hand in their classrooms. So who or what is this resource? Where do teachers turn to for assistance, guidance, through all the vast and minute problems involved in video production? Who are the knowledgeable people who are always there to provide advice? It is the students. Their knowledge has proven to be invaluable!

It is the teenagers who 'hack' away at night, play continuously on the computers, learn about the latest software programs and how they work, who are free from the thousand and one responsibilities that adults confront in a given day. And, it is the educators who are turning to their students for help, for guidance, and for instruction. This is the topsy-turvy relationship we find in schools today educators becoming students, and pupils becoming teachers.

Educators' Relationships with their Students

I found that students are assuming more responsibilities in the teaching-learning environment while teachers are shifting their role to become more like guides or managers. Mr. Kreighoff elaborates on what he believes is the teacher's new role: ... *the teacher still has the expertise and the control of the environment. They don't have to be the last authority on every aspect of every piece of equipment....the analogy is the bicycle. It's good to come back to very simple analogies and it's your responsibility to know that bicycle, to know that child can benefit or get hurt from it. You essentially coach the child on how to take the first pedal or the firsts steps and how to stop. After that, if the kid is going to do wheelies or tricks then it's time that they have to put in. That is something that you can't replicate. But you should know what that bicycle is capable of. You should make sure that it is in working order and that it is safe and you should be able to show it to the kid, either through demonstration or bringing in an expert or getting a video [to illustrate], how far [they can go] if they put in the time and the concentration.*

In tandem with teachers' shifting roles, students' roles shift as well. More teachers are relying on their tech savvy students to assume the role of teacher and teach their students. It happens formally and informally. In terms of the latter, I often saw, as a participant observer, teachers asking their tech-savvy pupils to teach less tech-savvy students when the educator did not have the answer. In addition, more formal situations are established in which students conduct workshops on software. An example of this are teachers who ask students knowledgeable about software editing programs, such as Final Cut Pro, to conduct in-class workshops. In the case of the private school, there were year long after school workshops using such programs as Adobe Photoshop taught by a select group of students. The Visual Art teachers not only set up these workshops but also took the workshops themselves, learning alongside their students. Not only are students teaching their peers but they are teaching their teachers as well.

Educators and their Pupils: Co-learning and Co-operative Learning

In describing the teaching of new media, many researchers often refer to the importance of constructing co-learning and co-operative learning environments (Gregory 1995; Jones, Valdez, Nowakowski & Claudette, 1995; Hartley, 1996; Hoffman, 1996). Researchers often used the terms interchangeably (Silverman, 1995; Sivin-Kachala & Bialo 1994). The most common discussions of co-learning and cooperative learning revolve around teachers teaching other teachers (Lai, 1993; Leino, 1991; Roland, 1990; Schofield, 1995) or students teaching other students (Bagley, 1994; Carey, 1993; Jones, Valdez, Nowakowski & Claudette, 1995). An important dynamic occurs in which teachers and students learn side by side together, tackling problems and finding solutions. Another important type of co-learning is one in which students know more and possess more skills in a particular area than their teachers. Nellen writes about this phenomenon in terms of his pupils being "student commandos who…train the computer-phobic teachers" (1998, p.105).

I find Weiss' definition of co-learning useful. He defines it as a situation in which learner and student "negotiate knowledge on equal terms" (Weiss, 1992, p. 5). The analogy is like a seesaw: sometimes students are the experts, sometimes teachers are, and yet, sometimes educators and pupils co-create knowledge together (p.6). The learning situation shifts constantly between students and teachers within a single relationship ranging from the traditional alliance of knowledgeable teacher and novice student, to the co-learning dynamic, and such roles in-between like the 'independent learner.' This is what I found often happening with teachers teaching videography; and, in so doing, they used new technologies in the classroom.

Teachers cautioned that in order for co-learning to be effective, students must be chosen carefully. They must not only be tech-savvy but also mature enough to handle untraditional, altered, new roles in which they have to relate to their educators differently, be able to handle responsibilities, as well as their new teacher role.

Educators work with students in these new situations both in and out of class. A teacher, Mr. Tyke, role plays how he would approach a student from whom he wants to learn. He will state, "Hey look at that—that's great. So and so has really helped us out here. Look at what he found!" He will proceed to ask the student to explain his findings. Another teacher tells of calling a tech savvy student for help as a result of being stumped at home over technological issues. She explains, "I'll introduce myself to his/her parents and say, 'Hi. Guess who this is? Is your son or daughter at home? They're helping me with a computer problem."

Educators perceive that an important component for teaching new technologies in the classroom is being honest. Do not cover up lack of knowledge: admit you do not know.

Pupils' Relationships with Their Teachers

Before conducting my research, I assumed students were disdainful of teachers who do not know much about videography and the technologies associated to it. I was, however, very surprised to be corrected. Students appreciate teachers who are honest and openly admit being unknowledgeable. To add to this surprise I found another: students openly accept being more technologically literate than their teachers. They explained the situation by stating that teachers were themselves not trained; that they cannot keep abreast of the quick change in new media and the quick obsolescence of the old; and that given all their other responsibilities educators do not have the time to learn.

These tech-savvy students are highly motivated, flexible, adaptable, good at problem solving, able to take initiative, enjoy exploring, are independent learners, and appreciate having more control over the learning process. Like their teachers, they assume a variety of roles, from learner to collaborator to co-learner.

Tech-savvy students are aware that they are taking a more active, more responsible role in the classroom and enjoy this new position. They teach others and welcome the feeling of empowerment. Joe states, "I like giving my knowledge out to people and helping other people do the best that they can do." Brian observes, "I think you should do whatever you can to help these people because they're trying to get used to this technology and it's hard for them to get used to it…You don't want to make it impossible because it isn't impossible." Danny comments, "it's kind of neat. It's different." And Dylan expresses the satisfaction he experienced when he co-taught a class with another student, Grant. Two of his peers who appeared uninterested in the lesson finally grasped what he was talking about. Dylan explains, "At one point about ten minutes before the class ends, the class is all quiet and one of them yells out, 'Yes, it's working!' Grant and I just looked at each other and laughed for the rest of the class. It was wonderful." Moreover, students also enjoy the empowerment they obtain from teaching their teachers.

Brian talks about the co-learning situation he had established between himself and Mr. Tyke in elementary school when they were preparing for an "Author's Day" conference: …I kept on having a problem because the programme that stops little kids from getting on the restricted sites was stopping the connection between the computers and the authors. So we had to extricate some people out from Glen Manor. I think it was Mr. Tyke who came out from Glen Manor and came down to Fieldhill to try to help to fix this problem. [We worked] two days straight and we finally got it fixed…We got it eventually…. I have his business card somewhere at home. I know that because I gave him mine.

Tom also discusses shared learning exchanges with his teacher: My computer teacher, Mr. Tyler knows the software programmes. He helps out and I'll figure out certain things, different ways of doing it and he'll say, 'That's great!' It will go back and forth…I think it's more of a reciprocal exchange.

Words such as 'exciting,' 'positive experience,' 'amazing,' 'wonderful' reflect student responses to their new dynamics in the teaching-learning relationships. Miriam reflects on the new relationship positively: You are treated as a colleague, almost. It's a workplace; it's a laboratory. You're treated as an adult and I believe that if you are respected as an adult, you respect back as an adult…Teachers get the respect back as well. That comes as well with the fact that they know that you know more than that and there is a lot of mutual learning that goes on because technology keeps growing so fast. It's up to both of them [teachers and students] to keep learning so you are in it together. That kind of creates a bond as well.

Students, like their teachers, express caution. One of the students, Sean, explains that in order for this new teacher-student dynamic to work well, certain factors have to be taken into consideration: I think first off you have to have the right type of student for it. There are broad varieties of students within a high school. You have students that aren't motivated, but yet they have the capability. You have students that are coming from broken home lives, students that are struggling to learn the language—stuff like that. It's good for them if they are into it, but they have to be given access to the technology to get to that level to switch paradigms between teacher and student. With the right types of students and the right types of environments in which, let's say, the student is brought up with access to the technology (which I was fortunate that I did) and has been brought up so that there is mutual respect between teacher and student, it basically changes the whole ideal of teacher and student in which teacher knows all and student knows nothing…

Joe views this new and pervasive model in an historical perspective. He reflects: I think what's important is just to understand that we are on a paradigm shift as far as the industrial revolution began in the 16th century. Now we're in a new revolution where computers are turning the way we do everything and anything around: jobs are completely *being turned around...What my point is is that education is going to have to take a huge turn...Because of technology (everything ties back to technology) the way anything is done is changing including education. I think that's very important to remember: we are watching and I am a part of what is going to be shaping the next hundred years of education. ...There's so much more knowledge that everyone is sharing with each other. So instead of school being, 'sit in a class and learn something,' in my opinion you're going to start seeing schools turn into a group of people who share knowledge and share experiences.*

This shifting role of teachers becoming learners and vice-versa, on the one hand, has been unusual in the school system but is becoming more prevalent where technologies are saturating educational institutions. On the other hand, teaching videography can be done solely through theory.

Teachers can cover such theory as camera angles and movements, lighting, the history of video, film or television and sociological issues and leave it at that. But if one wants students to experience the magic of production from planning the video and filming to editing using new, exciting, digital technologies, educators may want to rethink the teacher-student dynamic to facilitate flexible, co-learning relationships between themselves and their students.

References

Bagley, C. et al., (1994). *The shared-ownership technology model; Restructuring the classroom*. Minnesota, US: The Technology Group.

Carey, D. (1993). Teacher roles and technology integration: Moving from teacher as director to teacher as facilitator. *Computers in the Schools, 9*(2/3), 105-118.

Cuban, L., (1997). Foreword. In J.H. Sandholtz, C. Ringstaff, & D.Dwyer, *Teaching with technology: Creating student-centered classrooms* (pp. XI-XIV). New York: Teachers College Press.

Cummings, F.D. (1990). Introducing microcomputers in schools: a case study. *Dissertation Abstracts International, 51*, 4005.

Dalton, J. (1995). *Investigating co-learning: A life history of a classroom, focusing on meaning-making, relationship and knowledge production.* (Doctoral Dissertation, University of Toronto, 1995).

Gidney, R.D. (1999). *From Hope to Harris*. Toronto, Canada: University of Toronto Press.

Goodson, Ivor, Clark, R., Pitman, A., Rutledge, J., Mangan, M., & Rhea, V. (1990) *Curriculum and content in the use of computers for classroom learning: Interim Report 3*. (Interis Document No. ON05846). Toronto, Ontario: Ministry of Education.

Gregory, D. (1995). Art education reform and interactive Integrated media. *Art Education, 48*(3), 6-16.

Hannafin, R. & Savenye, W. (1993). Technology in the classroom: the teacher's new role and resistance to it. *Educational Technology, 33*(6), 26-31.

Hartley, J. R. (1996). Managing models of collaborative learning. *Computers Education 26*(1-3), 163-170.

Haycock, C.A. (1991). Resource-based learning:A shift in the roles of teacher, learner. *NASSP Bulletin, 75*(535), 15-22.

Hoffman, R. P. (1996). Levels of technology use and instructional innovation. (Doctoral Dissertation, The Claremont Graduate School and San Diego State University,1996). *Dissertation Abstracts International, 57*, 3797.

Jones, B. F., Valdez, G., Nowakowski, J., & Claudette, R. (1995). Plugging in: Choosing and using educational technology. *EdtTalk*, [Online], Available: http://www.ncrel.org/sdrs/edtalk/html.

Jordan, W. R., & Follman, J. M. (1993). *Using technology to improve teaching and learning. Hot topics: Usable research*. USA: Southeastern Regional Vision for Education.

Klier, D. (1992). Problems concerning the use of personal computers in secondary education. *Dissertation Abstracts International, 57*, 310.

Knupfer, N. (1993). Teachers and educational computing: Changing roles and changing pedagogy. In Robert Muffoletto and Nancy Knupfer (ed.), *Computers in education* (pp. 163-179). New Jersey: Hampton Press, Inc.

Lai, K.W. (1993). Teachers as facilitators in a computer-supported learning environment. *Journal of Information Technology for Teacher Education, 2*(2), 127-137.

Laino, J. (1994). Staff development in the age of technology: Recycling the experienced teacher. *Dissertation Abstracts International, 55*, 3368.

Leino, J. (1991). *Dynamic knowledge in school: An action research on instructional development with the aid of microcomputers* (Research No. 143). Finland: Department of Education, University of Helsinki, pp. 103-117.

Luke, C. (1996). Ekstasis@cyberia1. *Discourse: Studies in the Cultural Politics of Education, 17*(2), 187-207.

Nellen, T. (1998). Suring the Internet: Sink or swim. *English Journal, 87*(2), 105-107.

Pearlman, R. (1989). Technology's role in restructuring schools. *Electronic Learning, 8*(8), 8-9, 12, 14-15, 56.

Peha, Jon. (1995). How K-12 teachers are using the computer networks. *Educational Leadership, 53*, 18-25.

Pelgrum, W. J., & Plomp T. (1993). Educating the Educators. *In The IEA study of computers in education: Implementation of an innovation in 21 education systems.* New York: Pergamon Press.

Roland, C. (1990, May). Our love affair with new technology: Is the honeymoon over? *Art Education, 43* (3), 54-60.

Schofield, J. (1995). *Computer and classroom culture* (pp. 94-133 & 190-228). USA: Cambridge University Press.

Schultz, Y. K. (1995). Development and validation of a school leaders' guidebook for implementing multimedia in the classroom. *Dissertation Abstracts International, 56*, 3552.

Silverman, B. (1995). Computer supported collaborative learning. *Computer Education, 25*(3), 81-91.

Sivin-Kachala, J., & Bialo, E. (1994). *Report on the effectiveness of technology in schools.* New York: Interactive Educational Systems Inc.

Tapscott, D. (1998). *Growing up digital.:The rise of the net generation.* New York: McGraw-Hill.

Tinson, Lois. (1996). Teachers' vital role in bringing technology into the classroom. *Thrust for Educational Leadership, 25*(6), 10-11.

Wei, C.A. (1992). Instructional uses of computers in boys', girls', and coeducational senior high schools in Taiwan, the Republic of China. *Dissertation Abstracts International, 53*, 1862.

Weiss, J. (1992, June). *Dances with knowledge: Co-learning as a teaching/learning process.* Paper presented at the annual conference of the Canadian Educational Research Association on "Contemplating Co-learning: Teaching Learning Reconceptualized," Charlottetown, PEI.

Willis, B. et al., (1985). *Technology and learning: Changing minds in a changing world. Schooling and technology,* vol. 4. North Carolina: Southeastern Regional Council for Educational Improvement.

Feeling Legitimate in Teaching Filmmaking:

13

One Teacher's View

It is finally quiet on the street.

The neighborhood's need for lawn care with loud machines has subsided for the moment.

We are ready.

I stand beside the car, camera pointed into the driver's window.

"Okay- go!"

I am still trying to get used to saying the command 'action'.

One actress is sitting in the car waiting impatiently (my friend) and the other actress (my daughter) walks down the driveway and sullenly gets into the car.

As they drive away, I start to run backwards so that the camera will stay on the actors while the car is moving.

As the car begins to move faster than I can run backwards, I let them go and make an arching motion with my camera arm so that I won't fall over.

It's a wrap—even the arch shot makes it into the end of the film…

That was my first experience making real narrative film; a story of a girl who makes a magical bag that allows her to help friends and win the respect of her parents. I had written out a rough treatment, but came up with dialogue on the fly during shooting and often written on paper plates.

I had taken over the houses of three friends; the car of another; made use of many friends and family as actors. The 5-year-old kept her 'costume' under her bed so that she wouldn't wear it by mistake and not be able to film at a moments notice. I lost a whole tape and had to re-shoot a sunny hot summer day in 40-degree fall weather ad hoc because the sun had not been out on a weekend in 6 weeks. The summer basement band scenes had to be re-shot in an attic in the winter.

My first filmmaking experience was a 'fly by the seat' affair. Some people tell me it's still their favorite film ever. I have spent the last 4 years trying to recreate that freshness and whimsy that just seemed to happen during the first film. I'm getting closer. I make film/video for two purposes. I want to tell stories and I want to teach teens how to tell their own stories through film.

Film and television are the forms of cultural expression for this new generation of students—just like painting and sculpture were for generations before them. Moving images surround young people and influence them in ways that we adults cannot even begin to realize. Moving images are a constant in the teen world. The mimicking of movie and television themes guides how young people shape themselves. By having students learn how to create film and television, teachers are putting the tools of cultural discovery into the hands of those persons who need it most.

There are two things that I think are the most difficult for teachers to address when teaching filmmaking. The first is credibility or, 'how can you possibly know what you are talking about?' The second is the content of student films or 'How does an educator free up students to express ideas about their world when you, and administrators, can be called into account for the appropriateness of that subject matter as an in-school production?'

How do you approach the technical astuteness needed to be able to teach filmmaking to students?

The assistant producer has called for quiet. We've run through this crowded walking scene in the school hallway many times and are ready to roll film. Today I am a grip. I am carrying cable behind a dolly that travels along with the main character and into a crowd of people that swallows him. We will do this same scene many times to get it just right. It is day two on a project with film professionals that has a 6-day schedule of 15-19 hour days. By the end of the week, I can barely stand. I will learn so much.

At every mealtime, we talk and ask questions about how each of us came to work and learn at the same time. I have been taping interviews of the key people to take back to my students and all the professionals are happy to share their experience. The remarkable thing is how similar their stories are. The mantra is, 'get in there and get to work.'

The only way to learn to teach filmmaking is to start making films yourself.

These films do not need to be feature length; making a good short film requires the same preparation and learning curve as a long film does. A feature simply has more of everything. More characters, more plot twists, more locations, more setups, more, more and more. Think modestly for your first film.

Characters drive a story.

For your first short narrative script, think of a quirky little incident and the person that it involved and then build on that. My first film, *Evie's Bag*, was about those women you meet whose handbags always seem to contain the item you need to save a situation—be it a handy wipe, a candle, or a screwdriver. My son and his friend were talking about a girl from their school and all of the things she seems to have in her purse. I wrote a story about a girl who makes a large cloth bag for herself with the help of her little sister. She goes out into the world, helps out her friends and earns the respect of her parents by simply being prepared.

Sometimes it feels as though I've been preparing my whole life for this precise moment.

For me, stories are the reason for filmmaking; experience is the stuff of stories, cultural archetypes are the decipherable code. I learned the language of stories by reading to my children. Our family nighttime ritual included reading stories aloud to our children. We read fairy tales both classic and obscure; Andrew Lang's color coded fairy books; C.S. Lewis's *Narnia* series; Lloyd Alexander's *Book of Three* series; Patricia Wrede's *Enchanted Forest Chronicles*. Putting this together with Joseph Campbell's ideas on myth and archetypes and you come up with a vivid understanding of the standard story motifs that have been around for generations. Rebellious children who want to be independent; difficult and demanding parents who are afraid to lose control over said children; grandparents who are wise and are so happy that the grandkids are giving the parents as much grief as they gave them when they were young. Sibling rivals; bad influences; duty; honor;

love, and finally, magic; or wonder. The light that comes on and surprises us by showing everything is not as it first appeared. Good, Evil and how people deal with it.

After working in video in the late 1970's in art school, I went on to work in the realm of public access television. Mainly, I produced documentaries of dance work that my friends and I were performing. It wasn't until I turned 40 that I felt that I had enough life experience to look back and write a script.

I started doing narrative film because of a chance connection. I was introduced to a group titled Independent Student Media. Darrin Fletcher and Chet Thomas started this group in 1999 after the Columbine High School tragedy, as a response to high school students' needs to learn how to create the culture that was working to control them and teacher's needs for technical know how. I had stopped doing video when I went back to university to earn my teaching certificate. Now, with the help of these two men, I could test out teaching film to a small group of students. As the students were learning, so was I and I decided to make a short film of my own. That turned out to be the best way to learn how to make films—by simply not being afraid to do it. It was Independent Student Media's professional project workshop that I was involved with this summer.

No one really cares what medium you use, film or video. No one cares how well it's lit. No one really cares if the sets are fantastic. An audience will overlook many technical deficiencies of a film if the story is compelling. A compelling story, well told, will carry you past it all. No amount of special effects will get past a weak story line. Character motifs were my building blocks and personal experience, the mortar.

The two films made during the first session with ISM were *Anna* (the students) and *Evie's Bag* (mine). They can be seen on the website www.ismfilms.com, in the screening room.

The experience of making a film begins by simply taking some footage. It sounds so simple. A journey begins with the first step. (Can you hear the violins warming up?) It's true.

Having a simple story outline will get you through the first filming experience. Think of how to tell a story without dialogue. Where will the story take place?

My third film came into being because we happened to visit a co-worker at a small farm on a late afternoon. The light was wonderful. The sheep were resting in the field and the clouds were dramatic. I had to make a film at this farm. Who will the characters be? How do people look at each other? Use those expressions and the actions that drive them to tell your story. Take a walk; what could happen? What do you notice?

Having shot your first bit of footage with a goal in mind makes you miles ahead of all of those people who whine about how they wished that they could make a film and never get around to doing it. You do not need anything besides a video camera and a visual idea. It's the excitement of that first filming experience that will keep you, and students, hungry for more and so, on task.

Evie's Bag, my first film, was a relatively straightforward 8-minute project done on 8mm digital video with only one major prop and the help of a lot of friends and family. I edited using iMovie, a digital image editing software that came with my iMac computer.

My second film project was a suspense story. I shot on locations ranging from a local restaurant to the University of Wisconsin-Milwaukee. The story was a bit melodramatic but the experience of organizing a project of that size was extremely valuable.

Development (good screen writing, etc.) is important but it isn't going anywhere if the pre-production is not done thoroughly. Budgeting (people, places, and equipment on hand as well as money), location scouting, scheduling, catering and transportation are so important that without that groundwork, you can bet that your experience filming a larger project is not going to go smoothly.

Planning and preparation make a filming experience enjoyable for you and those working with you.

I have found that for myself, guerilla filmmaking does not work nor do I encourage my students to do this. I have found that by asking first and being a little flexible, I have had people, businesses, city governments and police officers all be happy to help me with my film projects. By not asking, the students give filmmaking students a bad reputation, making it hard for the other students whom will come after them to gain the cooperation of businesses and local government. Having a well-thought-out project also gives people confidence in what the students are doing. Filmmakers should always be polite, never arrogant and never take advantage of the people and places they are filming. Bridge building starts the first time you pick up a camera.

Keep working. Every project is better than the one before it.

I wrote the script for my third project, *Portrait of a Dog*, over the course of 8 months. It is a father and son story that actually started from seeing the film *Pollack*. I began a game of what if, what if Pollack and Krasnier had a child. What might he be like as a parent to an artistic son? I spent time researching character traits. I tried to put more subtext into the dialogue (saying one thing but meaning something else). I learned more about lighting; about technical aspects of filmmaking from a group from Denmark called *Dogma 95*, which puts emphasis on the script and does not add any extra lights and works exclusively on locations. *Italian for Beginners* is one of their films that has gotten international attention. After much deliberation, I came up with a bounce clamp light style that I could work with. I found real actors who would volunteer their time. I got permission to film in Milwaukee City Hall, a near by office building, two houses, a farm and a cemetery. My son drove the car while I would lean out of open doors and the sunroof to film the young hero running away from home. It was great.

How can you increase your production value?

Learning about how to light helps. Lighting for video is a little different than lighting for film, but as a rule of thumb, bouncing a light off a white surface will give a soft even light that is more flattering than aiming a light directly at someone. Shooting outside has the advantage of ambient lighting. Use a bounce card as a fill light on people faces. Shoot in the early morning or in the late afternoon—the Kodachrome hours—to get lovely light with good shadows and warm highlights. Look at films. Old black and white films are especially helpful.

Having a good understanding of composition will help enormously. Photographers create good-looking film images by using the golden square or division of thirds. Have students learn and locate this compositional technique in advertising photographs. Watch films where you have noticed good composition with the whole class and point out what you see. Have students take still images to practice compositional skills.

Think about sound as a descriptive element. Sometimes sound is more important than the visual image. Sounds will tell the time of day, fill in the blanks about location, and set the mood of the piece.

Try to use a microphone that is separate from the camera if you can and get the microphone as close to the speaker as possible. You can make a boom pole with a painting extender pole and a rotating head. Wrap the pole in pipe insulation to muffle noises from the hands of the boom operator. Also, make sure that the extending cords are taped together at the connecting points and have your sound person wear headphones connected to the camera so that they can hear the quality of the sound being recorded.

Now is about the time when you will begin to worry about equipment. Don't. If you have access to a video camera (preferably digital) and a simple editing program; you are set to go. I began working with a Sony Digital 8 camera and an iMac with iMovie. There are many other types of cameras and software, but keeping it simple will force you and your students to creatively think their ways out of problems. Focus on what is called "coverage." Coverage is making sure that you have enough shots to really tell your story well, and then some. It's the story about the characters that drives the film forward and makes people want to watch it.

There are many books and websites on making films. The Independent Student Media site (www.ismfilms.com) is geared for high school age and above. The quality of the site is extremely high. The information, interviews, and samples provided are extensive and helpful. *Matters of Light and Depth*, a book by Ross Lowell, has been helpful to me in learning how to improve the look of my films through better lighting.

Do not get loaded down with technique first. Students have been seeing images all of their lives. Basic composition and lighting experience will get them, and you, on your way.

Content

How do you teach students to look at their lives as a source for narrative and still have it be 'G' rated? Content is a big issue. First, because it's revealingly uncomfortable to write a screenplay for the first time. Students want to appear cool, but they also want their first venture out to be successful. I want them to be successful also. Nothing gets students on task more than success. Secondly, because high school students have often seen films in theaters and on television that have subjects I would not want to touch with a barge pole. Teen life may not be 'G' rated, but in the classroom, it needs to be—for your protection as a teacher, but also, to allow the students to creatively think and tell others about the world they live in.

To solve some of this initial problem, I have taught my students filmmaking through documentary and short narrative films. Going through the voluntary rating system for movies was an eye opener for many students. They did not understand the concept of a 'G' rated film. While trying to come up with a solution for the problem I was having with the whole content issue with an early class, I came upon my old Foxfire Project books and used that project as a model for my own class's work.

The Foxfire Project was one started in the Appalachian area by writing teachers who realized that their students had amazingly little appreciation for the rich cultural heritage that surrounded them. These teachers had their students do field research on the older people of their area, tape record their conversations, take photographs and then write articles in a magazine that started as a quarterly and soon developed into a book series. These wonderful books are filled with stories of everyday people and the things they do: farm, make soap, quilt, slaughter hogs, bake, fish, etc. These articles are really a wealth of information about not only the processes, but also the people themselves and their stories.

In my class, we watch documentaries in order for students to understand how a documentary is put together; the description of place with visual images, the narration, the history and the interview.

For the initial film, the class develops a project together. I find an in-school group that is working on a project or an instructional project that needs to be documented. We develop questions, production teams, assign jobs and go into the field to get footage. The teams then edit their footage and present it to schoolmates.

Before going into the field, I coach students on how to conduct themselves while interviewing someone and the importance of being calm and patient. With documentaries, that camera needs to run so that subjects have time to think about the questions they've been asked and then respond. For most students, this is a very different way of approaching people.

With narrative films, I play a game with my students similar to the 'Mad-Libs'™ word games of our youth. We used this as a way to start brainstorming story ideas.

Screenplay Game Chart on the Following Page

Screenplay Game

Where	Who	Does What	With Whom	And Learns What/ Moral
In a Desert	An Auto Mechanic	Learns to Ride a Horse	A Trapeze Artist	Life is to be Lived
While Driving Across the Country	A Young Girl	Discovers a Lost Goldmine	An Ancient Woman	The True Meaning of Christmas

The game answers are written down in each column without worrying about how each answer will relate to each other. When finished with the columns, students then work their way across and come up with story lines, no matter how absurd. It's a way to get out of the skateboard film rut. The film types have ranges from comedy to love story to tragedy.

Scripts need to be outlined and storyboarded before any filming is done. Shots need to be outlined and locations and equipment planned for. This may slow the students down a bit; they tend to be very excited about working right away on a film that usually involves danger or stunts. Not realizing that stunt work on a real Hollywood-type of film is extremely well thought out and planned to make it as safe as possible for both cast and crew. You will need to be focused, to keep them on track.

With documentaries, students will need to learn about the proper documentation demeanor: they need to become non-threatening or invisible. Teaching calm speaking by speaking calmly really gets students to pay attention. Teens all understand that frightened deer-in-the-headlights feeling of being put on the spot. As an interviewer, one must make a subject feel calm in order for the interview to be successful.

The Mechanics of Filmmaking

To teach techniques and jobs, the class will create a film from a script that I have developed in front of them in demonstration. From the screen writing game, I write a 1-minute script, 1-3 pages. I tear it down in class as far as story arc and get the students' input on what they see the characters actually looking like in both demeanor and costume. I then demonstrate how to storyboard, using the script and various types of shots.

We then shoot the film during class time; this can take as long as 2 weeks. I show students the film I made of the professionals at work. From this, they learn about the different jobs and how they all work together on a production set. They choose their job each morning, wearing passes that tell the position and a precise description of the responsibilities and the directions they are to give. I am the Executive Producer and all must do as I instruct. Production staff helps the producer and does the job of crafts (food). Associate Producer keeps the crew together, says 'quiet,' 'and,' and a final 'cut.' The Director works with everyone and says action and cut. The Director of Photography sets up the shots and directs the lighting crew, says 'set.' The 1st Assistant does a lot of things, marks the clapper and reads it for sound. Sound listens and says 'speeding.' The Gaffer is the head of the lighting crew. The Grips set up lighting. The Dolly grip wheels the camera around. Continuity is in charge of script and if shots that are done on different days line up. The Costume Master is for clothes. Vanity does hair and makeup. The Props Master is responsible for all of the props.

We look at the daily footage and discuss the success of the shots and sound. I teach them how to evaluate the shots and how they will edit them together into their short film.

Finally, the students create a film on their own. They must develop the project, researching and getting proper permission to film from the chosen person and the place where the filming is to occur. They have to pitch their project to the class, with script and storyboard on display, explaining why the subject they have chosen is worth a film. Students should also develop a shot list to make sure that they get all shots that they need. This is called "coverage."

The length of these films is about 1-2 minutes. The students only get 2 hours to do their full edit so having a plan helps. I encourage them to use music made by their friends, so that there will be no ownership issues.

I am always amazed and pleased with the final projects. They get a better appreciation for the work. The best part is when they start talking about their next film. Now they have credibility too.

Audience Appreciation

I walked into my local co-op food store where I shot a short film this past summer. It's titled *The Grocery* and is about the fantastic love that two older people have for each other and how that love influences others. I was so excited to do this film. I had arranged a meeting with the person in charge of community/media relations. This was a cold meeting. Though I had been a member of the co-op for many years, I had never been involved enough to know anyone in charge. I had prepared a notebook for her. It contained a script and a storyboard made with full color photographs that I had taken in the store. I talked with her about the story and about how the story came to me while I was shopping in the beautiful produce section. She said yes right then. I could have use of the store for 2 weeks before and after the doors closed for business and yes, employees could help—Wow.

Shooting was great fun. We had actors, a diva, dancers, produce and a fish.

I got a little bit of press coverage. The film is being submitted to festivals and I have plans for how to get it out to a wider audience.

My students come back each year asking about my summer film. When can they see it? The new students think that I know what I'm talking about because I've done it and I've met people who actually make films for a living and those people are interested in seeing the student's films.

A film really takes on a true life when others see it. When I do a project, I enjoy showing my early, or rough cut, to the actors, crew, and their families as a way of thanking them for their work and so that they can see how all the individual scenes fit together to make a whole story. It also helps to screen the film in front of an audience so that you can find out if it makes any sense at all.

With student films, we look at them as a class as they are finished in order to set a standard as well as get feedback. After the class has screened the students' films, we show them at a student film fest after school, so that parents can come and put them on the local cable access station. It makes everyone very proud. Pride is important for the kids and also for you as the teacher. Success breeds success.

I have been lucky enough to have a film on the Internet at the ISM site and to have also screened one at a local theater. Students really think that you know what you are talking about when your work is out there. In their eyes, you are no longer faking it. Now they might actually listen to what you have to say. Miracles can happen.

Filmmaking is a wonderful medium in which young people can express themselves.

Get a camera and get to it. Good luck.

Video Scrapbooks by Teachers and Students   14

At the princely campus of the Culinary Institute of America, overlooking the Hudson River in Hyde Park, New York, we tagged behind a tour group. Through kitchen windows we watched food artists in striped gray pants, decisively aligning carrots on a magnificent carrot cake. We observed the Zen of centering a torte, the elegance of a wine tasting class, and the interior of a satellite guided freezer. The Japanese tourists all carried up-to-date video cameras and listened to our guide while taking patient close-ups of the herb garden, the historic kitchen tools on the wall, and a bakery chef's practice board of involved cake decorations. They politely listened to our animated guide, occasionally fitting her into a picture, all while filtering the experience through their cameras. This habit of attending to life with a camera was their lifestyle. The Japanese students were not carrying inexpensive disposable cameras, but without exception cared enough about their task to have the most advanced digital equipment. They were very serious about camera work. Consider for a moment how wonderful it would be if art education could encourage Americans to carry a camera at all times, and students could become inquiring viewers and video collectors. In art teaching, I have used the video camera as a way of developing students' interests in making videotaping a part of their lives. The following "scenes" are edited from many years of carrying video cameras, from the first recorders that were as heavy as my child, to today's featherweights.

My videotaping habit has, in turn, shaped my art teaching and art classes.

Art teaching should encourage responding to our daily life with a video camera.

SCENE 1: Escorted from the school bus, Jacob is asked the customary question. "What did you do in school today?" "Nothing" he says, while waving a video box in his free hand. "I can't wait to show you the video I made in art class." Picking up his usual walking pace, his mission is to get in the house and pop the tape into the video player.

Of the framed pictures in a home, television is the most frequently viewed. When the family gathers in prime time to watch a child's video on the living room set, it receives unprecedented attention. Video is an art easily shared at home, a familiar media for a family to discuss and encourage. Digital videos from an art class played on sophisticated monitors with surround sound available in many homes make an impressive presentation. A child's narrative during the show adds a special flavor to the event. Video lives well beyond refrigerator art, or an art portfolio brought home, becoming a permanent library of the student's art. In videos, the art class goes home in a media likely to be further explored by students.

SCENE 2: Carrying five boxes, our neighbor Carol brings a wondrous gift. Her grandfather's model train collection consists of hundreds of tracks which now begin to wind around our furniture, creep under the bed, and rise over cereal boxes. Our youngest daughter, Ana, leads the one-person construction crew without knowledge of electronics, but lots of creative intuition. Her dolls are invited to play and receive a souvenir train schedule. The electric trains run on time, but sometimes need to be pulled to their destination. Before the artistic setup is put away, Ana asks for the video camera to record the final excursion along her intricate train-scape. My art class is accustomed to recording class plays and setups on the floor and will enjoy seeing her tape.

Video can become like crayons, one of many available media choices in an art room. And the video camera is there to be used even before the art lesson as a research tool to gather art ideas. Video updates the traditional show and tell—sharing kids' observations and collections from outside of school. During our classes, video is used to record art class performances, celebrations, and imaginary trips. It is a way of recording student art in progress. The video camera acts as an interested audience, an active viewer of child art. We use it after a lesson to conduct interviews with young artists who talk about their completed art. Many artworks children create are in temporary media, made from cards, sand, blocks, ice, or ice cream. Using video in art classes is a way to explore children's free mix of creative media in playing, while keeping tangible records of the process and final product. Videotaping in our art class is an important parting shot, a final visualization of a drive-in restaurant, a circus, a birthday party in class—all recorded in detail before the artwork is put to rest.

SCENE 3: Ana is walking on stilts, enjoying the balancing act required to clean the gutters. In her artistic approach to home chores, work is always stop and go. We stop this time as she carefully examines the abandoned wasps' nests we sprayed the night before. From the top of the tall 1920s wood ladder, she points out each white larva bulb still struggling to be hatched. She assists the newborn wasps

desperately using their stingers to saw their way clear of their cells. After finishing her chores, Ana carefully arranges a display of the handsome yield of wasps' nests on the kitchen table and rushes for the video camera. Part of her artistic display involves creating a beautiful video of nature's dramatic struggle.

Video allows children to save their collections when no one else wants them near the house or brought to school. The video camera saves valuable visual finds and experiences as a permanent and portable record—a record that, in turn, can be brought to an art class for appreciation.

And how do we prepare today's children for a life in art? We can begin by building on existing interests. In their teaching, art teachers need to emphasize student ideas and make the media they work in less important. Teachers need to focus on how to think about art, how to approach and communicate one's creative ideas through any combination of media. Adult artists have freely followed children's leads, crossing media boundaries, and including video as part of the artistic palette. School art can no longer consist of demonstrations of the finer points of each traditional art media. An art room has to become a young artist's think tank.

SCENE 4: All summer, the upstairs door of our cabin wears this sign: "Bank One—Woodstock Branch." Ana set up a bank in the attic, printing fun money, drawing picture checks, and repainting expired credit cards. The bank's ATM machine is an old computer monitor sitting on cigar boxes that store and dispense hand-painted bills. I climb the stairs to stand in a designated line, waiting to be called by the teller. Decorated transaction slips and a large poster of the bank's logo are tastefully displayed on a card table. All activities upstairs are monitored by our family's video camera, the bank's security system. I have already reserved the security camera's tape files to share with my art classes in the fall.

The video camera allows a celebration of the child artist before audiences of other children. I frequently screen great examples of children's home art for my art students.

Video helps in the promotion of student art—recognition which is seldom provided to young artists working at home. I curate videos of children's play creations or unique approaches to home chores. Artists in my video collection are seen wrapping presents, playing house, dressing up, creating an outdoor cafe, or redecorating a playhouse. Video tapes attest to the unique media, tools, and art forms invented daily by child artists. While examples of adult art are regularly featured in art classes, through video clips; children's fleeting, impermanent, and unheralded creations are recognized. I come to class with exciting examples of children's art each day and suggest art lessons which further the unique art the children see on tape.

SCENE 5: It is Tuesday evening, and Ana helps take out the trash while she stops to inspect the neighbor's curbside pile. She decides that, with some careful reworking, a tall wooden clothing rack would be perfect for her room. The physically challenged rack needs help to stand. Ana sees possibilities in its bentwood arms as she gently maneuvers the piece into my studio. Instead of telling the story, my students just watch the video of Ana "borrowing" my acrylics and best brush for repainting. They watch her using colored hot glue sticks for repairs and surface embroidery. They watch the video with great interest and freely offer their favorite rescue stories. "I was in a canoe and saved an old chair from a river bank." "My parents didn't want to stop for the old tires. I saw them on the curb in front of the bike store. But finally they stopped, and we put them in the car. Now I've got two bike tire paintings hanging my room!"

I always sing the praises of the innovative creations children make at home. I tell stories of home creations and occasionally bring in items kids have made. Using video in art teaching I can more convincingly show the story of the child artist who is observant and not ashamed to browse in a trash pile, someone who has wonderful art ideas and the determination to act on them. Videotaping highlights the collecting instincts of children who are always ready to pocket or haul unusual things to home studios. Video recordings document and celebrate this talent. Videos also reveal children as visual shoppers and capture how important it is to actively search for art ideas. The best ideas surface when artists find something special on their own. In the video above we follow a child's encounter with a special object find through its transformation into a handsome art work made for her room. The video states that making useful and beautiful things for one's room is an important form of children's art. My students were moved by the video, feeling it was close to their hearts and interests. They were very impressed that someone bothered to record it for an art class.

SCENE 6: This is grandma Ruth's apartment. We are visiting her in Florida this week. My grandma is 84 years old, and she is an artist and a collector. She would not say she is an artist. She says she just likes making things for people and saving the little things she likes. Since she does not give herself credit, I thought I would make this video to show her place. Above this stove is a museum of little figures made from tissues, dried apples, and shells. Her handmade frames, decorated and covered in pretty fabrics are everywhere. She even dresses up her spice boxes with souvenirs from her trips and displays them on top of the refrigerator. Just displaying things in a fun way is my grandma's art. The bathroom has knitted wall hangings with painted buttons and shells, and she made the tissue box into a sea creature. I bet there are many artists who are unrecognized because they don't make things in a regular art media.

There may be an artist in your family, or someone you know, who has never been recognized for their unusual art. While we can have students meet artists, these videos show the importance of creative people already in our students' lives. Through their videos, students often discover talent displayed in nontraditional art forms and art acts. The subjects of these videos are often surprised by the attention and by being called artists, often for the first time. The videos offer an unforgettable glimpse into students' artistic influences and promote important family talks about art. Student videos of art often record vital family treasures, including antiques and collectibles the videographer feels should be noticed and preserved in pictures. Video can become a child's voice, documenting his or her own view of art and visions of the world. Unlike written diaries which are private gestures that can be ignored, videos are public statements demanding attention, recorded for everyone to take notice.

I was in art school before I had the opportunity to visit an artist's studio. Children should not have to wait that long. Through my own videos, I take students into the studios of colleagues in a variety of art fields. We visit an architect's office, go along on a photo shoot, and enter the restoration suite of a major art museum. It is fine to have artists be seen on commercial videos, but it is not the same as an art teacher making a video designed for his or her art class. The artists in my videos talk about their works directly to us, and I take along some of the students' questions to ask our subjects. My videotapes represent artists who are alive, not only those existing on museum walls. Instead of looking at the works of artists in museums, we interview and record our local community artists while they set up at University galleries or local openings.

SCENE 7: In the early morning darkness, Big Chief, my pull cart, is loaded for the journey up the hill. By the time birds start chirping in celebration of a new day's light, the first leg of my climb is completed. I spread out stained pots and begin stirring colors to match the glow of the day. I greet the same old trees I have greeted for the past thirty or more summers, as I keep adjusting each mix to the morning's light. Finally, I pour the colors into used spring water containers with adjustable flow heads. For a springy canvas, I roll out long and soft white paper carpets over the delicate underlay of grasses. As morning rays of sunlight fill the trees, the search for individual rocks and twigs, my brushes for this day, takes a more urgent pace. Bottled up colors are ready for dispersal over a sensitive terrain, responsive to the touch and pressure of flowing paint. I free my colors over the white flooring, every so often pressing with sticks or stones to clear a natural passage. My landscapes paint themselves. Tucked in the corner of the pull cart is my video accomplice, silently broadcasting from the outdoor studio.

Video is with me to open up private art worlds, my outdoor and indoor studios, for my students to see their art teacher making art. Through the unique qualities of video, students have entered the many studios of my life and joined me on numerous painting expeditions. Each class viewing leads to robust discussions, extending students' notions of what painting is, what making art can be, and how they can learn unusual approaches to art from their teachers. I have always believed that art is taught through oneself, and it is important to show every aspect of my artmaking and art involvement to children. Taking students with me while I make art has been an important use of video. Bringing the outside art world, or the museum, the studio experience, to class would be difficult through words alone. I find that videos are able to take children anywhere, so they can share most vividly the art experiences in which I want them to participate.

SCENE 8: My first exhibit of this season transforms the New York gallery into a bookstore. Soho visitors are surprised to find bookshelves in the gallery, and the books they open are marked by a painted diary of climbing Woodstock's hills. Painted rice paper scrolls, which where used to line my summer floors, now cover the gallery's walls. The scrolls appear informally unframed, laid out in parallel rows, just lightly pinned to their new ground of white plaster.

Of course the opening is videotaped. I enjoy sharing the excitement of an exhibit with my students. Video has allowed students to participate in this event from the very beginning. They saw how the art was rolled to transport it home, how it was lovingly stored and later unfurled for the many stages of selection. I filled notebooks in planning the design of this exhibit. Students witness the behind-the-scenes preparation at the gallery, hear decisions made about furnishings, placements, and illuminating the work, including my concerns for maintaining the light and sounds of the country. Videos from the opening night are anything but silent, filled with background remarks and interviews. Students can match wits and impressions with other guests at the show.

After the show, it's a long drive home to Lexington, Kentucky, and I use the time to plan for painting indoors during the year. On the way home, I stop at a large art supply store, browse at a beauty supply wholesaler, and take the video camera to a plastics importing warehouse, documenting the shopping in preparation for a new classroom series. Video takes of a working artist capture the necessary planning, the supply shopping, and the relentless search for inspiration.

SCENE 9: Welcome to the giant community yard sale in Tivoli, New York, where the most unusual hair curlers, great aunts' buttons, and old post office stampers reside. Crazy and fun stuff is set out on driveways and front porches, waiting to be discovered. Let's follow the trail of an old box filled with pulleys and demonstrate how to bargain for a makeup case lined with vintage nail polish colors. The summer is an opportunity to stock up on amazing school supplies. Children are inspired by imaginative shopping, not by art supply catalogues. A great art class can be set up as a wonderful shopping place to which everyone contributes. To demonstrate how children's finds are welcome all year, I show videos of my playful shopping, uncensored purchases, and collections. My classes are with me wherever I go because I bring my own art excursions back to class through videos. Videos whet the appetites of young artists. They deputize kids to look for art supplies everywhere. I share with children my favorite shopping places and my dedication to the art of searching. I share my vision that anything found in the environment can become an art supply, found in the world's largest art supply store. Videos allow me to visually highlight interesting objects. I take a video camera to fleamarkets, yard sales, antique stores, thrift stores, and auctions. On videotape I cannot only show my many collections, but also how they got started and moments when they became enriched. In recent years, I have made few trips without my video camera. From my trips to the grocery store, to Target, or to the Met—through video, my students can come along. Video has enabled me to take my class wherever I go, to share the fun of idea shopping and not just talk about it in school. The video camera moves art instruction beyond classroom walls, to wherever exciting and beautiful things can be found, demystifying the process of creating art. As an art teacher I carry my video camera like an EKG halter, monitoring the visual heart stops of a day. In turn, students respond by bringing their own object finds to class in their pockets, lunchboxes, and lately on videos. These video finds come complete with stories about the search and the ideas that made the object special, worthy of saving on videotape.

SCENE 10: Look at the stained glass windows, not in a French cathedral, but at Joe Bologna's, a Lexington, Kentucky, Pizzeria. A magnificent light show showered the table and my plate and came complimentary with the lunchtime meal. The waiter explained to me that the windows had previous lives, inspiring Unitarians to prayer since1890, then sending heavenly colors upon Jews, when the building became a synagogue in the1920s. Luckily my small video camera is having lunch with me and can capture the light. I ask students in the video if they know of other places in town where one could film a light show?

Later, while introducing a lesson on stained glass art, students were fascinated by the video of a familiar place. Video is a powerful tool to point out overlooked art. It can inspire an art lesson with references to familiar sights and places. Yes, I also talked about the stirring lights of Chartes, but in place of reproductions on paper, commercial videos, or slides, the video lunch at Joe Bologna's made a powerful impression. Lecturing about art qualities and elements to children only abstracts the feelings we are trying to build towards art. After studying art history and aesthetics in college classes, art teachers often give college style lectures in school. Video is my art about art. It not only shows artworks, but expresses my deepest thoughts and feelings about it. Making a video focuses the artistic awareness of an audience. It translates art concepts into interesting and meaningful images. As a filmmaker I consider how information can be presented in a visually powerful way. While filming, I ask myself how the experience can be made unforgettable. Isn't this essential in teaching all art lessons to children?

It is not potato printing we are talking about in a printing demonstration, but the beauty of all surfaces. A brief video can move an art lesson from an abstraction into the world, from a narrow demonstration of a process, to showing its many facets. A video not only represents a lesson idea, but applies it to environmental situations and promotes new thoughts and dreams. And where do I go to capture printmaking on video? I follow young bike riders' tire marks after a rain, as they dip into puddles and print unusual markings on sidewalks. I film a printing demonstration in a supermarket produce aisle, inviting all fruits and vegetables, not just potatoes, to star. I film my mother turning pages from her old passport, stamped by sharp Communist and Nazi stampers, printers which enforced boundaries and sealed her fate. Lesson planning which includes video is an art and never a routine act.

SCENE 11: For some, cafeteria duty is a dreaded task. For me it is an important part of teaching art. Tied by school routines during the day, children break free with creative ideas in the lunchroom. I focus on the art that lives just outside my art class. This long shot, for example, is of a make believe cell phone call, with a child popping up his drinking straw antenna from a juice carton phone. At another table I need a ticket to film the show inside a student's lunch box. Lunch leftovers are great performers (applause) for the napkin-dressed apple core crooning into a foil mike held in her plastic fork arm. My videos catalogue the work of lunchroom artists, and I screen their finest moments as we prepare lunchbox theaters in the art class.

Video cameras can gather evidence of art in informal school settings. I collect samples of children's creativity during informal playing found in school hallways, playgrounds, and lunchrooms. To film a video about authentic children's inventing, one has to leave the confines of the classroom and find places where children can act as children. In a school where students live by instruction and ideas presented by adults, videos remind children that they have great ideas, often the most creative ideas in school.

SCENE 12: Race cars just arrived at our supermarket, and a lucky child will be first in line to drive. I just happened to be here with my video camera as the new shopping carts are unloaded. I interviewed the first test driver, wearing Matchbox car sneakers. Video recordings can bring to class the latest and newest in products and designs from any store. Perhaps, more importantly, these video reports convey the artist's enthusiasm about the future and the new. During "Back to School Days" events, I shop with the camera for the most interesting crop of folders, new pencil topper ideas, and the latest boom box pencil cases. Before Halloween, I file a report on K-Mart masks, the tribal disguises of our generation. You can see it in the art class first. My video camera was there to review the newest in children's character toothbrushes, candy dispensers, and the pool toys and beach towels for the summer season. Stores come to class in video diaries, showing children that their interest in playful artistic shopping has significance. Uniquely American objects are of interest to artists of all ages, and they challenge art room design teams. For me, lesson planning is no longer just paperwork, but an active state of searching for the video footage that best inspires and explains the art lesson. Instead of planning for a lecture, I plan videos for what the students will see and experience in my room. Video makes it possible to share how the art lesson inspired me in the first place, leaving some of the wonderment of discovery intact. Video reinforces the act of being an observer, of finding a lesson idea and seeing it develop on its way to becoming school art. The camera accompanies my daily journeys, ready to capture sights, events, and sounds which inspire the artist, but tend to be filtered out by school walls. The informality of the camera is a model for selective seeing, just like bending down and picking up interesting things all the time. Through videotaping I continue to be involved in fun objects kids notice and appreciate. When I videotape for a lesson, I think of planning as sharing something special with young artists.

SCENE 13: It's the mailman, delivering my large box. For the opening ceremony, I set up the video camera. The unpacking begins with the spilling over of annoying foam nuts, then newspaper, bubble wrap, and more bubble wrap. Then, finally, parts emerge from a white foam cloak and begin to show signs of the big bed I purchased.

The hand hewn oak beauty from the Arts and Crafts period circa 1900 has a lithographed headboard of dolls preparing for dreamland. I attended an antique doll collectors' show last weekend that had a wonderful selection of doll beds. I started filming this video at the show and decided to wait for the arrival of this doll bed I purchased on-line before I completed the project.

There are 364 beds on the wall...or was that bottles? Anyway, eBay has many more listings of unusual antique doll beds this week. Perhaps the finest doll beds anywhere are in the collection of the Indianapolis Children's Museum. Many of these wonderful pieces of furniture history appear in the video I prepared on the subject. My video sources from the museum, eBay, and my own collection were seamlessly melded, edited on a home computer. Curating the antique doll bed video is an example of bringing any historic object collection such as pull toys, cereal boxes, or coin banks to the art class. My prescription for art teaching is to show something beautiful in class each day. Videos made for the art class can import the museum to class in a memorable way. A teacher-narrated digital video is a crystal clear picture book, a sharply focused personal tour of beautiful objects. Next week's shooting will be inside vintage playhouses, expanding the history lesson on furniture to the history of architecture. Video becomes a personal invitation to young art historians, future curators, and antique collectors.

A Parting Shot

These are my scrapbooks, a vast video library filled with examples of children's objects old and new, creative plays, and my own art adventures, which continue to provide an exciting visual background to art lessons in my art room. I have films of my daughter Ana playing restaurant with her friend Jeremy on our porch. Ana was the creative table setter, menu board artist, and waitress. Jeremy, meanwhile, in a make believe kitchen, created special meals from rubber bands, paper clips, pencil shavings, and my shaving cream. Ana drew fancy menus and still remembers the receipts I never paid. Jeremy is now a famous chef, and my daughter is an artist-teacher. They are still friends, and appreciate my video scrapbooking, seeing their early art histories on film. My young students watch and relate enthusiastically to the same video. Video is a tool unlike any other, one that can observe and share special moments and events during the time they are taking place. It is an art form that thrives on action as much as children do. With a video camera you can travel to take in all the sights and actions which make finding and making art so much fun.

PART THREE

Video Art Projects in the Community

Street Level Youth Media

15

Street Level Youth Media *is a community-based media arts organization that puts youth at the center of community life, where youth voice and youth culture are valued assets towards negotiating differences, building community, developing critical thinking and artistic skills, and providing youth with the necessary tools to negotiate and decipher the media-saturated culture of the 21ˢᵗ century. The agency's 8 full-time staff members are artists and youth mentors. They guide young artists through artmaking processes in the media arts and spend an equal amount of time helping youth process what they see and hear in the world around them whether it is on TV, on the Web, in their homes, or on the streets. Youth, ages 8-22, produce, create, and design digital video, audio, web, and graphic art. In their artwork and through encouraged dialogue, young artists address personal and community issues such as identity, education, gentrification, violence, families, racism and history. As they progress in Street-Level programs, young artists begin to trust their own voices and aesthetic choices. However, the anticipated outcome is not only the inspired creative expression of youth but also increased youth civic awareness, civic engagement and the development of leadership skills needed to strengthen our communities.* (A. Vaidya, 2003)

The disparities of access and inclusion created a tension and hence a social and political need to deposit equipment (computers, cable and an occasional printer) in urban centers. With limited actual resources, individuals in these centers have made valiant efforts to meet the needs of targeted communities. Unfortunately, the image that "technology center" evokes in the context of an urban school or community based center setting rarely depicts innovation, student engagement or rarer yet, creativity. More often than not, in urban settings with limited access, Mavis Beacon teaches typing while Encarta provides the only window to the world. The use and creative exploration of multimedia such as digital photography and digital video is the exception and not the rule. The blind spot in educational practice further impaired by prescriptive and draconian district led initiatives is the inclusion of the lived experience of young people and the honoring of their authentic voices.

Street-Level Youth Media is a non-profit organization based in Chicago that strives to bridge the gaps between art and technology, and art and community based art practice that addresses the needs and concerns of young people. As a former Co-Director of the organization, I firmly stand behind its mission to "educate youth in media arts and emerging technologies for use in self-expression, communication and social change."

As an artist, I experienced first hand the transformative power of media and new technologies in the hands of young people. When entrusted, encouraged and supported in their vision and creativity, the work is powerful. Within the process, the teacher does become the student and the student the teacher. The experience forever changed my own art practice. As an arts educator seeking to support and promote the field, I advocate Street-Level's educational approach as an exemplary of good practice and a model for progressive arts education that is relevant and meaningful to youth and acknowledges the communities in which they live. Art education defies the notion that education is a separate practice of everyday life. Yet far too often that fact is lost in the context of a school. The art we practice is not the art we represent to students in classrooms. There is a critical need for an approach to arts education that is informed by the day-to-day experiences of youth.

An Approach to Arts Education

Street-Level's approach to arts education is informed by day to day experiences with youth on a grassroots level. S-L staff are trained artists who understand the critical role the arts play in our lives. The power of the arts to transform is acknowledged in the mission statement and experienced through youth media arts programming in and out of school. Youth are at the center of the work . Their lives and experiences are valued. They are treated with respect. There are high expectations and a presumption of knowledge and creative ability. Youth are given roles, responsibilities, decision making power, and choice. Instead of being the media content, defined, marginalized and marketed to, they are encouraged to create content and interpret their world for themselves. The notion that value and commodity are derived externally is replaced with the recognition of internal values of each youth participant, and real power and potential located within the untapped and unrecognized resources in the communities in which they live.

History

Street-Level's organizational history traces back to Tele-Vecindario, a project commissioned as part of Sculpture Chicago's *Culture in Action* public art program in 1992 and 1993. Artist Inigo Manglano-Ovalle sought to facili-

tate dialogue between residents of a West Side community in Chicago through a public art project that brought video as art into the street. Multiple video dialogues, or *Tele-Vecindario* as an art installation, would give voice to residents of West Town, a then isolated, marginalized and predominantly low income, Latino community in Chicago. The youth component of the project was named Street-Level Video and would later become Street-Level Youth Media. Through Street-Level Video, youth voice was given space and illuminated in a large public installation that placed 75 video monitors in multiple installations along a residential street. In an awesome display, the monitors glowed and lit the street as over 1,000 residents and non-residents, young and old, interacted with one another during the 12-hour event. Art emerged that evening as a public presence and a catalyst for discourse. The evening's events included live on stage teen performances and the creation of a peace mural. The block party was intergener-ational and cross cultural. It brought together gang-affiliated youth with grandmothers and civic leaders with graffiti artists.

Evolution

Street-Level Youth Media emerged in 1995, bringing together artists who initiated Street-Level Video and those who shared similar visions of community based artmaking, using media and new technologies as tools for creative expression. The organization was housed in a storefront studio that was named Neutral Ground. The name implied the studio's location within neutral territory in proximity to a corner where four gang lines converged. As well as conveying the spirit of open access, the name spoke to an encouraged dialogue the organization hoped to foster. One of the first Neutral Ground projects involved engaging gang-affiliated youth by providing cameras across gang lines. These youth created a series of video letters. Youth, who otherwise would never have spoken to one another, exchanged messages. The opportunity for gang affiliated youth to see each other differently also provided other community members with the opportunity to look at these youth in new ways.

The organization's focus on the use of computers, software programs and the Internet as tools for artmaking, building community leadership and fostering transformation, positioned it uniquely among technology access centers. The artists at Street-Level believed graphic art, audio manipulation, digital video and the Web in the hands of young media arts trainees, could forge new frontiers for technological innovation, artistic expression and community activism.

Today

The spirit and intent of the original project remains intact; public art and community activism are key components in the work. In 2003, Street-Level served 1,800 young people predominantly from low-income, minority backgrounds living within Chicago's inner-city limits. Street-Level employs artists of diverse backgrounds and experiences who are challenged to engage in meaningful work with youth and community. Street-Level programs incorporate peer-to-peer mentoring, apprenticeship, structured workshops, self-initiated projects, artist collaborations, group collaborations, focused project times, discussion groups and screenings to engage youth.

Three Areas of Focus

Programming has three areas of focus; mobile, studio, and professional development. Mobile programs bring media arts training for youth to partner sites at Chicago Public Schools (CPS), community-based organizations and other cultural institutions. The agency offers workshops and courses, ranging from day-long sessions to year-long residencies, in media production and media literacy, both during school hours and for after-school programs using arts integrated and project-based approaches.

Studio programming is implemented within a lab in the West Town community of Chicago. The lab, still referred to as "Neutral Ground," operates during after-school hours five days a week, and offers a variety of project-based media arts workshops in video, graphic design, Web design and audio. Projects and workshops change on a trimester basis. Youth also have open access to media technology and the Internet, so they can pursue personal media projects or complete schoolwork. The lab is a studio for innovation and a media hub

for other youth and community based organizations in the same neighborhood all over the city.

Through professional development, Street-Level offers training to Chicago Public School teachers, as well as other arts educators and youth workers across the city. The workshops engage participants in the practice of hands-on, applied learning. Street-Level aims to model best practices and promote youth focused approaches to art and technology. Professional development courses are based on the model of project based learning, address curriculum development, and implementation strategies as well as arts integration and technology training.

Public School Partnership

Street-Level's partnerships with Chicago Public Schools extends the mission and approach to arts education into the classroom. Street-Level has been effective in creating and implementing media arts integrated curricula that is consistent with fine arts standards, city and state goals, and learning objectives in the Chicago Public School system. The challenges faced by Chicago Public Schools, like in many other large urban centers because of national standards, place high demands and criteria on any initiative in the school. With the assistance of dedicated teachers, Street-Level has met and exceeded these demands. Street-Level's interest in Chicago Public Schools is in affecting overall school change through strong partnerships and collaborations with students, teachers and administrators. The programs in schools vary from one-day workshops to 6 to 12-week residencies in media arts and technologies. Students are encouraged to work as a team on creative projects, using tools such as digital publishing, video and audio production, script writing and animation. Both in school and out of school programming at Street-Level is project based. In schools, there is an intentional cross disciplinary approach that more accurately reflects how students experience and understand their world. The goal is to connect the curriculum to the real lives and experiences of youth and amplify their voices and perspectives through these media.

Strong partnerships in the schools requires real engagement and collaboration with classroom teachers in and outside of the art room. The role of a visiting artist should not be to further marginalize the resident art teacher in the building but to help leverage art as a curricular content. In fact, key to the success of S-L programming in Chicago Schools is the building of bridges across curricular areas and the prominent role of the art teacher as colleague and peer educator.

The Work

One art teacher, interested in further exploring collage with her students, reinforces basic concepts and pushes herself artistically by collaborating with a Street-Level artist to create digital collage with her students. Responding to the work of a well-known artist, Romare Bearden, students shoot and scan their own photographs and manipulate the images to represent their community graphically through collage. The collage unit is further developed to incorporate social studies curricula. In collaboration with a social studies teacher, students use video cameras as a tool for inquiry. Students interview elder residents in their community to experience first hand accounts of community history and gain understanding of the transformation of their neighborhood. The concept of layering images and sound in digital video is explored as another form of collage. Students work collaboratively, make choices and decisions and are encouraged to take creative risks. Another art teacher collaborates with a Street-Level artist to develop a unit on graffiti. Making signs or marks is examined within the context of community research and civic awareness. Graffiti is explored as a way to send messages, tell stories, document events and define identity. Historically, marks were made in some Chicago neighborhoods by immigrant population to offer directions and information for newcomers. In approaching the subject matter, student knowledge is recognized and honored. Students are given space to explain their understanding of the significance graffiti and other man-made marks and signs have in their community. Students make their own marks and learn layering techniques through the use of Adobe Photoshop to place those marks on buildings and other pictorial public canvasses.

In both examples, the final presentations are planned as public events or installations within the school building. Student work might be projected on wall surfaces. Sound and image could be separated to create layered sound or visual experiences. The intention is to engage the audience of parents, teachers, students and community members in dialogue and celebrate the work of the youth.

The environments in which young people live are often changing. Rarely are students given the opportunity to reflect and process those changes within school walls. Street-Level collaborated with the youth at another elementary school to create a digital photography exhibit. The exhibit focused on youth responses to the recent gentrification of Chicago's famed project housing initiative Cabrini Green. With the aid of digital technology, the class of 8th graders captured the changing face of their neighborhood and then used Adobe Photoshop to manipulate those images and create dynamic photographs. Over the period of a semester, the youth produced over 70 images on topics of violence, women in Cabrini, the greening of Cabrini and the changing topography of the area. This was followed by weeks of writing workshops where they put down their thoughts and ideas on paper, in the form of poems and essays, to be displayed alongside the photographs.

The Cabrini project bridged in-school and after-school programming. Unfortunately, after-school programming, even on school grounds, is disconnected from classroom activity. False distinctions between in-school and after-school activities reinforce unnecessary and detrimental distinction between life experience and daily school curricula. This exhibit was taken to a respected gallery space in Chicago where it was on display for 4 weeks. At the opening, parents, teachers, and students had deeper and more meaningful discussions than on typical "Parent Nights" at the school. Students were elevated and celebrated as artists and respected community members.

Street-Level's program areas are designed to flow naturally together to provide circular programming available to youth where they are during school hours, after school and continuing through paid art making opportunities.

The studio is the hub of organizational activity and provides opportunity for more in-depth art experiences such as residencies and one-on-one mentorship, an example of which was the Peace Signs Project. Through Peace Signs, Youth Anti-Gun Violence Billboard Project, six professional artists were paired with six young artists to design large scale billboards with messages that spoke out against gun violence. The young artists came from art programs at Street-Level Youth Media and Lill Street Learning Center. They attended group workshops where they discussed issues related to gun violence such as violence prevention, the role of the media in glorifying guns, and government action or inaction. They also studied the fundamentals of graphic design with an emphasis on billboards and political posters. Upon completion of these workshops each youth artist was paired with a professional artist for 8 weeks. The completed billboards were put up throughout the Chicago area for 6 weeks. A peace walk and vigil commemorated the project unveiling and engaged community members, promoting a public and open dialogue on gun violence with young people.

One final example of Street-Level work is the culminating gallery exhibit of a paid summer arts apprentice program. Fifteen youth were given the responsibilities of professional working artists. Youth artists worked with community based artists to create multimedia installations presented in a gallery show entitled "I CAM: Street Theories from Chicago's Youth". The work was conceived, produced and installed by youth. Youth addressed a wide array of subjects through video, sound, sculptural and 2-D graphic installations.

In one installation, the viewer encountered a monitor emerging from rubble and enclosed in a barbed wire fence. The piece was titled "Rezalutions: The Palestinian/Israeli Conflict" and was created by a 14- and 16-year-old artist in collaboration with an adult artist mentor. They documented their journey around the city as they posed questions to people on the street about the Middle East conflict.

Another teen wanted to explore difficulties and pressures facing young mothers. With assistance from her mentor

artist, this 17-year-old artist followed a teen mom for a day to create a video portrait. The installation was titled, "A Day in the Life of a Young Mother" The video portrait was placed within an elaborate sculpture of a pregnant woman.

The exhibit was inspiring and unexpected for an organization known for public outdoor exhibits. Formal gallery spaces are not typically receptive or reflective of urban youth culture or perspectives. Street-Level, in keeping with its mission, recognized that youth presence in the public and private sphere is relevant, vital, and should be promoted especially where it is least expected.

Summary

Technology is not just to be accessed but examined. It should be understood and applied within the context of everyday life. It does not lie outside of the arts, education or community. When properly employed to address the real needs and concerns of community and entrusted in the hands of young artists, the limited question of access is transcended. The question becomes one of inclusion. The issues of voice, representation and content emerge.

The fact of art practice as connected to and informed by lived experience should have implications within the art classroom in formal or informal settings. The artist collaborators at Street-Level support youth in making connection to their everyday experiences.

Critical to understanding artmaking and art learning is to appreciate the aesthetic experiences of youth. Youth are confronted daily with digitally enhanced false representations of themselves that place youth as a target market and youth culture as a commodity. At Street-Level, youth are encouraged to deconstruct and replace those false representations with images of their own making. New and emerging technologies bring forth new and emerging voices. Youth perspectives evoke and promote dialogue and community engagement.

Whether in school, in an after-school studio, in the public or private sphere at Street-Level Youth Media, youth are respected and their work is celebrated. Most importantly, youth find value and importance in their own voices. They begin to question and understand the world around them, and they learn to appreciate their role in shaping the future of that world.

Reference

Vaidya, A. (2003). *Street-Level youth media*. [manuscript] Chicago, IL: Unpublished.

Video Creativity for the Record: **16**

Documenting a Community-Based Art Project
in an Inner City High School

Mike was an average 10th grader who was well liked, self-confident, and a star basketball player. He always smiled when he came to class and was an avid cartoonist. Mike worked after school in a local grocery store and took care of his younger brother on weekends. On the way home from a party one evening he was fatally shot. Classmates wanted to honor his memory in a meaningful way. Under my direction, 15 high school sophomores organized, planned, designed, produced, and documented a memorial entitled *The Mural of Peace and Non-Violence.* The time was the late 1980s. The place was Bronx Regional High School, located in the South Bronx, in New York City, opposite abandoned buildings that doubled as drug dens and crack houses. Members of the school's community believed that Mike was a war victim, of a society that was not allowing young people to grow up in full and healthy ways, of a society that allows poor education, poor housing, and a lack of jobs to foster lives lost in drugs and without hope.

Prior to my teaching on the university level, I taught art for 15 years with inner city adolescents. Six of those years were spent in Bronx Regional High School (BRHS) an alternative high school where interdisciplinary art programs were effective with this high risk population. "The group of 10th graders I taught had truancy and disciplinary problems, records of dropping out of school, and some had experienced incarceration. This was their last chance to attain a high school diploma" (Asher, 2000, p. 33). BRHS had a population of 350 at-risk inner-city adolescents with 10/1 student/teacher ratio. These young people were not accustomed to using art to express their inner most feelings about violence in their lives. Most had after-school jobs or family responsibilities and initially viewed the "art class" as unimportant. As a community muralist, I know the positive impact public art can have on a neighborhood as well as for the people who create it. When a mural was suggested to this group, there were initial doubts and little enthusiasm. After a few days of discussion and seeing images of past murals, the entire class agreed to try. Eventually each class member transformed feelings of grief, frustration, anger, and despair at such a tragedy into a constructive and caring expression of hope. A video recorder documented it all.

Teachers who want to use visual recording to document their work with students will find the following pages useful. Although the focus is on documenting the creation of a mural, it can be adapted to any class project. Topics related to video as a documentary tool in classrooms include:

funding, maximum creative participation of students, sound and camera techniques, time allocation, and current teen video centers. I also offer suggestions for future projects and discuss video as a means of fostering community support for a school art program. This article is intended for those who want to impact the school environment and develop students' creative abilities to express themselves through collaborative classroom projects. Although murals can be seen as pure decoration, I understand them as more than that. For teachers, murals can serve as a way to reexamine the environments around them with their students and to integrate history into art. Through video documentation, students: (1) gain an understanding of ongoing participation by collecting evidence of their experiences; (2) are presented with opportunities to reflect on their learning while making recordings to be seen by their peers and community members; and (3) discover a hands-on approach to learning. A 10-year perspective on video in the classroom at Bronx Regional High School (BRHS) is given along with information about how four other organizations currently use video with adolescents. The purpose of this chapter is to discuss a 1989 video project, revisit the school, and report on current use of visual media by students there and elsewhere.

Video as Research

To conceptualize past and contemporary examples of nonviolent resistance, the class reviewed videos of the lives of Mahatma Gandhi, Dr. Martin Luther King, and Rosa Parks. Students formed study groups and linked research based on the larger theme of nonviolence and other civil rights activism. Illustrations were drawn, tapping into creative energies of all class members. Students analyzed causes and effects of civil disobedience and compared and contrasted what they knew with what they learned from the videos. They were able to separate fact from fiction based on further library research and formulated their own opinions and developed analytic skills in their ability to observe, describe, analyze, and interpret the videos. Part of the final design for the mural included an image of class members viewing a video about Martin Luther King, with a framed portrait of Gandhi on the wall behind him (see Figure 1).

Video as a Form of Artistic Documentation

Part of an educator's job is to teach students about accountability. Documentation records the progress of a mural project at all stages. The development of visual skills, composition, framing, and length of shots are all part of the learning process. A video is a visual essay, with a beginning, middle, and end. Video provided a valuable educational experience as a new way to document this artistic process.

Angelo was a shy student and uninterested in painting the mural with the rest of the group. Instead, he wanted to record it on his own; so he became the recording engineer. This opened up new avenues of interpersonal skills for him as well as providing a vehicle for creative expression. The school had access to minimal equipment which included a hand-held video camera with a separate VHS recording deck. Video instructor Al Jaccoma taught at BRHS for 15 years and with a small budget, over the years, built up a minimal system to teach video. Al worked with Angelo, as an Independent Study student; and so Angelo's role of documenter evolved. The project took place between February and May. In an interview, (January 31, 2003) Al described how he handled the documentation process of the mural with Angelo in 1989.

I encouraged Angelo to take simple shots with an old hand-held camera with a separate VHS tape deck. Angelo was diligent and prepared the video tapes carefully. At the end of each class, I viewed footage with Angelo to determine if any of the shots were good and which were not useful. If a shot was steady, or actually showed action, he noted that information. If clear and focused, it was considered a good shot. Angelo managed to keep track of what he did by numbering and labeling the good shots on a log sheet (see Figure 2).

These shots were edited together. Through class interviews and on-sight shooting, Angelo created an artistic piece using the video process. He learned how to manipulate time, space, and sound.

Approaching Video As An Artistic Process

A mural can beautify a public space. It can also convey a message. A teacher's objective for creating a mural must concentrate on eliciting images and ideas from the students' personal experiences of the world. The most effective kind of mural combines elements of line, shape, color and form as images that convey specific meaning, one that can be easily understood, symbolically by the community.

In the same way, Al and I encouraged Angelo to express himself in a short documentary within a 4-month project. With video there is a manipulation of time, space and sound. Al suggested taking simple shots. Angelo had to comprehend a range of camera, sound, and editing skills, including: (1) composition; (2) interviewing; (3) getting good sound; (5) lighting; and (6) adding appropriate music. Angelo learned how to use video as a *fixed canvas* and began to understand artistic concepts of space, movement, composition, time, and point of view. He dealt with the issue of not having a stable composition since movement is a large component of video-taping an art project as it happens. In the early stages, Al encouraged Angelo to compose the shots. After some practice, he became better at making technical decisions on his own.

Camera Aesthetics

Angelo mastered a variety of skills including: zooming in and out, panning, tilting, when to use close-up, wide, medium and long shots. He learned how to choose what was most appropriate to create visual information using a basic camera with no electronic zoom. This meant that he manually zoomed in and out for each shot, there was no automatic focus which actually helped him learn how to focus. Usually a tripod is used to support a camera. BRHS did not have one and Angelo hand-held the camera over his right shoulder so the record button could be reached with the thumb of his right hand. Less cumbersome than the tripod, it gave him more freedom of movement to interact with others and to be creative.

Audio and Sound

Although there is sound in the video, Al and Angelo were not concerned with the audio initially. It was in the editing stage that sound was explored. Angelo looked for good visuals to match up with the audio. In the Educational Video Center (EVC) Community Organizer's Guide to Video Production, there is a section devoted to tips in producing a short documentary. "Music sets the tone for any piece of video. . . selecting the right music . . . is very important because it will impact the way an audience *see's* a particular scene" (Gonzalez, Walker, & Mistry, 1994, p. 41). Encouraging Angelo to figure out the best way to tell a story, Al described the audio process: *There was some logging and notation on paper. We tracked footage with approximate numbers without time frames. Angelo used a lot of intuition, a lot of it was hit or miss. We laid down music of John Coltrane's piece Welcome from an LP recording (1965), Greatest Hits Years Volume III, since it had part of the Happy Birthday song on it, and the dedication was around the time of King's birthday. Angelo and I agreed to include a clip from a speech that King made the day before he died from The Reverend Dr. Martin Luther King: In Search of Freedom., (1968).*

When asked how the sequence was determined, Al explained: *With two Video Home System (VHS) editing machines and two monitors, we mixed directly onto the tape.*

The reason for two monitors is that one monitor allows you to see what is happening on the source tape (in the play-back deck), the other monitor allows you to see what is happening on the master tape (in the recording deck). Al continued: *We used analog VHS video. In 1989 the equipment was at least 8 years old at the time. We laid down the music, overlaid King's speech, then the pictures were superimposed, then the interviews of the students, then the audio. It's a pretty standard format.*

Problems and Surprises
Related To Classroom Video

One might expect to find problems motivating this group for such a long-term project; however, class members looked forward to getting the paints together and continuing where they left off in the previous class. For Angelo, problems with the task of documentation included making sure all cables and connections were secure and working.

According to Al, the main technical problems are the limitations of the equipment and its unreliability; for example, the camera's battery had to be recharged before each class. Although technology continues to change, even the most basic equipment has creative uses. Teachers do not have to let old equipment prevent them from doing creative work. In fact, the older equipment has some definite advantages, such as forcing the camera operator to learn how to focus manually.

A surprising outcome of the video component was the enthusiastic response from the entire class whenever Angelo taped them and their willingness to be interviewed. They enjoyed seeing themselves and watching the process unfold from class to class. A Citizens' Committee of New York grant covered the cost of mural materials. Upon seeing the finished mural, the Citizens' Committee director awarded a second grant in support of the school's art program.

Impact of the Final Video

A segment of the mural highlights Rosa Parks on the bus she rode in Montgomery, Alabama. At the time of the Mural Dedication, she was in New York City, and the class invited her to attend. Her secretary contacted the school, and explained that she was unable to attend, but agreed to videotape a short speech during a Press Conference. Angelo went to Manhattan with the school principal and recorded Rosa Parks live as she expressed her admiration for the students who painted the mural and sent best wishes for its success. Al edited the Parks video segment into the original footage of the *Mural of Peace and Non-Violence.* After many weeks of researching, planning, shooting, logging and editing, the first screening of the completed video tape was held in BRHS's auditorium for the entire school. Everyone who contributed to the making of the tape was invited, including people who were in the tape, and anyone who gave information and support. Mike's parents came and expressed their gratitude in a short speech. The class answered questions from the audience about the tape. They left the screening with a sense of accomplishment and pride, knowing that their message was heard by others. A few months later, I presented the video at a National Art Education Conference in Atlanta.

Personal Reflections

Children's video is well suited for populations and areas like the Bronx since video is one of the best ways for young people to express their opinions and feelings on any issue. Knight (2003) asserts that the "study of the visual experience must be approached from a critical perspective designed to empower the masses, particularly disenfranchised people, people of color or low income backgrounds, people who are disabled, gay or lesbian, and girls" (p. 46). Video can be used to help all youngsters understand or investigate an important issue and motivate them to do something about it. With these skills young video producers can make documentaries that can create change in their community, their city, or elsewhere.

Many times, students think that in order to make a video they must do something that resembles something they have seen on television. TV has a tremendous impact on the perceptions of young people — about themselves, their communities, and their environment. Watching TV is a passive means of entertainment. Through the art of making a video, people begin to ask themselves who is communicating what and why? (Andrews, Guzman, Harrigan, Roman, & Soto,1994). As video producers, they become more critical and better informed viewers; which, in turn, helps clarify their thoughts and raises awareness of production values, resulting in more effective projects.

If I were teaching this class today, visits to local cable news and television stations would be part of the syllabus, as would visits to college media departments and media art production facilities such as the Educational Video Center, Middletown High School, Harlem Live, and The LA Wilson Technology Center. I would encourage students to find out about video festivals and competitions, and arrange for public viewing of student projects. Local documentary artists and video/media artists would be invited into the classroom. Works of Nam June Paik, Ken Burns, Maryann DeLeo, Joan Grossman, Beryl Korot, Spike Lee, Michael Moore, John Toth, and Bill Viola would be discussed. For example, a segment of the film *Glory* was shown to introduce the context of Sojourner Truth's life during the Civil War. As a genre film *Glory* made history accessible (Asher, 1998, p. 18). Students can discover how artists have "humanized technology. . . [They] can carry home the videos they make and view them in their home VCR. With their families. . . discuss how they made their shots and how they used light, space, and action" (Wachowiak, & Clements, 1997, p. 285). It is important to learn basic technical skills necessary for this kind of project in order to keep up to date with the rapidly changing technology, and to be open to students who are more familiar with this medium than most teachers. This was a valuable learning project for me in that I continue to use video as a research medium as well as to document other murals, including the *Sojourner Truth Mural* at the State University of New York at New Paltz and the *Procession Mural* at Queens College, City University of New York.

Conclusion

The collaborative learning process at Bronx Regional High School transformed vision into action. Video documentation stimulated discussions for effectively exploring personal and collective issues. These young people asked questions about violence in their lives and searched for answers based on historical research of examples of acts of violence and nonviolence in the United States. Their search led them down roads towards understanding the American Civil Rights Movement, and the connections between civil disobedience, Gandhi, Martin Luther King, Rosa Parks, and themselves.

Video and mural art are both powerful mediums that can be used for change. Video and murals are excellent ways to bring people together, foster communication, educate, and motivate. They both require cooperation, collaboration, setting goals and time schedules, pre-production planning, research, interviewing skills, technical know-how, and experience with materials and equipment, composition, spatial concepts involving close-ups, managing the art elements of light and space, editing, and public presentations. Video is an important mural-like public medium. As New York University film professor George Stoney wrote in the Foreword of The Education Video Center Organizers' Guide to Video Production (Gonzalez & Goodman, 1994), "ideally, video for social change is a

device for promoting understanding and action. . .You are collecting evidence; you are encouraging witness; you are emboldening ordinary people to 'go public'" (p. 2). Murals effectively do the same.

Video can be an important accompaniment to mural artists as it records the process in an original and creative way. "Videos documenting the community's artists can be used as part of an art history/social studies curriculum" (Wachowiak, & Clements, 1997, p. 285). Through interviews, a muralist has opportunities to discuss his or her role in the process. Narration or voice-over can serve as a guide for the viewer to better understand what is going on in the piece. Music can set the tone of a mural video and can impact the way an audience sees a scene.

There are numerous elements that can be part of a mural video. It depends on the imagination of the creators and the intention of the piece. When young people pick up a paintbrush to paint a mural, they are making a public statement artistically. When they pick up a camera they are potentially bringing people together, to educate, and motivate others to express themselves. Both mediums serve to affirm human dignity and foster a future of peace and justice.

Illustrations

Fig. 1: Detail photograph of *The Mural of Peace and Non-Violence.*

Additional illustration on the following page.

Log Sheet

Project: Summary: Tape #

Counter	Description of Video	Description of Audio	Comments	Take

Fig. 2: Sample log sheet. Note: This Log Sheet is from The Educational Video Center Community Organizers' Guide to Video Production

References

Andrews, A., Guzman B., Harrigan, L. & Roman, C., & Soto, A. (1994). *Yo-TV production handbook: A guide to video by students for students.* New York. The Educational Video Center.

Asher, R. (1998). The Sojourner Truth mural: investigating african american history through art. In E. Sacca, & E. Zimmerman, (Eds.) *Women Art Educators IV: Herstories, ourstories, future stories,* (pp. 16-24). Boucherville: Quebec. Canadian Society for Education Through Art.

Asher, R. (2000). The Bronx as art. *Art Education. 53*(4), 33-38.

Barrett, T. (2003). Interpreting visual culture. *Art Education. 56*(2), 6-12.

Gonzalez, R., Walker, G., & Mistry, J. (1994). *Turn on the power! Using media for social change: The Educational Video Center community organizers' guide to video production.* New York: The Educational Video Center.

Kilik, J. (Producer), & Lee, S. (Writer/Director/Co-Producer). (2000). *Bamboozled* [Motion picture]. United States: 40 Acres and a Mule Productions, Inc.

Knight, W. B. (2003) Three approaches to teaching visual culture in K-12 school contexts. In Keifer-Boyd, K., Amburgy, P. M., & Knight, W. B., *Art Education, 56*(2), 44-51.

Wachowiak, F., & Clements, R. D. (1997). *Emphasis art: A qualitative art program for elementary and middle schools.* New York: Addison-Wesely Longman.Illustrations

Resource Guide

The following listing of New York arts organizations and schools offer video-training. For readers outside of New York, it may be beneficial to contact these places as they are probably connected with, or aware of media arts centers in your area. Also included is a funding agency for community improvement projects and national film/video festival listings.

American Digital Arts Festival
8595 Eola Ct., Ste. 1
Viera, FL, 32940
(407) 253-5866
www.digitalartsfest.com

Contact the Citizens' Committee for New York for a grant application:
Citizens' Committee for New York
305 7th Avenue
New York, NY 10001
(212) 989-0909
www.citizensnyc.org

Contact EVC to order a catalogue of EVC youth-produced videos, as well as the *YO-TV Production Handbook: A guide to video by students for students,* and *Turn on the power! Using media for social change: The EVC community organizer's guide to video production.*
Educational Video Center
120 West 30th Street, 7th Floor
New York, NY 10001
(212) 465-9366
www.evc.org

HarlemLive
1330 5th Avenue
New York, NY 10026
(212) 369-6275
www.harlemlive.org

KidFilm, USA Film Festival
6116 N. Central Expressway, Ste. 105
Dallas, TX 75201
www.usafilmfestival.com

Lewis Arnold Technology Center
Dix Hills, Long Island
(631) 667-6000
www.westernsuffolkbosces.edu

Middletown High School
Gardner Avenue Extension
Middletown, New York, 10940
(845) 341-5900
www.ecsdm.org

National Children's Film Festival
Children's Discovery Museum of San Jose
18 Woz Way
San Jose, CA 95110
(408) 298-5437
www.childrenfest.org

A r l e n e   J o r d a n

Dancing Across the Digital Divide

17

The Story of Digital Arts

To spark children's imagination, empower them to take on new roles and inspire them to collaborate, forge connections and create engaging products that blend art and technology. This is the vision of Community School District 25's (currently Region 9's) Digital Arts Technology Team in Flushing, Queens, and New York, where children come from over 100 countries and speak over 100 languages.

Background

CSD 25 had traditionally been recognized for its work in the arts on the city, state, and national levels. In 1996 the District received the Governor's Arts Award, in 1997 the School Board Award from the NYS Alliance for the Arts and in 1998 the President's Committee on the Arts and Humanities highlighted the District for its exemplary arts programs in *Gaining the Arts Advantage.* With the appointment of Superintendent Michelle Fratti in 1999, the District's *Areas of Emphasis* expanded to include the goal of making an effective use of technology in the classroom.

Year One: The Initiative

As Supervisor of Expressive Arts, I decided to work towards addressing Ms. Fratti's vision by collaborating with Teaching Matters, a nonprofit organization that focuses on integrating technology across the curriculum. In an effort to explore the possibility of creating programs that fuse art and technology, we offered sixth grade classroom, music, and technology teachers an opportunity to produce Digital Operas. Teams from four schools volunteered. Although there were no prototypes to guide them, the teachers were talented, professional, and excited about the possibility of participating in the groundbreaking Digital Arts Initiative.

In September, staff developers began to work with teachers and students simultaneously, using learning by an apprenticeship model. There were four parts to the process. First they engaged in the scriptwriting process—selecting a story, poem, or drama to adapt, analyzing the action of the plot, developing dialogue through drama exercises, revising the script, and creating storyboards. Next they composed music and used an audio mixer to record their voices. The most thrilling part was when the students drew and animated their characters on the computer, using the computer application HyperStudio. Some students chose to create artwork on paper and use a scanner to 'digitize' it. To complete the process, they assembled the artwork into graphic masters, making creative decisions about synchronizing sound, text and image and enriching the final version with 'cutaway' images (close-ups, wide views, etc.).

An unparalleled level of energy and enthusiasm emerged as students produced short animated musical theatre pieces that were charming, rich, and rigorous in content. The Chancellor at that time, Rudy Crew, stated, "teachers need to dream and take leaps, knowing that there is a community to support them." Teachers who committed to the Initiative were provided with any resources they requested, whether it was additional training, equipment, supplies or coverages for their classes so they could work intensively with small groups. The District created a line for a full-time Art/Technology Instructional Specialist.

This kind of support made the teachers feel honored, empowered, and validated, resulting in an unprecedented dedication to the project. Teachers and students started to work after school hours and on vacations. Classrooms started to transform into studios. Though by March, the Operas were still very much works in progress, we decided it was important to capture the learning experience and showcase the work.

We rented the theater at Flushing Town Hall and on May 25, 2000, four hundred students presented their work and engaged in reflective conversation with the audience at a Digital Arts Festival—*Dancing Across the Digital Divide. Orpheus and Eurydice, Myth of Zeus, Fanciful Fables* and *Cinderella* were acclaimed by all who viewed them, clearly demonstrating that teachers and students can embark on a creative learning journey they never imagined possible.

Year Two: Think Big

In the second year, after teachers proved that they were able to build capacity, several of us attended the Empire State Partnership Summer Seminar, a week long professional development opportunity that provided us with a think tank to bring more depth and breadth to the program.

We created a culture of inquiry that summer among the teachers by asking them to 'think big.' Conversations led to inviting teaching artists specializing in graphics, electronic music, and theater into the Initiative. Two teams

decided to create Digital Shakespeare productions. Others opted to cross the barrier between the live and virtual by infusing video and dance into the animated works. Teachers asked if they could learn blue screen technique, final cut pro, techniques for painting on video, and claymation.

Our response was, "If there's a dream, there's a dollar:" Teachers were willing to move forward because they were energized by the support, by the beauty of their students' creations, and by opportunities to acquire new skills. When students begged to continue the work, we expanded to include junior high schools.

Year Three: What Worked

In the third year, in addition to creating more sophisticated products, we concentrated on exploring ways to assess student learning. We created pre and post surveys, developed scoring rubrics, and started to use video to track student growth. At staff development workshops, we introduced action research as a way of giving greater voice to the teachers. Teachers learned to engage in reflective practice, using the Collaborative Assessment and Tuning Protocols.

We also initiated the practice of including a reflective period in each lesson where students engaged in conversations and wrote in their journals, addressing 'What worked?' 'What did not work?' and 'How can you make it better?' It became apparent from the triangulation of approaches that enormous learning and creative thinking was occurring in the process of creating a Digital Opera.

As part of the assessment process, we also looked at Standards across all content areas and discovered that they were being addressed. For example:

1 **Art:** #1 - Students will actively engage in the processes that constitute creation and performance in the arts; #2 - Students will be knowledgeable about and make use of the materials and resources available for participation in the arts in various roles;

2 Technology: #4 - Use general purpose productivity tools and peripherals to support personal productivity and facilitate learning throughout the curriculum;

3 English Language Arts: W2B-Students will produce a response to literature that advances a judgment;

4 Science: S12B-Students will produce evidence that demonstrates understanding of position and motion of objects;

5 Applied Learning: A3B-Students will use word processing, drawing and painting programs to produce reports and related materials.

Year Four: Creating Wonder

When asked how you can make people more creative, Professor Nelson Goodman of Harvard replied, "Give them harder problems." What's so unique about those involved in this Initiative is that they give themselves harder problems. They have embraced the philosophy—think big, stretch, and constantly engage in reflection and conversation.

In the process of creating the work, we also discovered that digital media isn't simply a creative tool for bringing new dimensions to artistic expression. It prepares children to think critically, develop strong work habits and meet the challenges of emerging forms of work. The project has become an example of how a community of learners took on an enormous challenge and experienced new roles—teachers as students and students as writers, designers, animators, dramatists, dancers, musicians, researchers and project managers who work hard, knowing how critical each of their pieces are to the success of the whole.

An essential part of this work is to provide venues for making the learning visible. Each spring, educators, arts partners, local politicians and sponsors attend our Digital Arts Festival. Schools include digital arts productions in arts events for parents. Curriculum fairs include digital artworks. Bulletin boards fill the hallways with samples of student work in digital arts. The Operas have been showcased on DCTV, WNYE, SONY Wonder, and the Brooklyn Arts Council's International Film and Video Festival and have been presented at art and technology professional conferences nationwide.

Dutch artist M.C. Escher said, "The purpose of art...is to create wonder in the audience." The wonder Digit-al Opera has created rich feedback that informs future work and motivates all involved to stretch even further.

Into The Future:
The Work Has Just Begun

In Spring 2003, CSD 25 presented the fourth annual Digital Arts Festival at Lexington School for the Deaf. The event opened with deaf and hearing sixth grade students performing a piece that incorporated live dance, video, animation and original student artwork to convey the genesis of art and technology. Other sixth grade students communicated their point of view in the creation of a digital documentary on a holocaust survivor. One class of junior high school students used 3D technology to produce *Robin Hood* while another incorporated artwork on 4 plasma screens into a live production of *The Crucible*. Fifth graders built a diverse, global community by paring the ancient art of theater with today's technology in an online project that linked them with students in London.

July 2003 the Department of Education restructured. CSD25 became part of Region 9 and district support terminated. The work, however, continues to grow. Some CSD25 classroom teachers gained sufficient skills to sustain the program independently. Several Long Island schools recently received funding to implement the program. I moved on to become the Education Director, Roundabout Theatre. The company's professional theatre teaching artists collaborated with a middle school in Flushing to produce *Digital Wizard of Oz*. Students learned to construct sets, plot lights, create sound effects, and sew costumes for the fully integrated production. Beginning January 2005, I will become the Education Director, New York City Center, where new resources and energy will add yet another dimension to the work.

Though it's been four years, the work in Digital Arts has just begun. Each step on the journey proves one more time, as philosopher Maxine Greene says, "Children need to affirm their own voices and need tools to express these imaginings."

Art/Technology Performance Standards

To specifically capture the learning that was taking place, we created Art/Technology Performance Standards.

Art/Technology Performance Standards reflect educational goals that are common to visual/graphic arts, music, dance, theater, video and animation and yet recognize the distinctive aspects of each discipline. Each area has unique methods, materials, history and content. The interdisciplinary approach provides students with rich and rigorous opportunities to solve problems and make creative decisions as they acquire new knowledge and skills. The work is anchored in the core curriculum, demonstrates sustained effort over time and promotes critical non-linear thinking, communication, and collaborative group work.

Creating/Performing/ Participating in Digital Arts

Students will assume various roles, in individual and group experiences, in the designing, producing, and showcasing of multimedia productions (dramatists, artist/graphic artist, musician, dancer, videographer, animator). Works synthesize audio, visual and textual material and blend live and virtual components in a variety of mediums, using current technologies, software and telecommunications networks.

Scriptwriting

- identify literature selection to adapt for digital arts production

- analyze central conflict, character development and scenes

- create story-board to describe elements of each scene

- use word processing to write and format script

- compose first draft and engage in revision process

- write final script

- complete Key-frame Inventories

Theater Arts

- use the elements of theater (language, voice, gesture, movement) in the development of characters for live performance or video

- communicate through non-verbal expression

- engage in improvisation exercises

- develop dialogue, analyze plot and adapt story

- develop acting skills and characterizations

Visual/Graphic Arts

- use the elements of art (line, color, texture, shape) to communicate ideas

- develop images based on literary themes, symbols and events through creation of two-dimensional and three-dimensional work

- scan flat artwork into computer and manipulate images

- create visuals for storyboard

- paint with HyperStudio

- use Key-frame Inventories to create graphic objects and backgrounds

- export artwork to be used in Key-frame images

- create graphic masters by assembling characters, backgrounds, and objects

- export assembled frames

- create animation storyboards

- create animation artwork

- add cutaway images to final animated movie

Music

- use the elements of music (pitch, rhythm, tempo, quality, dynamics) to create a score that accompanies sung, spoken or unspoken portions of the story

- use software to identify specific rhythms and harmonies

- use notation software (e.g. Melody Assistant) to create a series of short musical phrases based on script

- compose libretto for sung portion of performance

- use mixer to record dialogue, score, libretto, sound effects

- use computer and sound studio to digitize recorded audio

- use sound editing with sound studio to remove non-performance sounds and normalize sound files

Dance

- use elements of dance (time, space, force, energy) to improvise, create and perform dances for live performance or video

- choreograph and perform dances in two-dimensional and three-dimensional settings

- interpret and evaluate dance performance through written and oral language

- use theater and computer technology to integrate dance into performance experience

Video

- use the basic elements of the moving image (verbal/spatial language, sequencing, tuning, pacing, symbol/concept formation, manipulation) to create video

- use computer technologies to communicate ideas in visual medium

- use special effects (e.g. blue screen, mirroring, rotoscoping)

- edit video footage

- integrate video, animation and live performance for digital arts production

Using Materials and Resources

Students will make use of materials and resources available for the creation of multimedia productions.

- use a computer, scanner, digital camera and digital video camera

- use technology to develop creativity and thinking skills

- use technology to communicate visual ideas

- use Internet to create scores and research recordings to enhance original compositions

- use technology to research dance history and performance

- use HyperStudio and iMovie software

- use internet to locate primary sources (e.g. radio broad casts, archival drawings, photographs)

- share ideas with lighting/sound designers and stage manager in preparation for culminating performance

- demonstrate appropriate audience behavior at culminating performance

- use Internet to learn about different cultures and view points through online project in real-world setting

- use Internet to communicate via e-mail with professional artists and stream original plays (e.g. Webplay)

Responding to and Analyzing Digital Artworks

Students will apply thinking skills through responding critically to a variety of digital artworks, connecting individual work to other works and other aspects of human endeavor and thought.

- discuss ways the various disciplines connect in the making of a multimedia production

- use communication and critical thinking skills to reflect on, interpret and analyze works-in-progress and completed works as appropriate to audience and purpose

- view and discuss differences between live and video taped performances

- view and discuss performances that use blue screen technique to integrate live and videotaped components

Project Management

Students will learn to collaborate to manage a program.

- manage learning in a technology enhanced environment

- use technology to support learning that addresses diverse needs/interests/talents

- assume leadership roles (e.g. Project Managers)

- consult with group members to synthesize ideas and agree on common goals, work plan and time line

- consult with group members and agree on technical and artistic solutions to improve product quality

- demonstrate flexibility individually and collectively facilitate project as a whole

Assessment

Systemic assessment for the process and product are an integral part of this project-based approach to learning. Lessons will include a reflective period where students address "What worked?" "What did not work?" and "How can we make it better?" In addition, students will utilize a variety of tools/methodologies to assess their understandings and performances.

- complete pre-and post-surveys addressing attitude and skills maintain double entry journals and analyze video taped sessions

- use scoring rubrics to self-assess and assess peers' work in the areas of scriptwriting, acting, graphic arts, music, and video

Joanna Black

In conjunction with students:
Greg Kouts, Erin Murray, and Kar Wai Ng

"Cross-Curriculum" Community Venture:

18

Merging Art and Videography with Science

An exciting and motivating activity is to screen outstanding student videos in public venues, whether to students, parents, relatives, friends and peers or to the community at large, locally, nationally, and internationally. When pupils' works are juried into competitive screenings, it is exciting; when they sometimes obtain awards, it is exhilarating; and when they receive feedback while in the audience during public screenings, it is an invaluable learning experience. Some interesting ventures have resulted. Extending my teaching beyond classroom walls not only benefits students but has also brought about valuable yet completely unanticipated outcomes. One such outcome occurred last year when my students had their videos juried into a provincial digital multimedia festival. This resulted in repeated screenings of their videos over an extended weekend at the Ontario Science Centre (OSC) in Toronto, Canada. Shortly thereafter, I received a phone call from the Science Centre's Environmental Researcher/ Programmer, Julie Jones. Some of her colleagues had viewed my students' works and liked what they saw. Julie inquired whether any of my pupils would be interested in creating videos based on interviews with scientists.

Workers at the Science Centre were interested in ascertaining what teenagers might create if given the chance to interview professional scientists. There was a possibility that these video productions would later be displayed to the public as a pilot project. This appeared to be an out of the ordinary venture: I welcomed the opportunity for my students to produce videos for an international audience, liked the "cross-curricula" connections between art and science, and knew my new senior advanced video students could meet this challenge. Hence, I accepted the offer and in September 2002, 13 students became involved in the Ontario Science Centre's video production venture.

The key people involved in this project were my students, Julie Jones and the Hot Zone development team working at the Ontario Science Centre, and the scientists. Ms. Jones and three of my students have kindly offered their points of view.

Background:
The Ontario Science Centre

At the present time the Ontario Science Centre is undergoing a major transformation through a new $40 million revitalization initiative. My students' videos were a small part of the new order. Currently, the Ontario Science Centre provides hands-on, interactive exhibition sites for more than one million international visitors per year.

It has 13 large exhibition halls with over 800 interactive exhibits pertaining to science and technology. Based on attendance statistics taken in 1997, a study by Tourism Toronto suggested the Ontario Science Centre is one of the leading tourist attractions in this city (Ontario Science Centre, 2003). Since the millennium, people at the centre have been working on a major revitalization campaign and, to this end, in 2000 the Ontario provincial government granted the Science Centre $15 million. In combination with major foundation contributions and corporate donations from companies such as DuPont, the Science Centre's fundraising campaign has presently reached 82% of the $40 million goal. The future is to redesign and upgrade 25% of the centre through substantial building renovations, and extensive exhibition development. They have given this plan the dramatic title, *"Agents of Change."* Monies for this plan will be used to develop seven sizeable new exhibit sites based on the theme, "Solving 21st Century Problems." It is intended that by 2006 these sites will be open to the public with a focus on developing the skills, attitudes, and behaviors youth require to become innovative in science and technology. One of the seven new experience areas is called the "Hot Zone," and this is the exhibit my students played a small part in developing though their contribution of prototype pilot project videos for exhibition purposes in the Hot Zone site.

Currently posted on the Web is the following definition of Hot Zone: *The Hot Zone will be a dynamic, multi-faceted hub for celebrating, investigating and understanding current science issues and groundbreaking science and technology innovations. Visitors will encounter an eclectic array of timely and relevant information conveyed in unique and unexpected ways. Live presentations and Web/broadcasts by scientists working in the field can provide deeper connections for visitors on hot topics such as human cloning, bioterrorism and the latest mission to Mars.* (Ontario Science Centre, 2003)

Visitors entering the Hot Zone site will be enveloped by science and art multimedia integration. They hope to create an attention-grabbing, informative art/science installation site which first greets visitors. These installations are complete with kinetic and computerized sculptures and images. In addition, a multitude of various sized moving monitors, numerous multi-screens, and other "high tech" devices will emit ever-changing sound, texts, and images. The hoped for effect appears to be both experiential and educational, giving visitors a 21st century immersive, sensory, non-linear experience. Visitors will view a variety of media to facilitate access to information and science news. Video display monitors will provide 'hot' scientific topics through movable 'feasts' of eclectic digital multimedia. In addition to the moving screens and monitors, there will be temporary, hands-on exhibits, digital scrolling devices projecting messages, live camera feeds filming visitors and guests, and satellite links projecting up-to-the-moment live video footage on germane or "sizzling" scientific topics.

A Description of the Process

After some discussion, the Science Centre staff and I decided that my students would create six documentaries about the lives, careers, and work of scientists from the University of Toronto, with a running time of no longer than 5 minutes per video production. I would have six groups of two to three students working on this project, with each group striving to produce a different style of documentary. The objectives of this community venture were as follows: (1) to discover what young people would create when given the opportunity in regards to the specific subject; (2) to discover how youths and scientists would interact in an interview situation; (3) to discover what types of questions teenagers would ask a scientist; (4) to discover if they could capture the enthusiasm of a scientist for their work on video; (5) to discover if our visitors would find such a video interesting; (6) to discover what styles and length of video would be most appropriate to communicate to our visitors; and finally (7) to discover the quality of video production the students could create.

We began our project by asking students to select a scientific or technological topic of interest to them. Then specific scientists in these fields were contacted.

We believed it would be more exciting for students if we matched the appropriate scientist to a student's personal interests. Youths, interested in music, for example, would be coupled with an audio engineer; teenagers fond of cooking could interview a food scientist. Eventually, only some groups were coupled in this manner; others, owing to time constraints, were not.

When asked, two of the students described their initial reaction to the project as somewhat "overwhelming" and "intimidating" yet "wonderful," "and exciting." Even for senior year students it is a daunting prospect to approach a university professor, much less query her about her work. Yet the students were highly motivated. Greg, for instance, believes the experience was special. He reflects that, "the backing of the Ontario Science Centre would allow us to share our work with a large audience, and would prove to be a great learning experience."

A few weeks into the course, students had established liaisons with the professors and knew the topics for their documentaries. The following professors agreed to participate: (1) Dr. Kimberly Strong, a specialist in atmosphere physics and the ozone layer; (2) Dr. Peter Pennefather, whose research is in chemistry and pharmacology; (3) Dr. Robin Cameron, whose area of expertise is genetically modified foods; (4) Dr. Pekka Sinervo, who writes about high energy physics; (5) Dr. Andy Kenny, who concentrates on urban forestry and finally, (6) Dr. Gavin Clark a specialist in biological warfare, As an art educator, I was pleased with such a vast array of topics in which I, personally, had little expertise.

My next task was to provide my students with the necessary background information in science so that they could conduct an interesting and informative interview. I approached the Department Head of Science at my school and we agreed that two of her most outstanding senior-level students would research two areas: first the scientific areas in which the professors specialized; and second, the professors' own background. They would then write a report on the data, which would then be given to the student videographers. This data proved to be ex-

tremely helpful. It is not hard to imagine students feeling insecure about interviewing highly reputed professors with years of experience in their field, and so in way of thanks, we acknowledged the assistance from the Science Department by including the student researchers' names in the video credits. Thus, beneficial cross-curricula integration with the Science Department was formed.

We had a whirlwind program for a 5-month semestered course. Within this period of time we spent several weeks on preproduction studying theoretical issues, one day on filming, and a month and a half in postproduction, editing. Finally there were three screenings of the videos: one for the class, another for a final output to videotape with corrections, and a third screening for which we invited professors to view the videos at the Ontario Science Centre. During this final stage, students planned on modifying any footage based on the professors' feedback before the videos were put on exhibit. I will discuss the above process more fully in the text below.

Preproduction was a lengthy stage in which students studied different ways to capture images. The book, *Setting Up Your Shots: Great Camera Moves Every Filmmaker Should Know* (Vineyard, 2000) was extremely useful. My purpose was to have students gain knowledge of ways in which to achieve interesting camera actions, appealing visual art compositions, and exciting, creative ways to manipulate visual images using simple camera techniques. We looked at camera actions such as the "contract dolly" move in which both the actor and the cameraperson dolly toward each other, creating dramatic, action effects. We examined such shots as "dark voyeur" framing, an Alfred Hitchcock technique, in which characters are framed by bushes or inside closets to create suspense. Consciousness of the viewer as the "surreptitious interloper" is apparent in such works as Hopper's *Office in a Small City* in which he uses buildings to frame the shot. As with Hopper, Giorgio de Chirico uses this framing technique in his romantic, foreboding enigmatic street image, *Mystery and Melancholy of a Street.* Students learned about techniques such as making montages, which are not only used by filmmakers but by writers, musicians and visual artists like

David Hockney. As well, I introduced creative ways of capturing images such as filming reflections seen in Richard Estes's window painting, *Murano Glass,* in which glazed, clear glossy reflections play a key role. Likewise, Audrey Flack's still life imagery in such art as *Chanel* shimmers with gleaming reflections. We examined the use of camera techniques such as "whip pans" which blur actions to create works in the vein of Italian Futurist artist Umberto Boccioni. Connections between the visual art world and the filmmaking world abound.

I believe, making a documentary required students to approach the genre with a thoughtfulness concerning the role of filmmaker. Consequently, we discussed postmodern concepts regarding notions of truth and objectivity and from that posed questions regarding the students' own filmmaking intentions. For example, did they believe in the idea of truth? Did they intend to tell the truth through the documentary format? Moreover, did they believe objectivity to be a goal for which to strive? Is objectivity, indeed, even possible to achieve? Illuminating, interesting conversations arose from these questions.

Students read parts of *Making Documentary Films* (Hampe, 1997) in order to guide themselves through the planning of the documentary, the recording of human behavior, the interviewing through to the editing process. To this end we looked at the definition of documentaries and issues such as the filmmakers' power to shape the information through the way in which documentaries are created. Traditional techniques to convey information such as using statistics, reenacting scenes, and using voice-overs of interviewer's opinions were scrutinized. Each group made up their own interview questions based on (1) the research compiled from the students in the Science Department; and (2) the students' own interests in the scientific area. We used the semi-structured interview style discussed by Merriam (1998) as I wanted students' interviews to flow naturally. Merriam defines this style as one in which a list of questions are flexibly worded and utilized as guidelines in which the interviewer does not follow the exact wording verbatim or order (p.74). This format allows for a more natural, responsive, and spontaneous conversational

interview than the more formal, structured ones. I hoped that each interview would have a unique storytelling experience. Greg talks about the process of devising questions for the topic of biological warfare: *[We] tried to come up with questions that would be appealing to us as teenagers, since this was the audience the movie was aimed for. Although initially it was somewhat difficult to come up with questions that would interest the younger generation, after a good hour of brainstorming we had a list of questions that we felt were quite strong. We tried to use current events to our advantage (the Anthrax scare in the United States took place roughly around the same time as the filming of the documentary) and involve them in our questions. Although looking back at the project I feel that this wasn't the best idea, since the issue doesn't seem to be much of a concern anymore.* Erin adds that, "We wanted to make a film that everyone would like, even if they did not have a deep interest for science."

Typical questions asked of scientists were to describe what they do in their job, topics they research, contributions they have made to their scientific field, and opinions they have about their scientific area or the jobs they hold. Using the semi-structured interview style, some interesting digressions occurred when scientists offered off-topic, spontaneous opinions about such areas as women in the field of science or the attitude they have towards their day-to-day work routines.

To further their skills, the class analyzed different interview styles by examining key film documentaries and television shows. Later, students created storyboards to develop and help refine their approach. First, we looked at the movie, *Talk 16* paying particular attention to the way in which the filmmakers handled the interview process. In *Talk 16,* the interviewers are seldom heard and never seen. It appeared as if they do not have key roles in the film, and so we analyzed techniques interviewers' use to produce this effect. Second, we also looked at Michael Moore's, *Roger and Me.* Here, the interview approach is diametrically opposite to the first film discussed. Moore is far more confrontational and upfront; in other words, the viewer is aware of the interviewer's presence and opinions at all times. His voice as interviewer and filmmaker is heard throughout the film through techniques such as voice-overs and on camera interviewer shots during interviews. Third, we examined the new way of creating documentaries apparent on television, especially on newscasts in which split-screens show multiple films while text messages, symbols, and logos are flashed throughout. Fourth, another group based their documentary style on typical popular dating game television shows which have special text and images popping up on the screen to indicate the inner thoughts of the interviewees. The last two groups selected experimental film styles. Prior to the documentary project, the class had just undertaken a unit on experimental film for which each pupil produced a video. Students were well versed in the theories of Bordell and Thompson (1997) and were consequently well prepared for more innovative approaches. One group planned to use the experimental style from the beginning while another group turned to this style during the editing process.

After analyzing documentary styles, students submitted a description of the style they were planning to use well before the filming occurred. One example by student videographers, Vince Buensuceso and Zuzka Tatiersky, is as follows: *The project will follow an alternative method of execution, rather than the stereotypical and mundane style of documentaries. There will be an introduction and conclusion, where the interviewer will be engaging the viewing audience (speaking to the camera), [using] periodical time lapses, and various unique camera shots. The most important significance of the documentary will be the interleaves of humor and relaxed conversations. It will be informal compared to the conservative style of documentaries, which will reach out to a much younger and broader audience. There will also be experimentation on color, masking, and multiple camera views.*

Another student, Greg Kouts, discusses the process: *Another important element in the preparatory work on the project was our "style." Each team of filmmakers involved with the Hot-Zone project was assigned a unique manner with which to create the documentary—ours was experimental. Our knowledge about the subject was limited, but the beauty of an experimental film is that there is usually no wrong way to approach it. We created several storyboards to help us figure out how to shoot the documentary efficiently while still leaving space for creativity during the editing stage. This was the final step in the prep work, and once we completed it we were ready to meet the scientist...*

Knowing the style helped guide them during the crucial postproduction stage. Greg further reflects on this: *...once we actually sat down and reviewed the footage I had shot, we noticed that I made a crucial mistake. Since this was my first attempt at shooting a documentary, I gave in to the habit of having the camera in constant motion (just like in most of the narratives I shot) which created a problem, since the camera does not stay on Dr. Clark's face longer than 10 seconds in any of the shots. Fortunately, the fact that we were creating an experimental documentary saved us. We realized that we could get away with having the camera "look around" the room (similarly to a child who cannot concentrate), and I think it created an interesting atmosphere for the final cut of the film. This atmosphere also guided us into creating the light, "cartoony" outer shell of the movie. We were a little worried that the scientist would misinterpret the idea we were trying to convey, and find the manner by which we treated the footage offensive, however to our delight Dr. Clark enjoyed watching the film as much as we did creating it.*

The cartoon-like style Greg talks about is in fact very reminiscent of the Pop Art movement, particularly suggestive of the work of Andy Warhol. This was particularly effective when they also combined 1960s music with this imagery.

We originally planned for a two-camera shoot. Two groups undertook this approach. However, it proved impractical for the remaining groups, as time was limited and the scientists' labs and offices were scattered throughout the university campus. Consequently, 4 groups worked with one camera only, which limited their video footage.

The actual shoot occurred during a one-day period. For part of the day we filmed the scientists at the Ontario Science Centre: for the other part, students moved their film equipment to the University of Toronto and filmed professors in their offices, in their labs, and during classes. This effort provided interesting and invaluable footage.

My advice to students during the filming process was as follows: (1) to make the scientists feel comfortable; (2) to present your point of view as an interviewer; (3) to obtain stories and anecdotes engaging to the viewers; and (4) to work on developing the videostyle while taping. I reminded them that nobody wants to listen to self-conscious nervous interviewees talking about overtly technical, and therefore potentially boring material.

Unexpected occurrences took place as they always do during the shooting process. One group temporarily lost their camera; another group tried to slip into a lecture hall halfway through the class in order to film their professor in the act of teaching, only to find, to their utter surprise, that the doors were situated at the front of the room. In the student's own words, "two hundred plus pairs of eyes (including Dr. Clark's) were staring straight at us!"

For postproduction, some students edited at home and others at school. Most had approximately 2 hours of tape to condense into less than 5 minutes. I asked students to write a journal documenting this process. During this phase two key issues arose: the first was sound quality. The Ontario Science Centre has enormous modern exhibit halls that cause the sound to echo. Some of the university labs were no better. We were equipped with typical, inadequate, low-end school microphones. Should I attempt the project again, I would procure better microphones and test them prior to the interviews, using a variety of locations. One group, using an unidirectional mike, did not have problems. Another group that used the minidisk format also avoided the problem of poor sound quality. However, it proved to be difficult for many.

Kar Wai discusses his struggles: *As we moved out into the exhibit areas to do some more interviewing against visually interesting backdrops (such as some da Vinci drawings) I kept cursing at our school's lack of decent audio equipment. We were using the on-camera microphone (omni-directional as with most on-camera mics) and Dr. Pennefather's voice was fighting with the screaming kids [visitors at the Ontario Science Centre] in the background for dominance. Had we a good quality lapel mic or a proper shotgun microphone...we wouldn't have had any major audio troubles. Our struggles with audio would later have major repercussions on our project... Since the audio from virtually all our footage was terrible, with the exception of what we shot in the room at the OSC, we had to consider a change in editing styles by using less talking heads and more alternative visuals: we arranged with Dr. Pennefather to do some additional voiceovers in lieu of using the on-location audio. Our troubles mounted when these arrangements could not be accomplished; it was then that Ms. Black made the radical suggestion of abandoning the traditional documentary format [we planned to use] altogether and instead creating an experimental video, which could rely on the visual material we had.... We had a great deal of excellent content that had to be chucked out the window in favor of more interesting visuals that were more conducive to the experimental style. In a way, I felt as if the experimental route was the quick way out; however, with our time and resource constraints it was probably the only way out.*

The second issue was copyright. Showing the videos in a professional public venue meant we had to create original music or obtain permission from musicians to use their songs. I gave students a template of what a typical letter requesting the use of intellectual property should look like. My students either downloaded from the Internet already copyrighted works or wrote letters and obtained permission from artists in question. This was a time consuming task well worth the effort.

After approximately 2 months of editing, we held two screenings. One was at the school for some of the members of the Hot Zone development team. Shortly thereafter, we held a special screening at the Ontario Science Centre. Many of the professors attended this showing and provided their responses to the video: this proved helpful.

If the scientists were unable to attend, we sent them a copy so that they had an opportunity to respond before the project ended. We wanted to avoid misrepresentation: this was our way of establishing validity regarding the videos. Two of the groups had to alter their video, though for differing reasons. The students who struggled with sound problems, Kar Wai and Michelle, did not show any footage of the professor actually speaking: this the professor wanted to change. The other group, Vince and Zuzka, ran into trouble for the way in which they handled a highly contentious topic. The students had taken a position on the issue of genetically modified food. They aired their views during the documentary that, incidentally, were not those of the professor's. However, in order for the Science Centre to exhibit the video, these students needed to acquire authoritative quotes and references to substantiate their stance. Both groups took several months to make the necessary modifications to their video. The culminating act, the public screening of the videos, occurred in the springtime at the Ontario Science Centre. They were on display as part of an exhibit for approximately three weeks.

Analysis

The following analysis is based on the assessment provided by Julie Jones (personal communication, November 14, 2003) of the OSC's Hot Zone Development Team. Children under 13, as well as teenagers, and adults were questioned after watching the videos; not surprisingly they had quite different reactions. Youths responded quite differently to the ways through which the message was communicated and to the content. To them the content was "overwhelming" and "boring"; however, the medium, which was partly comprised of music and animation, was enjoyable. Teenagers' responses seem to vary depending on their genre. For instance, two groups of teenagers watched the video about Dr. Clark on bioterrorism. Concerning the female group, Jones (personal communication, November 14, 2003) writes that, *...in the video Dr. Clark makes a comment about women in science and how the numbers are changing. This they heard. So even though they did not appear to be listening when they heard something that was relevant*

to them it stuck with them. When asked what the video was about, their answer was women in science.

A group of young male teenagers, however, focused on the videos without distractions. When questioned later about what they had observed, these boys were able to answer the questions correctly. Adults, though, tended to be more critical about the production quality of the videos, concentrating on the fact that the sound was not up to par with the videos' music and pictorial qualities. Again like the younger children, older people differentiated between the content and the message but their response was the reverse of that of the youths: they enjoyed the content but found the music distracting.

The videos served as a prototype of the type of multimedia that could be placed in the Hot Zone Exhibition site. However, based on the results, the approach to the videomaking would be different. The people on the Hot Zone Development suggest three changes should they attempt this type of project again. The first recommendation is to establish a clearer understanding that the driving force behind such videos is student expression stemming from their own points of view and interests. It was found that the videos were not geared enough to young people's interests. Staff at the OSC stated that some of the videos appeared to have the OSC Hot Zone team and visiting OSC adults as a target audience rather than the youths. This could be true. One would have to examine the reason for the adult focus. One explanation is that interviewing scientists considered to be experts in the field is a serious topic and the pressure is there for student videographers to depict them in an accurate adult fashion. I also believe that by the very act of showing the videos at an established venue, the OSC made it more serious for my students. Finally, I would argue that the act of interviewing scientists is not only daunting but also pressure-ridden, and that this probably had an effect, not to be overlooked, in shaping the videos. Erin writes that, "I was a bit uneasy at first... ...We were both quite nervous when it came to meeting our professor. The fact that he is a doctor of his trade and lectures at the University of Toronto made him seem quite intimidating to us." In light of this, I believe that the Ontario Science Centre's new direction is beneficial: that is to change the theme of the videos. Rethinking the topics of the videos seems a logical direction. For this reason, the development team's second recommendation makes sense: that scientists or experts should only be on video if required. Furthermore, Jones (personal communication, November 14, 2003) explains that, "We discovered that even with student based questions and really good treatment many "experts" are still really boring on camera." The implications are that future videos be theme based rather than grounded in documenting an expert in science. Not making the scientist the subject of the film might engage more youths and teenagers and make the theme more interesting to this target audience. Thirdly, the development team suggests that they would ask students to pick topics from the current media such as magazines and newspapers. This definitely would be an interesting direction to explore.

So what was successful about this project? I will discuss this from three perspectives: (1) the OSC's Hot Zone Development Teams,' (2) my students,' and (3) my own perspective as an educator. From the Ontario Science Centre's standpoint it was found that all but one objective had been met, and this was to find out what length of video appeals to children. Personally, based on my experiences as a secondary school educator teaching video, as well as my experience as a museum educator, and museum researcher, I would recommend that short videos be approximately one to two minutes in duration if not sixty seconds or less. It was found that, on average, art museum viewers spend well under a minute with each art image they view (Black 1986). That said, more research by the OSC could be done regarding visitors' video viewing habits. All other objectives, however, had been met. The development team learned how youths and scientists will interact during interviews and they found out what type of questions youths would ask scientists. As had been discussed, the situation proved too intimidating, the interaction too stiff, and the questions not interesting enough, to capture the attention of youths and teenagers. This leads to the next objective,

which was to find out whether student videographers can bring out the enthusiasm of a scientist. Although achieved by one group in particular, this did not happen as a whole. The scientists are not trained actors: many of them tended to be stiff and awkward during the videotaping session. Further on the topic of video interest, what was particularly worthy of note was the difference between teenage males and females. Males were far more drawn to the subject of science than females and much has been written on this topic (AAUW, 2000). In future productions, I recommend a sensitivity to gender issues concerning male/ female teenage interests in science and technology. The challenge for the OSC (and for science and technology teachers) is understanding ways in which to engage female youths in this subject area. One of my female videographers admitted that it was surprising to her to actually be interested in the subject she was investigating. Another objective of the OSC was to determine what style of video is most effective in communicating to our visitors. It was found that children and youths, the target audience the OSC development team wanted to attract, responded well to the variety of entertaining styles that had youthful animation and music. The last objective, ascertaining the talent level of students, was fully achieved. On the one hand, as previously mentioned, the major detrimental aspect, which can easily be rectified, were sound problems in the videos. This is a purely technical concern. Procuring good microphones would alleviate the problem. This aside, many viewers were enthusiastic about the videos. For example, during a large gala event at the Ontario Science Centre, it was found that adults attending were impressed with and excited by what they watched (Jones, 2003).

Gray and Jones (personal communication, December 5, 2002) wrote the following to the students: *We send our thanks and admiration to you all for the incredible work you have done in creating video prototypes for the Hot Zone area of the Science Centre's Innovation Project. We were both impressed and delighted by the different styles of your videos, their energy and excitement...One of the key purposes of this project was to see what young people could do when given the opportunity to meet scientist and create scientific content using multimedia tools. We believe this endeavor has been an unqualified success.*

From my students' perspective, they found the project rewarding and challenging. Many learned much about the documentary process, having never made one before. It was found to be motivating and exciting to have their videos shown at the end of the production process to OSC visitors. Most students were proud of their work.

Kar Wai reflects on his experience: ... *I am very grateful for the opportunity to have been invited to participate in such an interesting project. It was also an invaluable opportunity to produce work as part of a contribution to a larger project. For many of us, the Hot Zone documentaries were our first practical application of our talent as filmmakers as well as our first exposures to the public arena outside of the usual student film festival circuits. The process as a whole was a great learning experience for all; both we, the students collectively and affectionately known forever as SuperFilm, as well as the innovation project team at the Ontario Science Centre benefited from this pilot project. Whether it be experience or research data, everyone ended up with more than we had going in.*

In addition, Greg writes: *When I look back at the Hot Zone documentary I feel that it was one of the most interesting films I had the pleasure to be involved in. This project truly pushed both my technical and artistic abilities to their limits, and although the production proved stressful and difficult at times, the final product made up for it all. In particular, for the students, the fact that the films would be displayed to the OSC's visitors rather than just their classmates was exciting, motivating and challenging.*

As an educator, I felt the process from preproduction to postproduction was successful. When I reflect upon how much we learned and the amount of material we covered, I am amazed we fit so much theoretical, practical and hands-on learning into such a short period of time. However, I would recommend two changes should this type of project occur again. First, more data collection should be

done to gauge the target audiences' reaction during the period the videos are shown in the OSC venue. This would further develop a more extensive analysis and help shape future video production in this specific venue. Second, I believe that the student videographers should be more involved in the final public video screening process at the Centre so that they can observe the type of reactions OSC visitors have to their works.

As an educator, I believe the joint venture with the Ontario Science Centre was an overall success. Students were encouraged to stretch their knowledge base and integrate Science with Technology and Art. I saw them challenged to create videos about experts in specialized scientific areas. Teenagers were also motivated to create works at a professional level that not only the multitude of visitors at the Ontario Science Centre would view, but that the Hot Zone Development Team and the scientists themselves would watch and judge. As well, the Hot Zone project has lead to exciting new ventures and community liaisons between Don Mills Collegiate and the OSC. One student who worked on the Hot Zone project is currently working as a videographer at the OSC through the school's co-op department. In addition, the OSC Hot Zone Development is planning for another video project venture with a new group of student videographers from Don Mills Collegiate. Even though this specific Hot Zone undertaking has been brought to a close and most of the students have gone on to higher educational training at community colleges and universities, they have left a legacy at the school. They have left a model of what can be achieved when one undertakes public community endeavors, when one merges Art and Technology with Science in cross-curricular pursuits, and when one tries their best, attempts to overcome obstacles and offers their work up to public scrutiny. These students experienced firsthand what it is like to be a professional videographer by offering up their work for criticism and appreciation in a public forum. We leave it to a future group of students to take up where these students left off: creating an exciting liaison between a school and museum.

Illustrations

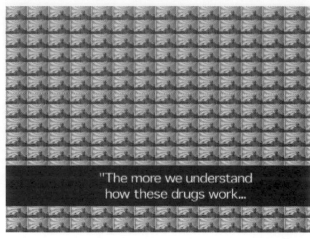

Still Images From Video

Still Images From Video

Student Conducting an Interview

Oct. 19/02.

Journal
entere 1

Editing

Today we are editing at Greg's house. Premeir is so different from Final Cut Pro (in my opinion it seems more complicated) Greg and I listened to the audio from our footage. These are all the time codes of the audio track of which we would consider using. That took awhile:

12:11, 11:36, 11:12, 9:17, 9:11, 10:37, 14:53, 14:24 16:52, 16:30, 8:10, 15:47, 13:20, 20:07 18:16, weapons. 20:09, 21:56, 28:43, 28:36, 4:16 28:13, 5:15, 6:12 (rearrange words) 26:45 21:14, make a difference

We discussed our opening shots and came up with videos, I wrote them down b/c I knew we would be forgetting them.

1.) outside 3 shot of building
2.) hallway
3.) fade to white when opened door.

-Greg used and showed me about After Effects this program we are going to be using for the special effects. Greg taught me about masks and we created the first few seconds of our film.

Example of Student's Notes

References on the following page.

References

American Association of University Women [AAUW]
Educational Foundation. (2000, April). *Tech-savvy: Educating girls in the computer age.* Washington, DC.

Black (1986). [Responses to museum atttendees' visits to art museums]. Unpublished raw data.

Bordell, D. and Thompson, K. (1997*). Film art: An introduction.* U.S.A: Mc-Graw-Hill.

Hampe, B. (1997). *Making documentary films and reality videos.* New York, U.S.A: Henry Holt and Company.

Lundman, J., Mitchell, A. (Writers/Directors and Producers). (1990). *Talk 16.* Canada: Alliance.

Merriam, S. B. (1998). *Case study research in education: A qualitative approach.* San Francisco, California: Jossey-Bass, Inc.

Moore, M. (Writer/Director). (1991). *Roger and me.* [Motion picture], United States: Warner Brothers.

The Ontario Science Centre (2003). *Ontario Science Centre's Home Page.* Retrieved November 20, 2003 from http://www.ontariosciencecentre.ca/about/aoc/default.asp" http://www.ontariosciencecentre.ca/about/aoc/default.asp.

Vineyard, J. (2000). *Setting up your shots: Great camera moves every filmmaker should know.* Michael Wiese Production.

M i c h a e l   F l o y d

Windsong Pictures

19

Introduction

In 1975, I established Windsong Pictures, based in Fort Wayne, Indiana, as a nonprofit educational motion picture company. The purpose of Windsong Pictures was to stimulate and encourage students, teachers, parents, and community members of all ages to explore the limitless potential that exists in the creative, integrated learning process of film production. Through the art of motion picture production, the Discovery Expo, the International Windsong Film Festival, and other project-based media programs, participants break down barriers that isolate learning, integrating skills from many disciplines in the creative art of filmmaking.

Windsong Pictures has involved students from as many as 300 schools and 39 universities, across 38 states, in the production of internationally screened short and full-length feature films. Students, along with adults, create, research, write, cast, costume, film, produce, edit, and market their original productions using state of the art digital technology. The company travels thousands of miles annually to shoot film productions on location across the country, to create authentic realism, and to provide a powerful learning environment.

Thousands of students and adults from many schools and communities are involved year-round in Windsong Pictures. The learning process of movie making, creating the Discovery Expos, and sponsoring the International Windsong Film Festivals for budding cinephiles motivates students to a level of commitment that most have not experienced before. History, culture, ethnic authenticity, period skills, and crafts come alive for participants. They develop a thirst for achievement, enrich themselves with an unparalleled self-confidence, and work tirelessly with a strong sense of teamwork and selfless cooperation. By joining a community of filmmakers, the lives of countless students, parents, educators, and audience members are dramatically touched.

Vision and Goal

Windsong Pictures serves to stimulate and encourage students of all ages to explore the limitless potential that exists in the creative and integrated learning process of film production. A staff of educators, students, and community members from across the country are actively engaged in Windsong Pictures. These are ordinary people who volunteer their time and work long hours to make extraordinary dreams come true. The primary goal of Windsong Pictures is to enhance the mental and spiritual outlook of people in a significant way—to reach out and dramatically touch others.

How It All Began

At the age of 5 in 1952, I saw my first film in a theater, a Hopalong Cassidy western. I was so taken with the experience that I remembered every detail of the film, and for the next 3 days, kids in my neighborhood were reliving the story by reenacting the movie under my direction. The film bug was permanently planted.

In 1971, I began teaching in Rogers City High School in northern Michigan after several years of acting and directing plays. That is when I met Bob Parsons, an incoming freshman. Bob and I, along with others, worked to develop an award-winning newspaper at the high school—and we always talked about making a movie.

In 1975, when Bob was a senior, the first film was born, *The Adventures of the Six Cent Man.* The 20-minute movie was a parody of the then popular television program, *The Six Million Dollar Man.* The film was shot with an old 8mm camera without audio. The film was a silent movie, and the subtitles were shot from a roll of freezer wrap paper. For music to accompany the film, a reel to reel tape recorder was used. To keep the film and audio in sync, someone kept their finger on the reel to speed it up or slow it down to match the projected image. The community of Rogers City poured into the high school gymnasium to watch the film for 25 cents admission. The proceeds were enough to purchase better equipment and the company was off and running.

In 1991, in Fort Wayne Indiana, David Habig, with a solid background in television production, video technology and the film industry, joined me. With the two of us at the helm, Windsong Pictures became the only student-based organization in the country to produce full-length motion pictures. These were shot on location throughout the United States and marketed around the world.

Windsong Pictures Programs

Windsong Academy Programs are hands-on cinematic learning experiences for students. Through the experience of working with students at their schools and at the Windsong Studio, barriers are broken down to enhance learning and to integrate skills from many disciplines. In filmmaking, we address contemporary and period social issues in highly creative ways. Windsong pictures is the only student-based organization of its kind that offers an extensive opportunity for young people to make films. Students from many schools create, research, write, cast, film, edit, and produce full-length features and short motion pictures involving thousands of students and community members. Besides local premiers, the students showcase the screenplays at national film festivals and distribute motion pictures around the world. Through its programs, Windsong Pictures provides expertise to enhance student learning, providing teacher training and support in a way that school districts cannot afford and with resources teachers cannot readily access.

The Feature Length Film Production Program is for both advanced students and adult cinephiles from the local community—and for people from locations where the films are shot. Students provide leadership, mentor new cinephiles, and take responsibility for the production, from inception to screening and distribution.

The Academy Program allows the Windsong technical staff to go directly into schools to train students and teachers how to operate audio and video equipment. Program staff provide training for producing videos and operating a television broadcasting program. One of the goals of the program is to help students learn to mentor other students to perpetuate the learning process. The Academy Program also facilitates the production of short films and documentaries using Windsong equipment and the support of the student technical staff. In order to participate in this activity, students must be active Windsong volunteers assisting with other productions.

The Educational Video Production Program was developed to create learning experiences through video production by students, and for students. The productions range in topics from science to art, literature, and dance. Students in elementary school, middle school, high school, and college participate in this program under the guidance of the Windsong student volunteer staff.

The Film Camp Program is an intensive program held during the summer months and is designed to teach students how to make their own short films.

The International Windsong Film Festival began in 2000 and is an opportunity to screen outstanding independent pictures from across the country and the world. Many of the films are award-winning productions, shown at a weeklong, family friendly film festival. The festival is also an opportunity to showcase the video work of students. The Windsong Film Festival is one of the few film festivals that is open to young students. Windsong Pictures takes pride in recognizing students for their productions as well as honoring independent filmmakers. The festival is also a teaching opportunity where students meet guest motion picture directors, producers, writers, and actors who participate in question and answer sessions.

The Art of Motion Picture Magic program is designed for students of all ages to foster cinematic literacy. Today most people watch more movies than read books. Through this program, students develop a greater understanding of film, a media that has become so influential in their lives. This program covers such issues as the history of motion pictures, cinematic elements and techniques, story lines through the eyes of the camera, and the use of sound and visual effects.

The Discovery Expo Program is a hands-on learning program conducted by Windsong staff and students in schools throughout Indiana and Michigan=. The Discovery Expo brings history to life. The foundation of the program is based on historical period films produced by Windsong Pictures on location at historic sites. For example, in 1998 Windsong Pictures released *Pirates in Paradise*, a 2-hour feature film. To create this film, extensive research was required to discover information about the lives of the Spanish at St. Augustine, Florida. The film covers the building of the fortress Castillo de San Marcos, and the enslaved Timucuan Native Americans. It also depicts the escaping African American slaves from the Carolinas and the destruction of the pirate haven Port Royal, Jamaica in

1692. In order to present the story at Discovery Expo, students built a 32-foot long pirate ship with 20-foot masts and sails. The ship was skillfully constructed in segments that could readily be assembled to move from location to location. The ship served as the focal point of the Expo, with other hands-on learning stations surrounding the vessel.

Other learning stations included period clothing, tools of the time, foods, and period crafts. In addition, full-scale models of the housing used by the Spanish and the Timucuans were constructed, depicting the Village of St. Augustine. To enhance the Expo experience, Windsong Pictures produced learning videos on the construction of the Castillo de San Marcos, highlighting Spanish life of the working peasants and Native Americans. At each Discovery Expo there is a stage show that highlights events of the period. To create the stage show, students make life-sized puppets and design special props for staging selected clips from the motion picture. Prior to participating in Discovery Expos, teachers receive packets of materials to help prepare students for the experience. There are also follow-up materials for teachers to use when they return to their classrooms.

Project-Based Learning

All Windsong Pictures programs involve project-based learning activities. The key is to actively engage students with adults in as many facets of film production as is possible—from the initial brainstorming through the production and marketing of the product. After establishing who the audience is, and solidifying the central idea for the project, the next step is to research the history of the people including their occupations, education, housing, food, art, music, dance, religion, and culture. This is followed by the writing process using teams of writers enlisting all the essential screenplay elements: establishment, exposition, plot, setting, character development, conflict, foreshadowing, irony, climax, and theme. While writing the film, it is imperative to keep the audience in mind. The next steps are screen-testing for talent, casting the characters, and training a technical crew. Each film involves collecting and making props, building sets when necessary, and gathering and making costumes. We solicit experts in the community in all of the above areas and seek parent involvement to optimize learning and create a believable and realistic motion picture.

For the actual production, a timetable for filming is established. Logistics for shooting locations, transportation, lodging, food, medical care, and technical support are other considerations. The technical staff includes the director, technical director, producers, assistant directors, production assistants, shot loggers, property controllers, prompters, and grips to name a few on-site jobs.

This is followed by post production which includes logging all the footage in a time code, selecting the best takes, editing clips, creating sound effects and video effects, and editing music. Music must be created by Windsong Pictures, or be in the public domain, and artist-approved for the production.

The marketing phase is the next step, which means skillfully composing letters, artistically designing flyers, posters, and a website to spread the word throughout the community. Contacting the media with press releases and public service announcements, and participating in television, radio, and newspaper interviews, requires tactful networking. Securing advertising, developing programs and tickets and displaying banners for the premiere are additional tasks. Following local screenings, the next step is to market the productions through established national and international networks.

Students are encouraged to actively engage in every aspect of these activities. Project-based learning involves every skill students learn in school and many more. In project-based learning these skills are not isolated like school subjects. Instead these interdisciplinary skills and activities are highly integrated and collaborative, reflecting the real world of film. For more ideas and support for project-based learning turn to the George Lucas Educational Foundation which provides monthly newsletters via e-mail with outstanding examples of project-based learning in action in schools across the country.

For a free subscription e-mail: e-newsletter-on@glef.org or edutopia@glef.org

How to Participate

Any student or teacher can participate in Windsong Pictures. There are no membership fees or dues. Windsong eliminates money as an obstacle for participants. To start, beginners fill out a talent form with some basic background information, undergo a brief screen-test, which is an enjoyable process, and go to work. Windsong provides the necessary training in all the tools of the film trade. Windsong asks two things of people—live up to your commitment and work hard as a member of a creative team.

Even though Windsong Pictures is located in the Midwest, it has helped educators and students worldwide. We provide on-site production assistance, ongoing advice, and a video on "How to Make a Movie." For those interested in working with Windsong pictures, submitting projects to the Windsong Film Festival, or learning how to create your own film program, please contact Windsong Pictures by e-mailing Windsong71@comcast.net or by visiting us on the Web at www.windsongpictures.com.

The Indispensable Teacher

20

Several years ago I had the opportunity to begin an educational filmmaking program for high school students. Not having attended a traditional film school, I did not have a formal background in educational filmmaking. My 15 years of working knowledge in the film industry was my guide. In an attempt to familiarize myself with the needs of students, I hosted several 3-month workshops in which high school students would produce their own films from start to finish. I had limited expectations, but to my astonishment the films produced by the teens were fantastic. They also cleaned up at several film festivals. Taking advantage of the success, I decided to take the program on the road and attempt a distance learning course over the internet. I rigged a camera to a computer and broadcasted live Web discussions everyday to our testing groups in various states across the country.

To my surprise, the program succeeded again. In one case a team of students from Wisconsin went so far as to produce a feature-length motion picture that they then screened in their local theater, selling out 1,400 seats for 2 days straight. These young filmmakers made $10,000, with which they paid their parents back for loaning them the budget for the project. The remainder was distributed back into their school filmmaking program. This team of students then graduated and moved away to attend college, leaving their high school with a gaping hole in its film

program. In the many testing sites hosted, this example repeated itself all over the country. These successes made me realize that I had taught students about filmmaking, but I had not gone out of my way to make certain their teachers were gaining a working knowledge of the craft. A new idea now dawned on me, as I realized that it was high school instructors who were the key to a successful filmmaking program.

Teaching the Teachers

To educate a vast number of high school teachers in filmmaking was not an easy task. It presented tremendous challenges which were extremely difficult to solve. Digging in, I decide to stand fast and tackle the problems head on. The primary solution was simple but had never been attempted before: to host large workshops on Hollywood sets where teachers from all around the world could come and participate for 6 days on a working film set. I did not want teachers to merely stand around and watch a movie being made; I wanted them to be a necessary cog in the wheel of the crew. The teachers had to understand all of the various departments, terms, conditions, and jobs of everyone involved in a film crew.

We broke a film crew down into six major sections through which we would rotate the teachers around various sections a day at a time. By the end of the last day, each teacher would have had the opportunity to work alongside each major department on a film set, thereby providing a basic working knowledge of what happens on a movie set.

I knew we would have to tackle all of the development, production and postproduction aspects of filmaking at another time. I remember looking at the plan on paper and thinking to myself how simple it was, but I also worried about how risky it was. I received a small grant for the first workshop from the Utah Office of Education and began pre-production in May of 2001. The State of Utah was fantastic in its enthusiasm and quickly helped to pull together 12 teachers for the workshop. The project was to be called, *A Kiss Remembered*. The teachers would follow a film about the true-life experiences of an American soldier during World War II.

The "Kiss Remembered" Project

The first day of production arrived, and I climbed into the first assistant director's car for the hour-long drive to our location in Heber, Utah. The location was doubling for a European countryside. While clutching the outline document of how the workshop was supposed to work, I reminded myself over and over again that this would indeed work. I turned to my first assistant director, with probably more than a little worried look on my face, and asked, "Am I going to have to figure out how to pay back the state of Utah?"

He smiled and confidently said, "enjoy it. This may be the most exciting part. After we succeed, and this works, you will never get back and enjoy the possibility of failure." I laughed. Somehow his comment lifted the burden from my shoulders. We pulled into our designated parking places. The sun was still hidden by the cold mountains as the teachers began to arrive. They were timid at first, unsure of what was going to happen, but excited by the prospect of making a movie. We pulled them together before setting up and briefed them as to the events of the coming week. I must say these were teachers who had absolutely no experience with film, yet each of them showed so much heart. They jumped in with both feet and ran. It was won-

drous to see how they were making our workshop successful. By the end of the week we had a hard time remembering who was a teacher and who were the professionals. Our concept worked, and we were ready to pull out all the stops and let loose with a much larger production. Moreover, there were now 12 teachers who were trained well enough to go back into a classroom and teach filmmaking. Those teachers would go forward to touch thousands of students, far more than we could ever dream of including in our previous workshops. The story of one of these participants follows.

Memoirs of a Participant
(Inner City Filmmakers Workshop#2)

Nothing I have imagined could have prepared me for the experience that I had in the second week of August 2001. Thinking that I was going to a small picture shoot, I found myself at the back gate of Universal Studios, looking at the address again just to make sure that I had come to the right place. It was the right place, and what happened over the next 4 days has now become one of the most fulfilling and memorable times of my life. I have truly lived out in reality one of my childhood dreams.

From the first person I met, Michael the assistant cameramen, to Chet Thomas, the director, everyone involved with the shoot was extremely welcoming and more than willing to help us learn the business. The first day of shooting I was assigned to Toni's crew and became a grip. I immediately found out that making movies was extremely hard work. During the course of the day I also worked with Chris's crew and did some lighting work.

I think I used up all my emotions during the day, to being overwhelmed, to being unsure, from extreme joy to extreme exhaustion, from frustration to satisfaction. Isn't show business great? During the day I had a chance not only to meet and bond with the cast and crew, but I also met some of the teachers and students that were part of our ICF program. We did not have much time to talk— movie making is a fast-paced occupation. By the time I had a chance to pick my head up it was already lunchtime.

It seemed as though the dust hadn't even settled from the morning session before we were back filming again. The afternoon went as fast as the morning, and I soon found myself at home intensely sore, very tired, taking a shower, and hoping the night would quickly pass so I could be back making movies again.

On the next day of shooting, I got a chance very few people get. I was able to shadow the director and work with him. After a period of time, he asked me if I would shoot still photos of the production behind the scenes. He gave me his digital camera and I spent the entire day shooting stills of the process of making a movie. By doing that, I learned as much about the process as I would have working the jobs. Along with shooting the pictures, I also helped the grips, or lighting crew, whenever they needed an extra hand. Teamwork is the name of the game in this medium. As one person told me, "This is not an individual art form, it only works when everyone is working on a common goal."

What a surrealistic week! I worked on the Universal Studios Lot making a movie. I worked with some highly professional craftsmen, some of the best in the field, who freely shared their special knowledge. I developed working relationships with some of the people, and I'm sure that I have established continuing contacts. I became much more knowledgeable about the process of making a movie. One of the students said it—and I was thinking it—"I used to ride on the trams and take the Universal tour; this week I was part of it."

Just like this teacher, other teachers in our program have gone on to instill an excitement about learning filmmaking in their students, which could not be accomplished through any other means. These instructors can now express in a realistic way their energy and love for filmmaking, which forever altered their lives. In turn, many future students will benefit from the confidence and excitement these teachers gained and now bring to their classrooms.

www.ismfilms.com

With the second workshop a soaring success, we decided to move on and give the teachers a tool with which they could bring the best filmmakers directly into their classrooms. We devised a constantly changing website to which schools could subscribe and use as their textbooks, testing centers, and filmmaking communities. In addition, the website included interviews from many of the very best filmmakers in the industry, so students and teachers could glean advice from professionals.

In subsequent workshops we developed, we concentrated on increasing an understanding of all phases of filmmaking that we may not have covered in the original sessions. We created development workshops that instructed teachers on how to write screenplays. Preproduction workshops dealt with preparing a crew for production and postproduction. These workshops also addressed issues such as editing and sound mixing. All of the offerings were established for one purpose—to make certain that teachers would not be intimidated by the filmmaking art.

Conclusion

In the final analysis, creating a successful school film program comes down to a single factor—the teacher. The one ingredient that cannot be duplicated or replaced is the energy, stamina, and excitement that a single teacher can instill in a group of students. We have now seen programs blossom under the sheer excitement of such instructors even when they have very little experience or equipment. We have also seen well funded and equipped programs suffer and die due to a lack of teacher interest, or the removal of an enthusiastic teacher. One thing is certain, young people will not cease to enjoy the movies and will continue wanting to understand how they are made. Some of these students will make films whether we teach them or not. The punishment for us not teaching them the difference between good cinema and trash is overwhelmingly important. The job needs to be filled by an excited and ambitious instructor with a love for filmmaking. Nothing else will suffice.

Mentorship and the Media Arts:

21

Children's Media Project

Perhaps no one can describe the impact of mentorship on the young participants at the Children's Media Project better than 18-year-old Eileen Kennedy. "There's not one person at CMP who would close the door to you," she says, as she reflects on her many experiences over the years with the organization's programs. "At CMP, instructors are strong role models who are very vocal and open. They're not so much our teachers as our friends." Children's Media Project, located in Poughkeepsie, New York, focuses on developing young people's confidence by helping them express themselves to others through the media arts. Process, not product, is a main focus of the organization's mission, and media making is the means to building positive outcomes in the lives of children.

This process of developing confidence and self-expression in youth is driven by the unique definition and practice of mentorship CMP has developed and refined over the years—a definition that emphasizes a combination of feedback, self-reflection, and leadership. Such mentorship comes in many forms at CMP and infuses all levels of the organization's activity. The central tenet of teacher-to-student mentorship exists alongside equally important student-to-student peer mentorship, staff-to-staff

mentorship, and at times, and in no small way as the children inform their instructors of their needs and feelings—even student-to-teacher mentorship.

This case study investigates how mentoring can facilitate long-term learning and social skills by instilling the spirit of independence and self-awareness in its young participants. Combining technical video making skills with these important foundational lessons can further enable young people to become more sophisticated consumers and producers of media. In the end, the skills obtained through CMP's program are especially useful for those who may not go on to pursue a career in media: they may never pick up a camera again, but lessons about independence and self-awareness and what it means to be a leader will carry through to other pursuits in their lives.

This is a particularly interesting time to explore the role that mentorship plays at CMP. As the organization becomes more established, it is able to hire more staff and acquire better equipment—computers, video cameras, and other essential high-tech tools. This expansion is allowing them to provide resources for all of the young people interested in participating in its programs and to develop new programs to serve the community's needs.

But growth and expansion present their own challenges and suggest several questions for the future: as CMP introduces greater structure into its programs, what impact will this have on relationships between its mentors and the young people they seek to influence? As the organization grows, is it possible to serve a larger number of young people with the same proven mentorship methods and to preserve the personal relationships that have made CMP a success thus far?

The Background

Executive director Maria Marewski, an experimental filmmaker, founded CMP in 1994 with the goal of "teaching young people to 'read' and 'write' in the increasingly dominant language of image, word, and sound." In its early years, CMP's offices operated out of Marewskis' home, and then moved to three rooms at a small private school. Workshops were conducted at off-site locations throughout the Hudson Valley. Marewski worked closely alongside board members and part-time workshop instructors to shape the early direction of the organization.

Since its founding in 1994, the Children's Media Project has experienced a steady rate of growth. That growth increased dramatically, however, in 2000, when its budget increased significantly and the organization moved to a new location in downtown Poughkeepsie. The move allowed CMP to begin working with an expanded community of at-risk youth, both through the city's public schools and through drop-in programs at the organizations new downtown Media Arts Studio Space. This newly named community media center now houses the majority of CMP's programs, which include a wide range of media production workshops and exhibitions for young people, ages 8 through 20, from the city of Poughkeepsie and surrounding region.

Poughkeepsie, located 80 miles north of New York City in New York's Hudson Valley, is a post-industrial river town. Recorded decreases in yearly school enrollment suggest that at least forty percent of Poughkeepsie's entering public high school students drop out before graduation. The economy has been significantly jolted in recent years by major downsizing at IBM, the city's top employer. Still, the character of Poughkeepsie is on the upswing. The downtown area has reopened to traffic after a failed 30-year experiment with a pedestrian mall, and new businesses and organizations, like CMP, are moving into the area, providing a much-needed resource for the city's young people.

"Our move (into downtown Poughkeepsie) was the first major commitment to the community," says managing director Ben Kalina. "We've made ourselves available on a daily basis to the kids, and given them informal access to our staff. A program is one thing, but interacting with adults on an informal basis in a positive way is one of the most important things a teenager can experience."

The Philosophy of Mentorship

Children's Media Project builds its programs around teaching the "inner process," a concept executive director Maria Marewski says was influenced largely by the mythological texts of Joseph Campbell; a version of his work *The Hero's Journey* is incorporated into many of CMP's programs. By approaching the role of mentor as someone who guides teenagers through the stages of a journey, the staff at CMP gives young people the agency to shape their own creative visions and to direct their personal paths through life's challenges. "I would consider us extremely successful," Marewski notes, "if we were able to bring to life in each staff member and each student an internal mentor that guides them through life." This inner process is at the heart of CMPs artistic vision: "The nature of being an artist is that you go against the grain," Marewski reflects. "And you need that internal strength to go against the grain."

CMP uses videomaking as a tool for engaging young people in this creative process, and in so doing exposes them not only to risks and challenges but to the opportunity to examine those risks and the concept of "process" in general. "Whatever process you engage in will change you," Marewski points out. But videomaking is an especially useful example of process: the creative solutions teachers and kids discover in the mutual journey of making a video together have concrete and visible results in the final project. Kids can actually see how the process has made the piece better. In making a video project, she argues, "You will always find allies, and allies are mentors—people who can reflect back to you who you are."

It is especially important in working with at-risk youth, she emphasizes, to remind young people what the process looks like. "If you're the smartest person in the world, you're still going to have obstacles, there's no way around that." The process of creative problem solving that mentorship in CMP's programs helps children develop is almost surely universally applicable to future challenges in their lives.

Building Leadership Skills

Given the population of at-risk youth it serves, CMP faces a number of challenges in implementing its vision of empowerment through the artistic process. Most important, perhaps, is redefining and recontextualizing young people's notions of success and leadership. "Being an artist is not the vision of success that is most often presented in mainstream media," Marewski says. Everyone knows what success as an athlete means, but conveying the importance of less heralded values is much harder to achieve.

CMP applies media literacy techniques to help young people develop the skills to decode the visual messages the popular culture is sending them and to gain a better understanding of media influence in their lives. "By teaching them to decode the images that they see on television and in advertising, we are trying to show them that there are a lot of ways to make it in life, that success and power is not just about the glamour and the glitz," Kalina says. "It's about gaining the skills you need to navigate successfully through life."

Often, this includes the "soft skills" that relate to emotional intelligence: the capacity to work as part of a team, the ability to resolve conflicts, the development of self-awareness and awareness of others; leadership abilities. This last skill is defined uniquely in the CMP vision. "Leadership," according to CMP education coordinator Penny Lane, "is being able to help someone else achieve something." The definition is built into the programs themselves: as youth become more skilled as media makers, they are encouraged to serve as mentors to those who are younger or have less knowledge or expertise in a particular area.

By completing the majority of CMPs programs, youth producers Eileen Kennedy, Ryan Sullivan, and Willie Wright have all matured into leadership positions at the organization. Sullivan and Wright served as peer mentors for the younger kids in CMP's Media Guild program last summer, even though they, too, were a part of the program. "CMP has given me the focus to be a leader," Sullivan says. Whenever I get the chance, I step in and say, "I can do this." Kennedy became an actual instructor for Video Diary for Girls, the program that had first introduced her to CMP as a student. Together with instructor Penny Lane and a college fellow from nearby Vassar, she helped coordinate the lesson plans, leaving room for the participating young people to add their own elements to the curriculum. "Eileen's only a few years older than some of the girls in the program," says Kalina, "but she has been in a direct mentoring relationship with Penny, and so her experience and understanding of what it means to be supported as a younger person has translated directly into her ability to care deeply about the young women in the program and support their growth as well. And that's exactly what we want to see in all of our programs."

Mentorship has been the means for achieving these leadership success stories. Wright and Sullivan developed their confidence to lead under the guidance of instructor Tim Sutton, who became a "friend" right from the start. "Tim's always joking about how he raised me, about how I'm his son," Wright says with a smile, noting how he learned to be a cameraman by watching and working alongside Sutton and gained editing skills from Joy Reed, a CMP workshop instructor. "My success is based on their teachings," he says. This personal connection with students, Sutton says, enables him to "plant seeds" with greater meaning. "It builds trust and respect . . . two of the most important things.

And it becomes more than TV Production 101. You get to know the students and can use real experiences from their lives to empower them."

Process-Oriented Programs

CMPs earliest programs, animation workshops for elementary school students, explored the "inner-process" by asking young people to animate their personal journals. Marewski believes that this approach—"asking young people to tap into their inner life"—is critical to the mentorship process.

After seeing what a tremendous motivator the animation workshops represented, CMP developed teacher-training programs that offered both the media-analysis and film-making processes as a tool to teachers. These programs have taken many forms at CMP, including the most recent incarnation, Smoke Screens, an in-school media-literacy textbook that teaches young people how to critically analyze tobacco advertisements. Thus far, 1,400 Poughkeepsie public school students have completed the program, and a second edition of the textbook is on its way.

Two other early programs—Hidden Heroes and Finding Your Future—allowed Children's Media Project to work with at-risk youth from both urban and rural communities in the Hudson Valley region. The programs used Campbells' *The Hero's Journey* and the physical challenge of daunting ropes courses to engage young people in "positive rites of passage" and to introduce them to the idea of risk-taking in the creative process.

These early efforts laid the foundation for one of CMP's most recent programs, which addresses a specific challenge facing many at-risk youth in the Poughkeepsie area: the lack of positive role models in the community. Talking Walls: Transformation from the Inside Out, which received a MacArthur Foundation media center's grant in 2000 and 2001, was the result of months of discussions and workshops with a group of offenders inside New York's Green Haven Correctional Facility, a maximum-security prison in the Hudson Valley. Originally intended to include a com-

ponent that would take place inside the prison walls, the program was altered because of unexpected administrative decisions by the New York State Department of Corrections, which denied CMP access in the end. But CMP followed through on a primary concern the prisoners expressed: namely, that the high percentage of men from low-income communities incarcerated has left few males in the community to mentor kids.

While CMP doesn't try to fill that role precisely, it does aim to close a gap that the group identified. Managing director Ben Kalina, who joined CMP 3 years ago to co-direct the Talking Walls program, explains: "When they are not sure who to rely on, who to ask, we encourage students to see obstacles as teachers, not barriers. The program asks kids to look inside themselves, to find what they're gifted at, to figure out who their allies might be—maybe a friend, teacher, or adult mentor." The program's success influenced the organization's decision to move to downtown Poughkeepsie and devote more of its resources to young people in that community. "Mentorship is a long-term commitment," Maria Marewski explains, "and we realized that if we were truly going to make an impact on the kids lives, that we had to be there."

One of the features that makes the Talking Walls program significant within the scope of CMP's programs is that teaching young people to make videos is not the program's primary objective, even though CMP identifies itself as a youth media organization. Video Diary for Girls, a media-intensive program for girls ages 12 through 18, also follows this model. Marewski says that the program aims to lessen the gender gap in media, and derives from CMP's early and continuing emphasis on exploring the personal memoir. The curriculum includes graphic-design projects, spoken-word poetry, drumming, and a final project, a video self-portrait. This is the only video project produced within the program.

"We use the media arts as a vehicle for self-expression, but giving young people the vehicle isn't enough," explains Penny Lane, director of Video Diary for Girls.

"We're trying to teach them to communicate their ideas, help them find their voice, and then give them the vehicle so that they can actually say something." At-risk youth, she says, are in particular need of such process-centered mentoring. "In most of their life situations the kids aren't actually empowered to have anything to say. Some of these kids have never been asked, 'What do you think?' So you can't just hand a video camera to a kid and say, 'Go ahead, make a movie.'" Lane says that the "process work" creates an environment in which young people feel safe being honest, sharing ideas, and speaking up for themselves. "If you don't do that then they just mimic what they see on television. They'll all make ninja movies, all day long. That's really boring for the staff, and for [the students], it's not as meaningful."

Video Diary for Girls expanded from 4 girls in its first year to 12 girls in its second; each was paid a stipend to participate so that, for young people from low-income households, the experience could take the place of a summer job. The Talking Walls program had been set up in a similar way in previous years, but did not run in 2003 due to a lack of funds. CMP hopes to continue the program.

The Learning Curve

As they teach the students, staff may be building the initial lesson plans of a program or learning how to light an interview or use the latest equipment themselves. "(Young people) get the brunt of our inconsistencies," says Tim Sutton, director of the Media Arts Studio Space. Sometimes, though, the staff's learning process can be a critical component of mentorship at Children's Media Project.

Eileen Kennedy reminisces with her former instructor and now co-teacher, Penny Lane, about when she was a student in Video Diary for Girls herself. "You seemed like you were very much on our level instead of above us, teaching down to us, which was cool." Lane and Kennedy imagined how different it would be if Lane were an award-winning filmmaker, for example. "It would be very difficult for me not to be intimidating," Lane surmises, "or for you to understand how you could get to where I was." Kennedy nods in agreement.

Learning, for staff as well as students, involves taking risks and trusting instincts. Physical and emotional risks, in fact, are built into CMP's programs. In Talking Walls, Ryan Sullivan had to soar down a zip line suspended 50 feet above the ground, despite his fear. So did staff members Kalina, Sutton, and Lane. In Video Diary for Girls, Lane performed in the drum circle, despite reservations about her talents. Kennedy read her poetry out loud in front of people she had never met. "A challenge for the staff as well as the students is to become comfortable with uncertainty," Marewski explains. "If you already know everything, there's no room for anything new or different to happen."

Because youth producers Kennedy, Sullivan, and Wright have participated in CMP's programs through stages of major growth for the organization, they are greatly affected both by its learning curve and by changes the organization has undergone. But this trio of students-turned-mentors has helped shape the direction of the organization as well. Often, such highly active and involved young people are the primary catalyst for curriculum changes or for developing new programs and ways of teaching.

Since the three students have made their way through almost all of the programs that Childrens Media Project offers, the organization has continued to develop ways to challenge them at higher levels. They are able to continue to work at CMP on an informal basis on their own projects, but the organization also tries to challenge them in their personal development and in their ability to assume leadership roles and positions. As Kalina explains, "It's been really important for us to figure out how to create a ladder in the organization for them so that they can move along in their own ability to mentor younger students. . . . That's what we envision as a critical element of the mentorship structure at CMP."

Kennedy, Sullivan, and Wright have built strong relationships with one another and with the staff, as well as an extensive portfolio of PSAs, documentaries, and experimental videos. All three have represented Children's Media Project at numerous regional conferences. Their progression through CMPs programs mirrors the arc of CMP's proposed solution to the challenge of creating more experiences and "earning curves:" The Media Guild.

The Media Guild:
A Framework for Learning

"The idea behind the Media Guild is that it will provide incremental programs and opportunities, from entry level to professional level," Marewski says. An individual's "trajectory" through the program will vary, based on his or her experience and interests.

For CMP, the Media Guild provides a cohesive framework for the multiplicity of programs and workshops the organization offers, especially those serving the local community. The concept is still evolving, and this year marks its official pilot program. Ultimately, CMP aims for it to become a "progressive series of workshops and programs that are designed to introduce young people to advanced le-vels of video and media production." Young people are ex-posed to four components of media making: media production as art, as activism, as education, and as entrepreneurship.

The Media Guild hires local young people to produce media projects that CMP has contracted, and they gain valuable job skills in the process. Mentorship is the very essence of this program as well, with students working closely alongside four team leaders. Kalina describes the Media Guild "as a medieval blacksmith shop, except with video." The first week of the Media Guild is called "Video Boot Camp," and, as its title suggests, involves a week of intensive training on the basics, including composition, interviewing, and critiquing. It also serves to let young people know what will be expected of them for the rest of the summer. For many of the young people, this is their first paid summer job.

In summer 2002, 19 young people from the Poughkeepsie area, ages 12 through 18, were paid to produce video PSAs and documentaries and to learn graphic design and animation. They were the primary producers on a range of projects: the design of a brochure for the Dutchess County Youth Bureau's fall conference; instructional videos for other kids titled "How-To-Make a Public Ser-

vice Announcement" and "How-To-Make a Stop Motion Animation," both to be distributed by the Noodlehead Network; ten public-service announcements for county-wide broadcast on cable channels including MTV, BET, and the Family Channel; and a documentary about the revitalization of the city of Poughkeepsie, which is funded by the federal Weed and Seed Initiative.

Video Diary for Girls and Talking Walls, Marewski says, "will serve as the introductory levels of the program, and will create the context for the Media Guild so that (young people) understand the creative process and begin to become exposed to alternative media, in terms of evaluating and viewing as much as in terms of gaining the basic skills." After taking on more advanced projects and making their way up the ladder, students will ideally attain a level of expertise that will enable them, like Eileen Kennedy, to return as junior instructors in the programs.

The Feedback Loop

CMP's mission does not end with the promotion of life skills and the production of videos. Public exhibition, critique, and evaluation feed back into the programs to complete the cycle. The organization's outreach is broadened by its connection with the Hamptons International Film Festival. In addition to curating the festival's "Young Videomakers" component, a program of works made by young people, CMP coordinates and facilitates panel discussions and presentations for young makers. Youth producers played a role in curating this year's festival program, which took place in October.

As part of a program supported by the Open Society Institute, CMP is currently training young people to critically evaluate their peers' work, in much the same way their own work is evaluated by CMP's staff. Each video accepted to the Hamptons International Film Festival receives written peer evaluations. All accepted films screen at the festival, and competition-winning films screen as trailers before regular festival programs. Professionals, including actor Bill Murray and HBO's John Rikkers, participate in the final judging process, alongside youth producers like Eileen Kennedy.

By evaluating their peers' work, CMP hopes that young people will learn to think about their own work and its merits as well. Ben Kalina says that by emphasizing this feedback element, the program also helps young people to become comfortable with receiving both positive and negative feedback from their instructors, "which can be difficult when you're trying to maintain a comfortable, friendship relationship between mentor and student."

The administration at CMP believes that true mentorship requires a willingness to learn from and respond to criticism and suggestions from every direction. This "feedback loop" applies not only to the students but to the staff. "There's always something to learn." Marewski says, "We don't know all the answers. As we move along, the kids are telling us where we were strong and where we need work. Its a dialogue."

Kalina stresses the usefulness of this student feedback: "If we are being inconsistent or hypocritical, Ryan [Sullivan] lets me know that, and I want to know it," he says. Indeed, most young people say they feel CMP is truly their organization. Ryan Sullivan and Willie Wright say they have often made suggestions about how to better work with the young children who come in to CMP—how to relate to them, how to keep them interested, and, of course, how to keep their astounding energy levels in control. Tim Sutton says he often relies on students informing him of what equipment and resources they need to take on the projects they're most interested in.

Staff must also play a role in CMP's mentorship culture by offering feedback to and accepting it from other staff members. This philosophy strengthens the staff's ability to create change within the organization. "(CMP) is organic," Sutton says. "We're making it." Kara Janeczko, a summer director of the Media Arts Studio Space, explains the process: "Everybody has a vision of how they think their connection with the kids should take shape." By providing regular opportunities for feedback, she says, staff members can help one another improve their relationships with students—when "its getting too sarcastic, or when a students having trouble with a particular teacher's authority,"

for example. "It's hard to have that vision of how you are [interacting] yourself. We really try to do check-ins with each other, and we usually know where those points of disconnect are."

The staff talks openly about how they, too, benefit from CMP's mentorship philosophy. Martha Dewing, CMP's special projects director, is the former editor and publisher of Children's Video Report, and a former board member of Children's Media Project. She says one of CMP's greatest strengths is the concept of staff development. "CMP is interested in developing the kids and the adults who come through our doors." Media Education Coordinator Penny Lane identifies a major difference between basic staff training and CMP's version of mentoring: "Training is in the best interest of the organization," she says, "while mentoring cares about and is in the best interest of the individual and their personal growth."

Lane's desk at Children's Media Project is positioned directly across from Dewing's. Such proximity, in the typical office, tends to breed more familiarity than coworkers often expect or even want. But Lane, who came to CMP right out of college, and Dewing, who joined CMP after years of experience in the media education industry, offer one another feedback from their differing perspectives willingly. Both say this mentorship culture is intrinsic to CMP, that the benefits are constant, and that the pathway for sharing such knowledge is circular.

Growing Concerns and Looking Ahead

As greater numbers of young people take part in CMP's programs, participation has increased to levels the organization considers desirable. After CMP's move to downtown Poughkeepsie, it took time for word about its programs to spread in the community and for enrollment to reach its current levels. Before that—when youth producers Kennedy, Sullivan, and Wright first came to CMP, for example—programs often had a student-to-teacher ratio as low as three to one, and students benefited from that opportunity by forging strong mentorship bonds with the staff. Now that ratio has just about doubled, and more often than not, teachers and young people interact mostly during structured program time— something that has challenged the mentorship process for both staff and students.

The staff tries to ensure that young people play a role in the rules and structure being introduced. "In the Media Guild this summer," says Kara Janeczko, "we're trying to set up a community where the kids feel really safe and it is very student-driven, where they get to come up with a lot of the rules and regulations." Some contradiction, she fears, is inherent to that process. "It's hard," she says, "because we're also trying to prepare them for the real world, and as a mentor, it's hard to cultivate these skills in the kids and to help them make their own decisions but know in your mind that [outside of CMP] it's not always like that—things aren't always fair, and you can't always control the situation that you're in."

Just as the changing roles and relationships between young people and staff creates challenges to be solved, staff sometimes finds adjustment difficult, and the issue must be addressed. It is not uncommon for employees at such evolving organizations to feel burned out or confused by ever-shifting responsibilities. Alafaka Opuiyo says that when she started working at CMP she thought the environment was a little "chaotic," because she didn't know her place. "With every growing organization there tends to be the appearance of disorganization," she says. Nevertheless, she likes the "work-in-progress" nature of the place.

Shifting some staff members from their roles as workshop instructors, where they interacted closely with the students, into administrative positions, where they work primarily on fundraising and curriculum development, can pose potentially difficult adjustment problems. To fill the occasional creative void that ensues for these workers, CMP developed its Staff Movie Nights. Every other month, a staff member suggests a broad theme around which staff can create personal projects, such as "shoes" or "relationships." For the many artists on staff, this provides extra motivation to find time to work on their own projects. Kara Janeczko says working on the "Movie Nights" was a great way to improve her technical production skills. Plus, she says, "it was something that really sealed our mission for

what we think video is capable of doing—both entertaining and bringing people together."

The three students who were brought together through CMP's programs—Ryan Sullivan, Willie Wright, and Eileen Kennedy—all went in different directions this past September, and each attributes their success, in large part, to the guidance of CMP. Sullivan still has one more year of high school to finish. Since his first program with CMP, he's been mainstreamed out of special education classes in half of his subjects. Wright has gone on to Dutchess Community College, in Poughkeepsie, and promises to remain a familiar face at CMP. He and Sullivan have started a graphic design company, RAW Visuals (Ryan and Willie Visuals). And Kennedy has started as a freshman at the SUNY Purchase College Conservatory of Theater Arts and Film, a highly competitive program.

Executive Director Maria Marewski says that to this point, Children's Media Project has been focused on creating a metaphoric space—a teaching and learning environment, a place for young people who are artists to connect with one another. The Media Guild adds structure to that space, and by this winter, CMP hopes introduce an ideal home for that structure.

The organization plans to move into a 7,000-square-foot, three-story firehouse, also in downtown Poughkeepsie. This will consolidate CMP's office and classroom space, which is now split between three locations, and will expand the number of permanent classrooms and exhibition space. "The physical space is really important because its the container," says Marewski. "It makes us a part of the revitalization of downtown Poughkeepsie, which is really exciting. It really increases our capacity to serve the community."

CMP's new physical space will be vital to its ability to provide feedback, structure, and, ultimately, further opportunities for young people to advance their careers as media artists. The move will redirect the administration's focus toward a new set of challenges, whose outcomes will be dependent on the strength and focus of CMP's vision.

Mentorship remains at the center of that vision. The organization's mentorship culture has given staff a major role in directing both the vision and its path for the future. Young people will continue to shape it as well. Serving as mentors in many capacities, they help CMP both learn from and reflect back to the community's needs. "The function of the mentor is to be an ally and help people see themselves, because we all have blind spots," Marewski says. "Mentorship provides opportunities for us to support one another's growth "as artists, administrators, and, of course, as human beings."

This paper is reprinted from *A Closer Look: Media Arts 2002*, by permission of The National Organization of Media Arts and Culture (NAMAC). For more information on our media arts publications, visit www.namac.org.

Tuning in Video Art

22

Marshall Weber is an interdisciplinary artist who is best known for his work in video art, performance art, installations, and artist books. His work often explores issues of social justice, peace studies, linguistics, and theories of representation. Over the last 15 years, Marshall has also been committed to educating children, youth, and adults through art. The two artist collectives that he co-founded, *Artists' Television Access* in San Francisco, California and the *Booklyn Artists' Alliance* in New York City have a strong educational component. Marshall's work as an artist has informed his exemplary pedagogical practice that offers what Paulo Freire calls, pedagogy of possibility. And, in turn his work as an artist educator has shaped his work as an artist. Working in a truly collaborative manner with his students in a unique high school after-school media program in East Harlem, he has created a space for students to explore issues that are relevant to their lives through video. Recently, I talked to Marshall at this home in New York City about his work as an artist educator in video art.

DD: Marshall, I have followed your work over the years in video art and performance art, but I also know that you have taught video art extensively to middle/high school students in public and private schools since the late 1980s. Why video art?

MW: Well, there are many reasons for using video art — personal, pedagogical, and social or situational. Personally, I have always been interested in video art. In the early eighties, it was an emergent art form with relationships to experimental film and independent broadcast journalism. So, it was an interesting medium for me as an artist. I was using video in my own work, exhibiting it, and my videos were being collected. I was familiar with video as a medium. In terms of the situational reason, in 1983 I co-founded a non-profit arts organization that focused on emerging media arts called *Artists Television Access* in San Francisco. We provided an exhibition venue for video artists and helped them make video art. We also had VHS production facilities and we taught classes and trained people to use the equipment. Then, in the mid-80s we started to partner with schools, mostly area high schools. We had a partnership with Mission High School in San Francisco doing a media art program with their special education classes. This grew and led me to become more involved with high school level art programs— planning curriculum and designing programs nationally and later doing adjunct work at the university level.

DD: What is the relevance of using video art in art classes?

MW: What is interesting to me about video art/media art is that there are some really obvious reasons to use it as a pedagogical tool. One, students are living in a world of television and media. Secondly, they are living in a world where they can make their own new media. Some can buy cameras or they can use their parent's video camera, or they have access to cameras through schools or youth organizations in their neighborhood. In addition, most students do use interactive video media such as "Game boy," computer games, arcade games – and so there is equipment everywhere. Furthermore, there is also public access television that is available to anyone. Video art is not only very contemporary, but popular and comprehensible to students. Video is a very creative medium to put into students' hands and one that is relevant to their daily lives. In addition, electronic media at its best is a tool that allows for a critique of itself. By teaching students how to use tools of media, you are also teaching them how to be critical of media. And, you know, therein lies the whole media literacy movement. I think all these things address the issue of why video art and media art are relevant in the classroom.

DD: "Media literacy" is certainly the current buzzword and there is a growing body of published work on it. I think the link you just made regarding the value of video art as media and medial literacy is important to clarify.

MW: Here is my short, truncated history of the media literacy movement, in terms of it being an ideology, practice, and pedagogy. Simply put, media literacy is giving people and students, whether youth or not, the tools to deal with media propaganda. Media is a primary method of social control. It influences popular aesthetics and it is a primary tool of advanced capitalism—as it controls the physical distribution of information and is easily manipulated by political forces. So, media literacy is a way of revealing the fabrications of the corporate media and governmental communication system. It is also a way of revealing the vocabulary of media as a communication tool; showing how television works, how film works, how editing works, how soundtracks work, how camera angels work. Mainstream media literacy in this country has become obsessed with the critique of mainstream media and therefore in some ways it has become very self-limiting.

Ironically, the origin of media literacy movement in the United States is different from the other primary originating countries of Canada and Great Britain, where it emerged from the discipline of English and Film Rhetoric. Artists working in independent media and independent journalists working in alternative media prompted media literacy in the United States; both these groups were using politically informed leftist critiques of liberal and right wing controlled media. They were definitely making a statement that media is to be opposed with media—the "fight fire with fire" method. Artists and independent journalists were saying: "we are going to make our own television, and we are going to make television that critiques corporate sponsored commercial television." What happened with media literacy movement in the United States is that it was appropriated into a mainstream market and linked to the commercial educational media industry. This appropriation developed into anti-media phenomena that simplistically proclaimed that television and other forms of media entertainment influenced children negatively. Mainstream media literacy for the most part is now controlled by a conservative agenda that is obsessed with how bad television is and with the problems of electronic media as a content-bearing form. The critique has moved from the structural elements of media as a politically controlled communication network to the content of media as a form of entertainment. My analysis, (which is greatly simplified) points out the general trend of content critique now replacing the critique of political and economic structure. For example, you have the constant amorphous critique of violence on television as opposed to a specific critique of military propaganda on television. Content critique is displacing the critique of our unequal political structure. Media literacy has also become part of the educational video market with horrible commercial-style videotapes that simplistically critique television content. It is no surprise then that both liberals as exemplified by Tipper Gore and conservatives as exemplified by Jerry Farwell, join together in a critique of how bad television is. This critique of content I think has unfortunately filtered down into mainstream art education pedagogy as a resistance to using media as an art form. Of course, the ironic exception to all this is computer arts.

Computer use successfully has been introduced as a vital media in classrooms, but devoid of content and structural critique. Computers are seen as simple tools that do not carry the same moral evaluations that are imposed on television and therefore there is no analysis of the superstructure of computer media. However, that is another story....

DD: True. Let's not embark on that story. Can you talk a little more about this relationship between the media literacy movement and video art/media arts?

MW: My pedagogical relationship to video art is somewhat complicated. As media literacy develops a conservative philosophy focused on critiquing commercial media (as if it were a hegemonic structure), video art and media art practice becomes oppositional to media literacy because it is about self-expression. It is not about evaluating or moralizing about the content of media; rather, it is about making something else. For me, teaching video art to students is about teaching students that they have an incredible range of expression and technique available, which is both similar and different than Hollywood, commercial television, MTV, documentary, and independent film. I think it is great to offer students access to all these different aesthetics strategies and forms as well as to ones that are not as popular, such as using video as a self expressive art form, that is similar to painting, sculpture, and drawing. Now, I do not think that there is any inherent or static relationship between the media literacy movement and video arts. Rather, wide spectrums of relationships exist with many blurred borders. I think that the media arts and video arts are very flexible, growing, and are a ubiquitous phenomenon that is not monolithic but fragmented and heterogeneous. This is apparent in popular culture, academic culture, and the arts culture—as the line between mainstream video and art video is blurred. What is unfortunate is that the grip the mainstream media literacy movement has on pedagogy and art education has limited the use of video and media arts as a part of more flexible, creative, and aesthetic curriculum and practice.

DD: How do you use video art in your classroom?

MW: I try to define video art as an extension of the traditional media that students already have mythologicalized for them. They know about traditional painting, and sculpture as well as popular forms, such as graffiti. I try to make the bridge between traditional and contemporary art and popular culture more visible. Students often see media as being an inherently commercial medium, not that it matters to them, since they are immersed in a popular culture, which is predominantly commercial. As an alternative, I teach video as a form of creative self-expression. Class work is about student expression and is not directly modeled on external forms. Of course, there are instances where external models are followed, for instance, students may make the conscious decision to enter into a contest and produce a video tape that adheres to the structure of the contest requirements or students on their own initiative sometimes mimic commercial television or film. My approach to video art pedagogy is experimental and very much a student-directed process—where students are responsible for the concept, design, execution, and, to an extent, distribution of their work. I discuss video art as both a fine art and commercial art. I bring in media art pieces for students to see, students bring in commercial movies for each other to see, and students look at the work of their peers.

Currently, I teach art as part of the after school program at Heritage High School in East Harlem, New York City. I think it is useful to give you some background of this particular school because it is different from most public schools and allows me more freedom to teach in a more fluid manner. The Heritage High School in East Harlem, New York City was a collaborative project initiated by Judith Burton of Teachers College-Columbia University, the New York Board of Education, and the Taller Boricua/Puerto Rican Workshop Inc., a Puerto Rican artists organization founded in the 1970s. It is a small progressive school that is committed to integrating the arts to all areas of the curriculum. The school culture creates an environment that supports creativity and collaboration. The video/media art program is an after school art program where students receive one credit in art for successful completion of the course. The classes are small with 10 to

18 students. Because it is an after school class taken as an elective, students are relaxed, open, and sociable. They want to be there either because it is the easiest thing to do that afternoon, or they are actually interested. There is not a lot of academic pressure, but nobody wants to flunk the class, nor is anybody overachieving. Class leadership usually goes by default in terms of technical skills. What is interesting about Heritage is that the group dynamics are much more important to the local culture in that neighborhood (East Harlem) than the kind of hierarchy that may be associated with other high schools. Students do not opt for individualized video projects, similar to the solo video artist tradition. One aspect of the program that is wonderful is that over a 3-year period of offering video art, there is now a library of student videos. In each new class, I screen student work that came out of previous classes. The students really respond to that and then pursue their own direction.

DD: What kind of work have students produced in your classes?

MW: The work that students have done covers a wide range of techniques and aesthetics and is more often modeled after commercial and popular media, than after video art seen in the art world. Since my classrooms are so student directed there is a very interesting relationship between whatever work I present and the composition of the students in the class, in terms of the kind of culture they bring with them and their interests. In any given semester, I am presenting students with a lot of externally motivated possibilities. I introduce video festivals that we can participate in or contests. I always give students the option in terms of how they are going to produce their work. One approach is systematic, where nothing is left to chance—one begins by brainstorming the idea and then students work on the story line and dialogue. Later on they create a storyboard with all the details in terms of shooting, dialogue, and action. After creating a storyboard, they pick up the camera and start shooting. The other approach is much more fluid where the students just pick up the camera and start shooting and then look at the footage and edit it—pen never hits paper. I let the students decide which

working method (or a combination thereof) they prefer. For example with the video, *Sugar and Spice* (2000) the production was all on the fly. Students were very focused on social interactions during shooting. They saw it as being a simple production and the editing to them just seemed obvious. They mostly worked in committees in terms of editing, and it really was just a matter of: "No, don't use that, use that." They laid a kind of a character structure over it. It was not edited on paper, there was no storyboard—it was all very much in the cinema verite style.

DD: Could you describe the process students engage in your class in terms of conceptualizing and producing a video?

MW: We begin projects by brainstorming. I stand in front of the class and go: "Okay students, what is this semester's tape going to be about?" We get all the ideas on the blackboard and students argue it out until it gets down to the least amount of ideas. For example, the *Sugar and Spice* video explored the topic of dating.

The semester this video was produced was unusual because students in the class knew each other well. The class was primarily composed of students from the very first class to be enrolled in the school and they strongly identified with Heritage. There was strong sense of school solidarity, and because of this they also had this unique social sophistication. They had very intense relationships and did 2 months of roundtable discussions on issues of sex, sexuality, and relationships. They gravitated towards emotional and confrontational material with gender relations becoming the most obvious concern. The end result was a very intimate tape that was extremely volatile. The tapes directly reflected the students and their interests and not an externally motivated autobiographical documentary style. I think something happens in the realm of freedom of expression where I as the teacher function as more of a facilitator than an instructor. The video has an artful quality in terms of the way it was shot and in terms of the facile nature of the discussion. However, it is still classifiable as an informal documentary about gender conflict in a high school environment.

The next semester students worked on similar topics. The resulting short videos were collectively titled as *Sex and Consequences*. They were specific studies of dramatic incidents involving adoption, abortion, and abandonment. Students were again dealing with intimate issues. This class was divided into social cliques and so I allowed each clique to produce a tape. Now, I know this flies in the face of some social dynamic theories concerning classrooms that advise teachers to avoid perpetuating social cliques. Perhaps it is my laisse-faire attitude, or maybe it is my concept that within sincere social relationships comes a generosity toward sharing creative expression that prompted me to allow them to remain in their cliques. In *Sex and Consequences* students started with scripts, storyboards, etc.—everything was planned out. Production was along a traditional dramatic film production method and in some ways produced similar results. It was obvious, however, that they were dramatic productions, though each one was different stylistically.

The following semester, WNET a public television station in New York had a contest on local community art. I presented the contest to the class. Three of the students were interested and wanted to enter the contest. They decided to make the video on a local artist De La Vega who owns a small store two blocks from the school. This artist does a lot of public artwork and has a very complicated relationship with both the local community and art world. For this video the students did not do a script, but they did a scene study and a proposal for what they wanted, so that it would adhere to the contest. Then they went out shot and edited it. Now, you are talking about students who had already been in the class for a few semesters and so this video was quite sophisticated. I have noticed that students who have taken video for more than one semester gradually begin to get more involved in technical aspects. I let the students' interest in the technical aspects guide my teaching in terms of the technical instruction of video production in other words, introducing students to techniques at their request. I allow students to decide if they want to work in groups or on individual video projects. Most of the students prefer to work in groups rather than individually.

Other video pieces made by students range from music rap videos to videos that mimic Hollywood movies, but even this is done with mixed intentions. These videos both emulate and critique movies that the students love. High school kids in the inner city love movies like *Scream, Austin Powers*—movies that have incorporated a satirical self-critical element into them. I mean, it is a very postmodern pallet in New York City in general and these kids are not against that. They are totally into it.

DD: Do you watch the video they make and then give them feedback, which they can decide to consider or not?

MW: Exactly! To give you another example: yesterday, I had this group of young women arguing with me about the editing which I saw as a lazy editing job. They were describing their editing to be intentionally stupid— "No, it's stupid. It's supposed to be stupid." I told them; "Well, yeah, it may be stupid, but there's a difference between stupid and boring and lazy." I mean, you can work much more on this and it could still be "stupid" but it could also be more interesting and certainly more coherent.

DD: Since young people are so familiar and comfortable with media today, do you find that it has influenced the way they make art?

MW: A phenomenon that I see more frequently these days is that students are going on-line and they're downloading anime films and they are editing them to other pieces of music that they download. There is this on-line remix film phenomenon that is hitting youth culture. Students are creating a kind of collage and montage works at home independently. Some students will come in and show this work and I see that we are getting to the point where there is an independent body of work that some students are bringing into the classroom. I can show them work that is similar to documentary video or the video art tradition, but what is interesting to me is that not everything is derived from classroom instruction. Students often have plenty of opportunity to make or reflect upon media art outside school and bring that work into class.

Students are acutely aware that electronic media like video requires distribution. It is necessary to have an audience to view the video; it is not just made for oneself. It is special for students, for instance, to go to an art gallery, but that experience does not afford a sense of inherent conclusion in the manner in which a video does. You know, the student who is doing these anime cutouts does not necessarily think he is making video art. Rather, it is like a hobby; it is like a sport; it is like play. And so, that play is shared and the sharing of it is natural. One, because of the ubiquity of the medium in their everyday lives and two, because of the social structure of the group that I mentioned earlier, even the media work done at home alone is shared.

DD: Earlier you mentioned the fact that video art has an audience. Do students consider the audience when they are making video art?

MW: I like to make it apparent to students that whatever their motivation may be, that they are probably going to show this video to their friends and family. I am not the only one who is going to look at this and give them a grade. This is going to be public. Yesterday afternoon, as I mentioned earlier when the young women were arguing about the intentional "stupid" look of their video tape, I said, "Well, how do you think the rest of the school is going to feel when they look at it?" They were like, "Oh, you didn't tell us you were going to show . . ." Knowing that their work is going to be shown is a great motivator for students. Media, especially in this country is typically a shared experience. Students know that their work is going to be shown in school. They also know that work is selected to show in various youth video festivals. Currently, we are developing a relationship with the Manhattan Neighborhood Network to start showing videos on cable television. This is certainly a motivating force, but it is not a requirement in the video class. If students feel strongly that they do not want their work to be publicly shown, they do not have to show it. They know that their work has the potential for being public. Today, anyone with access can have a website or send something into cable television—distribution is just inherent to the media.

Every year we take students to the American Museum of the Moving Image youth media festival in New York and it is extremely exciting. Not only do they get to show their videos but they also get to go up and speak about them in front of an audience of students from other schools. Students get to view really good work made by their peers. I think this sort of activity is beneficial because students are directly connected to the world outside their school. After all, there is no practical difference between their distribution systems and the distribution systems they are going to participate in when and if they decide to become professionals.

DD: Marshall, given your knowledge and expertise, I think it would be helpful to conclude our discussion with resources you think are important for art teachers interested in video art.

MW: The following are excellent resources in video art:

www.artiststelevisionaccess.org
A grassroots media center for innovative emerging media artists; home of Other Cinema, an important venue for underground and experimental film and video. Located in San Francisco.

www.evc.org
One of the oldest media literacy and student media education center, an award winning and major distributor of student produced video. Located in NYC.

www.dctv.org
A primary media education and alternative news production center in downtown NYC.

www.fair.org/fair/
Fairness and Accuracy in Reporting, a primary source for critical analysis of corporate media-massive links.

www.freespeech.org
Free Speech Television, an alternative media distributor. Great links to many alternative news sources.

www.imc.org
The Independent Media Center, a huge worldwide network of alternative media and journalism.

www/moderntv.com
Possibly the best media website, incredible design work, great links.

artcon.rutgers.edu/papertiger/squat/
Paper Tiger Television, one of the first alternative video production collectives, great media work, fabulous links. Located in NYC.

www.Videomachete.org
An activist art education media collective organization; located in Chicago.

www.Videodatabank.org
A primary distributor of artists' video and alternative media; located in Chicago.

www.gkids.com
New York International Children's Film Festival.

www.hrw.org/iff/2003/
Human Rights Watch International Film Festival. Features youth films and classroom activities.

Here, I would like to conclude with some of my thoughts based on this interview. Today, visual images dominate our daily lives and all of us routinely read these images consciously or unconsciously. These images on the media, in the streets and in schools shape our understanding of the world in particular ways. As Marshall has indicated in this interview, increasingly children and youth in the United States develop their identity based on visual culture. Furthermore, growing up in a media saturated visual environment they are both consumers and producers of images. This radical shift in the ways children and youth come to understand their world and themselves can no longer be overlooked by art educators.

Video art is an obvious pedagogical tool that should be part of our art practices in schools because it is relevant to students' daily lives and is comprehensible to them. They live in a media saturated world and they know all about it. As Marshall convincingly suggests, video art opens a space for children and youth to communicate their ideas, feelings and thoughts in a visceral manner. The process of making a video inherently involves re-presenting images

and that process in turn requires students to become critical of media images and the forms of knowledge media shapes about our world. However, as a form of self-expression, video art in schools needs to be antithetical to the particular form the media literacy movement in the United States has taken.

Marshall's pedagogical philosophy of video art that focuses on the collective process of both making a video and evaluating it, I believe is an important aspect of art education. Although collaborative art practices are gaining some ground in art classes, the tendency is still for art projects to be individually driven. The ubiquitous mural project is for some students the only time in their art education career where they work in collaboration with other students. The final video reflects the collective voice of the students. Moreover, the audience evaluates their work in the real world when they put it out in public. This is a fundamental difference from many art class projects where often the only person evaluating the artwork is the art teacher. In my experience, student motivation shifts radically when artworks are made for a larger public audience. Students then want to spend time working on their art project as it will be displayed in the community and not just in the school.

Video art as we have tried to show through this interview is an interesting medium precisely because it blurs the boundaries between the art world and popular culture. By occupying this in-between space, video art forces us to engage with issues of visual representation that are fundamental to pedagogical practices in art education. It is a medium that we art educators need to embrace as it forges new ways of knowing and seeing.

Illustrations on the following page.

Illustrations

 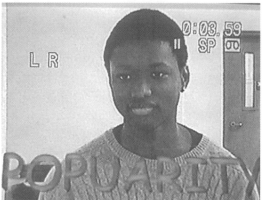

(above) Stills from video: *Sugar & Spice*

(above) Stills from video: *De La Vega*

Final Take

23

Ilona and I are clearing out the last remains of our family darkroom. We spent a lot of time in this room. She joined me here as soon as she was old enough to be captivated by the magic in the photo trays. While we package the items we've sold on eBay, we reminisce about our early photography days and toss out ideas for how we will convert the generous counter space for our digital work.

I remember Ilona's first serious camera, the old Nikkormat, purchased for the children's summer program in Ulster, New York. We browsed through the summer program's large course catalogue each year, hoping there would be room in the popular photo workshops. This past summer we met a parent in the village post office, lamenting at the difficulty of getting her daughter into the digital video class of the same summer program. Ilona asked the parent about photography classes. The parent said they were no longer offered. All the darkrooms had been converted to classrooms. As we moved ahead in the line, we talked about the change of guard in media and how children today are flocking to filmmaking and digital video classes.

Community-based video art programs are thriving across the nation. Our anthology offers a modest sampling of the exciting video work being created in community funded studios and the important connections they are building to

school art programs. On-line, or in the community, art teachers have a wealth of digital video experts to which they can turn. (As our authors noted, these experts often include students in our own classes.)

Our anthology research also indicated that many art teachers are on the forefront of video art education, and exemplary school programs exist in every state. We conclude this manuscript with the distinct impression however, that to truly turn the tide towards video becoming a significant part of every art program will depend on the leadership of those who train preservice art teachers. The extent to which teacher preparatory classes are structured to provide the skills, advocate the importance, and encourage participation by new teachers will determine the future of video in the art room. Most art teachers learned to see and capture decisive moments by taking the photography requirements in their foundation art classes. Today, video needs to become a fundamental art course.

Our authors are dedicated to the importance of advancing video art studies in the nation's schools. Every author noted that video artistry is natural, relevant, and invaluable to our media-nurtured youngsters. They generously contributed their writing with a strong belief that appearing in this volume sponsored by the art teaching profession will make a difference. Contributors would like you to look at their websites for more information and student video galleries. They further extend a warm helping hand to colleagues interested in starting, or advancing, their video art courses. Please don't hesitate to write an author who sparked your interest or inspired your thinking. Invite our experts to speak at your school or professional meetings, or share your own successes and students' videos with them.

Betcam-Professional Component video, in a 1/2-inch recording format.

Digital Video-Refers to the capture, manipulation, and storage of video, in a digital format. A digital video (DV) is a video camera that captures and stores images on a digital medium such as a DAT.

Dub-A copy of a master tape, usually at a low resolution for off-line editing.

GIF-Short for Graphic Interchange Format. Unlike JPG, GIF format is a compression technique that supports only 256 colors. GIF is better than JPG for images with only a few distinct colors such as line drawings, black and white images, or small text, that is only a few pixels.

Generation-The number of steps between an original recording and a copy. A second generation duplicate is a copy of the original master. A third generation duplicate is a copy of a copy of the original master. Each new generation loses signal quality, hence the term generation loss.

Hypertext-A special database system in which objects, text, pictures, and music programs can be creatively linked to each other. When an object is selected, all other objects tat are linked creatively liked to each other. When an object is selected, all other objects that are linked to it can be viewed. One can move form one object to another even though they may have different forms. Hypertext systems are particularly useful for organizing and browsing through large databases tat consist of disparate types of information.

Jog-To move a video tape forward or backward a short distance of one or two frames, in a search for the "perfect" place to edit.

Jpeg-Abridgement for Joint Photographic Experts Group. A compression technique for color images. Jpeg can reduce file sizes to about 5% of their normal size, with some loss of detail in the compression.

Layer-Part of a computer image, separate from other parts, which can be changed independently. For example, changing the background behind an animated figure.

Overlay-Adding a graphic or text to (usually on top of) a video image.

Pixels-Picture elements of tiny dots that make up the picture. In a camera, pixels represent the tiny light-sensitive transistors that store the image.

Quicktime Movie-A file format that takes a series of individual files (pictures) and combines them into one file. Quicktime movies can play pictures in a sequence, creating animated motion.

Storyboard-A series of comic-book-like sketches showing what video scenes will look like. The corresponding audio is noted at the bottom of each sketch.

Streaming-A technique for transferring data, processed as a steady and continuous stream. With streaming, one can browse or "plug in" and start displaying data before the entire film has been transmitted.

Rikki Asher is director of Art Education at Queens College of the City University of New York. She has taught middle and high school art in New York City, and has been a Teaching Artist at the Lincoln Center Institute, working with the Museum of Modern Art and the Whitney Museum in New York City. Asher has produced several video works, including *The Bronx as Art* (1991), *Children's Literature as Art* (1990), *The Sojourner Truth Mural Project* (1998), and *The Making of the Procession Mural* (2000).

Joanna Black worked for 12 years as a secondary art teacher in Toronto, Canada. She was a museum educator at the Montreal Museum of Fine Arts and the Cobb Arts Museum in Georgia. Black is currently an Assistant Professor of Art Education at the University of Manitoba in Canada. She has worked with high school students to create award winning videos.

Dipti Desai is Director of the Art Education Program at New York University. Desai has taught elementary and middle school in India, New Zealand, and the United States. Her professional interests include the social context of contemporary art that includes various forms of media art. Desai interviewed Marshall Weber, a nationally recognized video artist and educator. Weber founded the Artists' Television Access in San Francisco and now serves as resident artist in the Taller Boricua/Puerto Rican Workshop's Media Lab.

Darrin Fletcher is a veteran filmmaker and founder of Independent Student Media, an organization which assists and encourages students and their teachers to make film and video art.

Michael Floyd has been Director and Executive Producer of Windsong Pictures for the past 30 years while David Habig has been the Technical Director and Producer for the past 14 years. Floyd and Habig have taught film and video production to all age groups, from kindergartners to college students. Windsong Pictures, a nonprofit educational film company, has produced over 100 films and videos and his students have won more than 200 state, national, and International awards.

Arlene Jordan has devoted 30 years to creating innovative arts programs with the Department of Education in New York City. During her tenure in District 25, the district was recognized by the President's Committee on the Arts and Humanities as a model arts district in the nation. Since then she has worked as the Education Director, Roundabout Theatre Company. January 2005 she will begin to serve as the Education Director, City Center. As a pioneer in the world of digital arts education, in each of her positions Jordan has mobilized teachers, teaching artists, and students to produce widely acclaimed Digital Operas.

Donna Learmont has been a video production instructor in Bloomfield Hills, Michigan since 1986. Her students have won over 300 awards, including 15 student awards from the Michigan Chapter of the National Academy of Television Arts and Sciences, the Emmy organization. Learmont is currently serving as one of ten teacher advisors in the country for Cable in the Classroom Magazine.

Susan Lehman teaches video at the John Still Center for Creative Expression K-8, in Sacramento, California. Lehrman's students have been regular participants in the annual Panasonic Video Festival. The Center has received several grants and awards from the Panasonic Corporation Outreach Program, honoring student video productions.

Corrinne Militello is a freelance writer and video artist residing in upstate New York. She has authored many articles on media arts.

Harold Olejarz teaches digital imaging, digital video, and television production at Eisenhower Middle School in Wyckoff, New Jersey. A performance artist who has created wearable sculptures, he has moved his art since 1990 to new digital directions. In his recent digital images, Olejarz treats the flatbed scanner as his stage on which he performs during the scanning process. Olejarz has served on the Executive Board of the Art Educators of New Jersey.

Ralph Raunft is currently a Professor of Art and former Chair and Director of Graduate Studies in Art Education at Miami University of Ohio. Raunft has served as Editor of the Ohio Art Education Association Journal and his edited book, *The Autobiographical Lectures of Some Prominent Art Educators,* was published in 2001 by the National Art Education Association. He has had his creative work exhibited in over 40 exhibitions including he Corcoran Gallery of Art and the Pennsylvania Academy of Fine Arts.

Karen Lindholm-Rynkiewicz is a teacher of Art, Design, and Technology at Muskego High School in Muskego, Wisconsin. Her most recent video project is a short film entitled *The Grocery.* Lindholm-Rynkiewicz is working on three new scripts which involve the interplay of American Sign Language and English. Her desire to see films that focus on an intergenerational audience that appreciates creativity led her to start Get Off the Couch Productions.

Deirdre Searcy is a media artist and educator. She is a former Co-Director of Street-Level Youth Media in Chicago, a media arts organization that educates youth in media arts and emerging technologies for the use of self-expression, communication, and social change. Ms. Searcy led the organization's efforts in positioning media arts as a catalyst for change in Chicago's inner city schools.

Mary Sheridan has been teaching visual arts at the elementary level in Pickerington, Ohio, for 14 years. She is the initial developer for *Changing Places,* a school wide initiative, which received an Outstanding Project Distinction by the Environmental Education Council of Ohio. Sheridan was also the director for *Saving Our Wetlands,* for which she received an award from the United States Environmental Protection Agency.

George Szekely is area head and senior professor of art education at the University of Kentucky. Szekely has been a pioneer in developing creative methodologies for art teaching. He is the author of such classic texts in art education as; *Encouraging Creativity in Art Lessons, From Play to Art, The Art of Teaching Art, A retrospective: 1973 - 2003 Essays for Art Teachers*, and a new book, *From Home Art to School Art.* Szekely has served as Regional Vice President of the National Art Education Association and received the Manuel Barkan and Victor Lowenfeld Awards.

Ilona Szekely is an elementary visual arts teacher in the Arlington, Virginia, Public Schools. She has taught video art classes in New York City and Northern Kentucky. A prolific artist Szekely has had exhibitions and screenings in Cincinnati and New York City. Szekely's most recent videos are a series about the passing of her grandmother. Ilona Szekely was director of the Northern Kentucky Region, of the Kentucky Art Education Association.

Erin Tapley is an associate professor of art education at the University of Wisconsin, Oshkosh. Making videos has become a regular activity in her methods classes as well as in her work as an installation artist. Tapley actively exhibits her work and was a recent resident fellow at the MacDowell Art Colony where she researched interdisciplinary artforms.